Library of
Davidson College

ENGLISH POETRY
IN A CHANGING SOCIETY,
1780-1825

English Poetry
in a Changing Society
1780–1825

A. D. HARVEY

St. Martin's Press
New York

All rights reserved. For information, write:
St. Martin's Press, Inc., 175 Fifth Avenue, New York, NY 10010
Printed in Great Britain
First published in the United States of America in 1980

Library of Congress Cataloging in Publication Data

Harvey, Arnold D
  English poetry in a changing society, 1780–1825.

  Includes bibliographical references and index.
  1. English poetry—18th century—History and criticism.
  2. English poetry—19th century—History and criticism.
  3. Romanticism—Great Britain.
  4. Great Britain—History—1789–1820.
  5. Literature and society—Great Britain.
  I. Title.
PR575.H5H3   1980   821'.7'09   80-20221

ISBN 0-312-25502-0

In studying the history of literature, it is not enough to attend to the mere names and characters of Authors; we ought also to be acquainted with the form and pressure of their times, and should know the moral atmosphere and light of their age and country, in order to judge their size by the shadows of their reputation.

(Thomas Campbell, *Letters to the Students of Glasgow on the Epochs of Literature*, 1827)

They owe their existence not only to the efforts of the great minds and talents who have created them, but also to the anonymous toil of their contemporaries. There is no document of civilization which is not at the same time a document of barbarism.

(Walter Benjamin, *Theses on the Philosophy of History*, c. 1940)

Genius is native to the soil where it grows — is fed by the air and warmed by the sun — and is not a hothouse plant or an exotic.

(William Hazlitt, Commonplace no. 27, *Literary Examiner*, 13 Sept. 1823)

Contents

		Introduction	1
		PART ONE. PRELIMINARY STAGES	
CHAPTER	1	English Poetry In The Eighteenth Century	17
	2	The 1780s	44
	3	The Age of Lyrical Ballads	58
	4	The Great Age of Rural Poetry	77
		PART TWO. THE CRUCIAL YEARS	
	5	The Metrical Romance	95
	6	Lyric Poetry	120
	7	The New Poetry and the Reading Public in the 1800s	132
	8	The Renewal of Interest in Elizabethan and Jacobean Playwrights	142
	9	The Dethronement of the Augustans	148
		Conclusion	166
		Notes	171
		Appendix: Numbers of editions of poetry published in British Isles 1795-1825	186
		Index	191

Introduction

> But a history of poetry, for another reason, yet on the same principles, must be especially productive of entertainment and utility. I mean, as it is an art, whose object is human society: as it has the peculiar merit, in its operation on that object, of faithfully recording the features of the times and of preserving the most picturesque and expressive representation of manners.
>
> (Thomas Warton, *The History of English Poetry*, vol. 1, 1774)

Of all periods of English literature, it is perhaps the early nineteenth century, the Romantic Period, which has experienced the greatest retrospective abandonment of its literary values. Samuel Rogers, Thomas Campbell, Thomas Moore were much more famous then than Wordsworth and Coleridge, but no one reads them now. Walter Scott is remembered only as a great novelist, though he was once revered as a great poet. Byron, who in his lifetime was likened to Homer, survives on the merits of a misunderstood and over-dramatized personality, and owes his modern acceptance as a poet to a work which, though characteristic of the man who wrote it, is not at all typical of the poetry with which he astonished and delighted his contemporaries. Wordsworth, Keats, Shelley and Blake, however, have come to be regarded as epitomizing the period which neglected and misunderstood them. Not that the Romantic period was something which occurred only in retrospect: the contemporaries of these men were well aware that they lived in a new poetic era. They spoke of it frequently; but it was the era of the greatest posthumous fame of Thomson, Cowper and Burns, the heyday of Moore, Scott and Campbell, to which they referred.

The relationship between poets like Wordsworth, Keats, Shelley and Blake, on the one hand, and Moore, Scott, Campbell and all the other forgotten versifiers, on the other, is of great interest. The major Romantic poets were not culturally isolated figures; they were working in the context of changing literary fashions. Important aspects of their achievement will be misunderstood so long as they are seen apart from the great literary changes which influenced them and to which they contributed. Even the most original mind will be influenced by its surroundings, will work against, or in accordance with, the prevailing taste; and this was certainly true of the great Romantic poets. This fact has long been admitted, even taken for granted, and there have been a number of excellent studies relating individual poets to their cultural tradition,[1] but no adequate attempt has ever been made to understand the general change of literary standards to which the better-known Romantics made only a partial contribution. The basic fact about any culture, which tends to be neglected by students of literature, is that the contributors to a cultural environment are to be numbered in scores and hundreds, not in ones and twos. The purpose of the following study is to bring the scores and hundreds back into the picture.

The literature of the Romantic period suggests itself for historical treatment perhaps more than any other, for perhaps more than any other it is reckoned to have been fundamentally influenced by the "historical" — i.e. political and social — developments of the time, and particularly by the French Revolution.

There was some near contemporary support for the view that the French Revolution was a vital stimulus to the new poetic fashion. T. N. Talfourd wrote of the French Revolution in 1815: "one of its immediate effects was to raise and darken the imagination, to deepen the shade of serious contemplation and to fill us with a delight in strong emotion."[2] Three years later Hazlitt wrote that the Wordsworthian school "had its origin in the French Revolution, or rather in those sentiments and opinions which produced that revolution; and which sentiments and opinions were indirectly imported into this country in translations from the German about that period".[3] In the same year Leigh Hunt referred to the "political convulsions" as one of several causes of the change in taste[4] and in 1821 he asserted: "it remained for the French Revolution to plough up all our commonplaces at once; and the minds that sprang out of the freshened soil set about their tasks in a spirit not only of difference but of hostility."⁵ In 1819 Shelley described Wordsworth and Byron as "deriving from the new springs of thought and feeling, which the great events of our age have exposed to view, a similar tone of sentiment, imagery and expression".⁶ Hazlitt, born in 1778, was eleven when the Bastille fell, and sixteen when Robespierre was executed, and may, as an adolescent, have been impressed by events in France, but in his attribution of the new poetic style to the influence of the French Revolution he was clearly copying Talfourd, who was not born till 1795, the year after Robespierre's death. And it is interesting to note that Hazlitt actually shifted the emphasis from events in France to the general intellectual climate of the times, a piece of subtle redefinition in which he was followed by Shelley though not by Leigh Hunt. Thus the chief responsibility for ascribing to the French Revolution the major influence on Romanticism rested with Talfourd, who had no first-hand knowledge of what he was talking about, and with Leigh Hunt who, born in 1784, had only a childhood memory of the period in question. Their opinion received no corroboration from the older Romantics who actually experienced the French Revolution as adults. The course of the French Revolution undoubtedly left an indelible impression on the minds of Wordsworth, Coleridge, Southey, and others of their age group; but they never pretended that it was the strongest impression their young minds received. The only poets whose major work was principally inspired by the revolutionary upheavals of the period seem to have been Josiah Walker, author of *The Defence of Order* (1802) and George Sanon, author of *The Causes of the French Revolution; and the Science of Governing an Empire* (1806); they were both hostile to the revolutionary cause. It was the next generation's thoughtless projection of present feelings on to a past they had not properly understood that was the origin of the myth of the French Revolution's place in English literary history.

But the case for the French Revolution's vital role does not, of course, rest on near-contemporary testimony alone. There is a coincidence of dates — the revolution occurred in the formative years of Wordsworth's, Southey's and Coleridge's early adulthood. (Blake, who was sufficiently impressed by events in France to begin a poem entitled *The French Revolution*, had commenced his poetic career earlier.) But a coincidence of dates is merely an adventitious circumstance. More important is the argument derived from the commonly accepted view of the French Revolution's impact on British politics, and British society in general. If the revolution had a great effect in enlarging horizons in politics and society, it is argued, it must have had an equally great effect in enlarging cultural — including poetic — horizons.

This view is derived from a fundamental misunderstanding of the nature of British politics during the 1780s and the early 1790s. It is too often assumed that Britain before 1789 was a well-ordered, rather stagnant but secure political society, and that after 1789 the floodgates opened, sedition and dissent became widespread, and nothing was ever quite the same again. This is almost the complete opposite of the truth.

England in the 1780s was already in the grip of an extensive movement for reform. The division in the House of Commons of 174 in favour of Parliamentary reform against 248 opposed, in 1785, gives an idea of the strength of the movement. In Yorkshire reformers had won a considerable success against the great landlords in the 1784 election; among the allies of their reform cause was William Pitt, the prime minister. Of Pitt's ministerial colleagues, the majority were still lukewarm or opposed to reform, but the Duke of Richmond, who represented the army in the cabinet, had particularly progressive views, agitating for manhood suffrage and annual parliaments. (It was Richmond, incidentally, who later presided over the Quarter Sessions which acquitted Blake in his trial for sedition.) The hundredth anniversary of the flight of James II, in 1688, saw the establishment of the Revolutionary Society, pledged to the agitation of parliamentary reform. Its president, Earl Stanhope, was a cousin of the prime minister and of two other cabinet ministers.

Naturally, the growing movement was given tremendous encouragement by events in France in 1789, not least because the French seemed to be copying English principles of constitutional government. But as the French Revolution moved towards violence, terror and regicide, many people in England suffered a revulsion of feeling. The more populist elements of the reform agitation were repressed; perhaps this would have happened eventually in any case, but the fears aroused by developments in France brought on the event. War broke out with France, and Earl Stanhope, opposing the measure, found himself in "a minority of one" (it was he who coined the phrase). The tutor he employed for his sons was prosecuted — the earl himself was too grand a personage for his relatives in the government to touch. The Whig party split down the middle; Burke, whose political philosophy was a major influence on Coleridge, was a spokesman of those Whigs who set their face against reform. Among his followers was a young barrister named Edward Law who later, as Lord Chief Justice Ellenborough, came to epitomize the repression of truth and liberty to Shelley, Byron and Hunt. On the government side too, the many advocates of reformist ideas, including Pitt and Wilberforce, became committed to a policy of repression at home and counter-revolution abroad. Young men, born almost at the same time as Wordsworth and formerly sharing his political sympathies, such as Canning and Huskisson, rallied to Pitt's government. The number of M.P.s in favour of parliamentary reform fell to 91 against 256 in a division in 1797. It is against the background of these events that the vexed question of Wordsworth's and Southey's apostasy in politics is to be understood. Nor were they particularly bold apostates except by the standards of men like Shelley, who had no personal knowledge of the time which had caused Wordsworth and Southey to change their minds. Though Southey soon gave up the absurdly unrealistic scheme for a utopian settlement on the banks of the Susquehannah he clung to his almost equally naïve belief in parliamentary reform well into the early years of the nineteenth century, long after the subject had been dropped from normal political discussion. Wordsworth, in his pamphlet on the Convention of Cintra could still, as late as 1809, condemn the British government's "presumptuous irreverence of the principles of justice, and blank insensibility to the affections of human nature".

It is probably fair to say that, far from being a great liberalizing influence on Britain, the French Revolution provoked a massive swing to the right and delayed many overdue reforms till the 1830s. Society in the early nineteenth century showed the same obscurantist characteristics as society in the eighteenth century, but some of them to a more advanced degree. The powers of borough-mongerers increased during the period, as did the power of large-scale employers of labour, through the agency of the Combination Acts. The establishment of the yeomanry gave the upper classes a new weapon with which to oppress the lower. To be a gentleman, however poor, meant that one belonged to a completely different world from that of one's social inferiors, as several incidents in de Quincey's autobiographical writings testify. Even literary patronage continued to flourish, in spite of the opinions of A. Beljame, J. W. Saunders and A. S. Collins to the contrary;[7] and at least one foreign observer in the 1800s regarded noble patronage of literature as a characteristic feature of English society.[8] Wordsworth for example was a dependant of Viscount Lowther, later Earl of Lonsdale, and dedicated *The Excursion* to him. Campbell was a protégé of Lord Minto till the latter's departure to India in 1807. Thomas Moore attached himself to the Earl of Moira, later Minto's successor as Governor-General of Bengal. Southey was a pensioner of his old schoolfriend, Charles Williams Wynn (who took the opportunity of office to transfer the expense to the government). Crabbe owed his career as a comfortable rural clergyman to the favour and ecclesiastical patronage of the fourth and fifth Dukes of Rutland. It was largely because society was still organized on these lines that Byron, Shelley and Hunt became political dissidents twenty years after the French Revolution; and it was precisely because Hunt resented having the same relation to Byron as any other impecunious writer had to his noble patron (while having to submit to the egalitarian charade of pretending they were on terms of social equality) that the two men quarrelled.[9]

Of course, the French Revolution is not the only sociopolitical event adduced to explain Romanticism. As long ago as 1915, G. F. Richardson in *A Neglected Aspect of the English Romantic Revolt* linked Romanticism with the social changes of the industrial revolution; but it can only be said that his exposition showed a remarkable ignorance both of the social history and of the literature of the period. Of course, it *can* be argued, for example, that Wordsworth and Byron knew something about the industrial revolution. There was the letter Wordsworth sent Charles James Fox in 1801 with a copy of *Lyrical Ballads,* which argued that social change was causing a "rapid decay of the domestic affections among the lower orders"; there were the passages in the eighth book of *The Excursion*; and there was Byron's speech in the House of Lords on the Luddites. But the changes Wordsworth discussed in his letter to Fox had been taking place, in one area or another, for generations, and the peculiarly novel conditions of the industrial revolution became known to him only after he had written most of his best poetry; and whatever Byron thought about the Luddites and their ilk as a tyro politician, he showed no sign of it in his verse. As for the mass of social-comment poetry in the 1780s and 1790s, it was not directly linked to contemporary social developments, and much of it owed more to literary convention than to direct observation.

That there is a relationship between culture and society it is impossible to deny, but we must beware of supposing that such and such a social change automatically equals such and such a cultural change. Merely intermixing a potted history of social change with a few samples of contemporary comment, as in the work of Raymond Williams, does not satisfactorily explain the mechanisms of cultural response to socio-economic developments.[10] Only after we have isolated the two sectors of change and analysed them separately can we state with any certainty what is the connection between them.

This process of separation is perhaps objectionable on the grounds that it breaks down the organic, indispensable links between socio-economic conditions and their cultural superstructure. At the same time it may be that the cultural superstructure has in some degree an autonomous dynamic of its own. The development of art depends to some extent on developments in public receptivity and on the emergence of new talents, but the essential dynamic comes from within, from the continuing dialogue of individual artists with their cultural heritage and the contemporary cultural scene. Consequently, the most important factors to be considered in any cultural history, in the history of any form of art, are the characteristics of that culture or art form. With regard to poetry written in 1800, the most important factor to be considered is the corpus of poetic writing existing in that year — in other words, the poetry written before 1800.

In this study I do not ignore non-literary factors but I do try to distinguish between a direct response to non-literary factors and a response to an established literary tradition. Several purely literary factors in the Romantic period have hitherto been underrated, and a true assessment of the changes that took place can only be made with a working knowledge of these factors. They can only be restored to the picture by, at least temporarily, turning our backs on non-literary considerations. If there is indeed an equation of literary and socio-political change, it will be better understood if the two sides of the question are first to some extent separated.

It is so obvious that there are difficulties in lumping Wordsworth, Shelley, Byron and Keats together in one poetic school that it is not nowadays usual to bother even to point this out. And yet the attempt is still made to show that the great Romantic poets had in essence something in common, whether it be esemplastic power, a new view of society, or a similarity in their modes of imagery. Northrop Frye for example writes, "The great achievement of English Romanticism was its grasp of the principle of creative autonomy, its declaration of artistic independence",[11] but elsewhere he points out that the characteristic of Romantic poetry is that its metaphors "move inside and downward instead of outside and upward".[12] Exiles, breezes, lost travellers and serpents have all been identified as characteristic Romantic symbols, though some critics prefer to stress the common symbolism less than the common attributes of the great poets. M. H. Abrams refers to the "concern with the eye and the object and the need for a revolution in seeing which will make the object new... the Romantic categories of freshness of sensation, revelatory moments, and the rectified outlook which inverts the status of the lowly, the trivial and the mean."[13] And even when fundamental divergences between different authors are being illustrated, the divergences are often shown to be a matter of viewing the same characteristically Romantic topics differently, rather than of viewing different topics. Thus M. H. Abrams again, who explains that he omitted Byron from his study *Natural Supernaturalism* "not because I think him a lesser poet than the others but because in his greatest work he speaks with an ironic counter-voice and deliberately opens a satirical perspective on the vatic stance of his Romantic contemporaries".[14]

Such attempts at exegesis derive from an assumption that the essential oneness of Romanticism will be found at the level of symbolism, metaphor, philosophy or prophetic stance; symbolism, metaphor, philosophy and prophecy all being things which the Romantics are quite good at. Yet similarities of this kind do not inevitably strike the reader's attention; they may be there, but they have to be searched for (and *search, and ye shall find* is a dictum held in justifiable suspicion by social scientists). Characteristics which may be difficult to discover are, so to speak, a high common denominator. There are, however, other similarities in Romantic poetry of a cruder and more obvious kind — a low common denominator — which students of literature tend to take for granted, perhaps because they are intrinsically less worthy of discussion. Yet in the history of changing taste, these cruder, more obvious resemblances are of the first importance, for as Wordsworth pointed out, "The qualities of writing best fitted for eager reception are either such as startle the world into attention by their audacity and extravagance; or they are chiefly of a superficial kind, lying upon the surfaces of manners."[15] It was the superficial aspects of Romanticism, or certain of its aspects rendered superficial, that established the new type of poetry in the popular esteem. And the less these superficial aspects appeal to the mature and receptive intellects of literary scholars, the more they may be assumed to have delighted their original readers, not one of whom had the benefit of a university degree in English.

The low common denominator characteristics of Romantic poetry were

A. Subject matter:
   1. Nature, and the sensations of external reality.
   2. The supernatural (i.e. the divine, the mythical, or the magical) and the praeternatural (i.e. visions, insights, heightened reality).
   3. Strong feeling (e.g. love, grief, melancholia, hope).
B. Diction:
   1. A more varied and vehement metre, more suitable for handling the subjects above than the measured heroic couplet.
   2. A vocabulary and imagery that aimed at *immediacy*. Instead of being concerned with general statements that might refer to anyone's experience at any particular time, as was the case with Augustan poetry, Romantic poetry was more concerned with the experiences of one particular person in one particular set of circumstances; so that the reader was, so to speak, swept up and involved in what he was reading.

Romanticism's rediscovery of the past was a part, rather than a cause, of the new type of subject matter. All of the Romantic poets wrote at least one major poem about the more or less remote past: even Wordsworth produced *Laodamia* and *The White Doe of Rylstone,* and of course the passages about the past in *The Prelude* are among the most striking in his work. The past provided scope for supernatural and praeternatural effects; involved characters with strong, unsophisticated feelings, who were in close touch with external nature; and suggested vehement verses loosely based on antique measures.

When I imply that even Romantic poems about the past were more *immediate* than Augustan poems about the present, I intend no paradox. What I am referring to is the difference in the way they operate on the reader's sense of participation. During the eighteenth century, artists (painters as well as poets) actually suppressed their most individually intimate experiences in order to provide a generalized picture for public consumption; instead of trying to capture the uniqueness of a single experience, they attempted to bring out what it had in common with all such experiences. As Norman Callan wrote, the typical Augustan poet "merges himself in the general consciousness of his readers, pointing to what they have in common and ignoring what separates them".[16] Samuel Johnson encapsulated this view in chapter ten of his novel *Rasselas*:

> The business of a poet, said Imlac, is to examine, not the individual, but the species; to remark general properties and large appearances: he does not number the streaks of the tulip, or describe the different shades in the verdure of the forest. He is to exhibit in his portraits of nature such prominent and striking features, as recall the original to every mind; and must neglect the minuter discriminations, which one may have remarked, and another have neglected, for those characteristicks which are alike obvious to vigilance and carelessness.

Whereas the Augustan poet stressed community of experience, the Romantic confronted each reader individually, with a representation of the poet's individuality. By communicating a sense of his own self, the Romantic poet enhanced his reader's own awareness of self; and the way in which this sense of individuality was communicated was through a stress on the uniqueness of specific experiences.

From the mid-eighteenth century onwards there was a striving for the more specific but it was some time before writers learned to distinguish between uniqueness and mere detail. It is significant that when Joseph Warton praised Thomson for the specificity of his evocations of nature,

> What poet hath ever taken notice of the leaf, that towards the end of autumn,
> Incessant rustles from the mournful grove,
> Oft startling such as, studious, walk below,
> And slowly circles through the waving air?
> Or who, in speaking of a summer evening, hath ever mentioned,
> The quail that clamours for his running mate?[17]

the evocations Warton cited are general and idealized, rather than referring to specific occasions — "*oft* startling *such as,* studious, walk below"; "*the* quail" rather than "a quail". Later on Warton praised the lines,

> at his evening watch
> The village dog deters the nightly thief;
> The heifer lows; the distant water-fall
> Swells in the breeze.[18]

Yet how many village dogs did have occasion to howl at nightly thieves, outside the severely edited and improved countryside of Thomson's imagination? It was Cowper who was perhaps the first to achieve a genuine specificality, and during the generation following Cowper nearly all poets became much more particular in their evocations. Coleridge wrote of the typical poet of the 1800s: "Both his characters and his descriptions he renders, as much as possible, specific and individual, even to a degree of portraiture".[19] This is most marked perhaps in Wordsworth and Keats, but it is evident even in the early work of Southey, whose anxiety at the beginning of his career to imitate the style and subject matter of Thomas Gray and Joseph Warton did not prevent him from being far more precise than either of the earlier poets in his handling of detail:

> Faint gleams the evening radiance thro' the sky,
>   The sober twilight dimly darkens round;
> In short quick circles the shrill bat flits by,
>   And the slow vapour curls along the ground.
>
> Now the pleas'd eye from yon lone cottage sees
>   On the green mead the smoke long-shadowing play;
>   The Red-breast on the blossom'd spray;
>   Warbles wild her latest lay,
> And sleeps along the dale the silent breeze.
> Calm CONTEMPLATION, 'tis thy favorite hour!
> Come fill my bosom, tranquillizing Power!
>   (*To Contemplation.*)

This kind of detail, which brings to life the setting of the poem much more vividly than the generalized scene-painting of Thomson, was of course an important ingredient in the appeal of narrative poetry, though as can be seen from Cowper and Southey the development predates the rise of the verse romance.

A similar movement towards increased immediacy also occurred in the use of language. Most eighteenth-century verse is written in the same idiom as the extremely one-dimensional prose of the age; words have each a rather small individual value, and are used most effectively in bulk. Early in the nineteenth century there was a rediscovery of the weight and resonance of the individual word. The prose, not just of over-conscious artists like de Quincey but of writers like Thomas Jefferson Hogg, Edward John Trelawney and Leigh Hunt, is much more vivid than that of earlier generations; and the same is true of poetry. It is sometimes assumed, from a misreading of Wordsworth's *Preface* to *Lyrical Ballads,* that "poetic diction" was a feature unique to the eighteenth century. In reality authors in any age attempt to write in a language which seems appropriate to their subject, and it was not *falseness* or *artificiality* which was the especial feature of eighteenth-century language, but its lack of resonance. As F. W. Bateson wrote, "Their words were to be counters of an agreed value which could pass from hand to hand and from one context to another without changing their meaning".[20] There was indeed a degree of artificiality in their language in that they had attempted selfconsciously to regulate it, but it was not their selecting, but the *way* in which they selected which occasioned that blandness of flavour characteristic of eighteenth-century language.

As an analytic framework for a study of the great Romantics, my low common denominators of subject matter and diction may be beneath contempt. Their value is that they link the greater with the lesser, and bring Wordsworth, Coleridge, Shelley, Keats together with their contemporaries Campbell, Rogers, Montgomery, Hunt, Moore and many others.

The features I have indicated are remote from what is often assumed to be the characteristic preoccupations of the eighteenth century, yet all these features are evident in some of the most popular poetical work of the period 1720-90. The classic Augustan authors — Pope, Johnson, Addison — who might be termed the satirico-didactic school, enjoyed less popular esteem than men like Thomson and Young, and others of what might be termed the evocative school. Taking the period 1720-90 as a whole, it can be said, very approximately, to have been a period of equilibrium between these two schools, the evocative school enjoying the greater sales and influence, the satirico-didactic school the superior critical repute. If anything, the balance was already in favour of the evocative school. During the so-called Romantic period three things happened which totally destroyed the equilibrium.

1. The satirico-didactic school came under theoretic attack. It had had hostile critics before, such as the Wartons, but the theoretic opposition increased after 1800. It continued to produce a great deal of bad verse, not only till the 1820s, but even after, but its vitality was gone. At the same time, the evocative school gained ground, partly as a result of an increasing volume of good work being produced, partly as a critical rehabilitation of the pre-Augustans, but mainly as a result of a general shift in taste in favour of the more melodramatic and emotional.

2. A number of great poets emerged, all, with one partial exception, members of the evocative school. The partial exception was Byron — if indeed he can be called a great poet. He first won acclaim with his *English Bards, and Scotch Reviewers*, and his swan song was *Don Juan*, both satirico-didactic poems. He was a fervent, if uncritical, admirer of Pope. Yet, such was the current of popular taste, he spent most of his career writing verse of the evocative school, and his enormous popular success was the major individual contribution to the subversion of the cause he really favoured.
3. There developed a general awareness that the period was one of dramatic innovation in poetry. In the 1780s and 1790s it was customary to refer to poetry as in decline. After the turn of the century it became commonplace to assume the very opposite. *The Edinburgh Review* condemned the innovations of Wordsworth and Southey but also referred to the time as "a period when we have more eminent poetical writers than have appeared together for upwards of a century".[21] *The Eclectic Review* called it "this age of poetical experiment".[22] The innovators were at first mentioned with disparagement, thus *The Edinburgh Review* in 1802 referred to "a *sect* of poets, that has established itself in this country within these ten or twelve years ... *dissenters* from the established systems of poetry and criticism."[23] With the great success of Scott and Byron, however, innovation became respectable.

The period of transition from the old to the new era was variously put at the mid-1790s or the 1780s. *The Quarterly Review* thought *The Pleasures of Memory* (1792) appeared "when the old school ... was drawn almost to its lees, and before the new one had appeared",[24] whereas James Montgomery wrote:

> between the school of Dryden and Pope, and our undisciplined, independent contemporaries, Cowper stands as having closed the age of the former illustrious masters, and commenced that of the eccentric leaders of the modern fashions in song.[25]

Having identified an old and a new school, critics were at great pains to emphasize the differences between them. The following elaborate rhetoric of the Rev. George Gilfillan, written in the 1850s, merely rehearses what had been the generally accepted view during the four previous decades:

> It is like stepping, we will not say from the frigid, but from the

> temperate into the torrid zone. In the one class of authors you will find the prevalence of strong sense, flanked by wit and by fancy, but without much that can be called imaginative or romantic. In the other, imagination or fancy is the regnant faculty.... The style of the one is clear, masculine, sententious and measured; that of the other is bold, unmeasured, diffuse, fervid, and sometimes obscure.... The temperature of the two races is as distant as their sentiment and style, that of the one seeming somewhat curbed, if not cold, while that of the other is ardent always, and often enthusiastic and rapturous....[26]

This is a travesty of criticism, in that it totally ignores, or inverts the role of, some of the most widely-read and seminal poets of the eighteenth century, such as Blair and the Wartons. It is an early example of the enduring practice of overgeneralizing the eighteenth century. But this practice of overgeneralizing, though objectionable in modern literary historians, has to be acknowledged as a vital factor in the poetic movements of the early nineteenth century. The impact of Romantic poetry on its first readers was not entirely due to its excellence and novelty, though some of it was excellent and novel; it was also partly due to the belief that it was much more novel than was really the case. The somewhat dislocated view of the Romantic period which still prevails was to some extent a necessary part of the Romantic period itself.

This study attempts to repair some of this dislocation. I am afraid I do not offer any new critical interpretation of the handful of poets who have become accepted as the "major authors" of the period I discuss. My aim is neither more nor less than to set these "major authors" in their literary context and to suggest ways in which this literary context relates to the socio-economic context. By discussing figures like Hurdis, Campbell, Grahame, Rogers, Montgomery, Kirke White, I am in no way pretending that their poetry *as* poetry has been unfairly neglected; but I do believe that a study of them will help our appreciation and understanding of the great writers who were their contemporaries and of the times in which they — and their first readers — lived.

PART ONE:
PRELIMINARY STAGES

1
English Poetry in the Eighteenth Century

> These three Writers, Thomson, Collins, and Dyer, had more poetic Imagination than any of their Contemporaries, unless we reckon Chatterton of that age. I do not name Pope, for he stands alone — as a man most highly gifted — but unluckily he took the Plain, when the Heights were within his reach.
> (Wordsworth to Dyce, letter 12 January 1829)

In 1816 the critic Francis Jeffrey wrote in *The Edinburgh Review*:

> When we were at our studies, some twenty-five years ago, we can perfectly remember that every young man was set to read Pope, Swift and Addison as regularly as Virgil, Cicero and Horace. All who had any tincture of letters were familiar with their writings and their history; allusions to them abounded in all popular discourses and all ambitious conversation; and they and their contemporaries were universally acknowledged as our great models of excellence, and placed without challenge at the head of our national literature. New books, even when allowed to have merit, were never thought of as fit to be placed in the same class, but were generally read and forgotten, and passed away like the transitory meteors of the lower sky; while *they* remained in their brightness, and were supposed to shine with a fixed and unalterable glory.[1]

This statement fits in with the still current view that the central tradition of eighteenth-century poetry was sophisticated commentary on the attitudes and activities of the English upper classes and their literary hangers-on, the tradition of which Pope is perhaps the best exponent. But like many of Jeffrey's most confident assertions, this passage I have quoted is somewhat misleading. His testimony as to the syllabus at the High School in Edinburgh may be believed, but it does not prove that boys were set to read Pope, Swift and Addison in the classrooms of England, Wales and Ireland (see below p. 149). In fact it was afterwards a complaint that schools taught all about Latin and Greek but totally ignored everything else, including English literature.[2] And though — for those who did not ignore native authors — Pope, Swift and Addison may have been regarded as classics, it does not therefore follow that they were either the most popular authors, or the greatest influence on literary taste, which is what Jeffrey wished to imply.

In terms of popularity, as gauged by numbers of editions published, Pope was ahead of Addison and Swift, but considerably behind Shakespeare, Milton, John Gay, Isaac Watts, Gray, Young and Thomson. What this position on the scale of popularity means in terms of influence on literary taste, however, is difficult to assess. It might be argued that Pope had a much narrower appeal than his rival best-sellers, that he was the favourite author only of a certain class, but that this class was the better educated and more cultured section of society. The extreme rarity of references to Watts and Gay by other writers, and the nature of their work (Watts was best known for his hymns and Gay for his doggerel fables) does indeed suggest that their popular esteem was among the poor and ignorant. Shakespeare was already established as a national classic and therefore, for many readers, placed beyond the need for critical appreciation. Milton was often regarded as principally a religious writer. Thomson, Young and Gray had an appeal to readers of all levels of sophistication. Thus, it might be argued that as Pope suited the taste only of the well-educated reader, his position as eighth, or ninth, or tenth in the best-seller lists, close behind national classics and poems of mass appeal, showed how thoroughly he had impressed the country's intellectual élite.

There are two counter arguments to this. First, Pope's very reputation for sophistication and polish might have ensured that he was purchased by many who could afford to buy books but were not otherwise equipped to appreciate poetry. His resemblance to the Latin classics might well have endeared him to readers whose true poetic allegiance was to his Roman prototypes. His elegant translation of Homer might have made him seem indispensable to any respectable household that aspired to raising its sons to read Homer in the original Greek. In short he might have been a best-seller for reasons other than his merits as an English poet. Secondly, even if he did have an ascendancy over the minds of sophisticated readers, this does not necessarily mean that he had an influence on the *writing* of poetry. Poets do not always come from the most sophisticated

ENGLISH POETRY IN THE EIGHTEENTH CENTURY 19

backgrounds, and even when they do they quickly tend to transcend the values of their immediate cultural environment.

To place the readers of Pope in their cultural context, it would be necessary to analyse the nature of the eighteenth-century reading public at large. In this chapter, however, we must confine ourselves to a couple of points. Anyone who read anything in the eighteenth century read a great deal of verse. *The Edinburgh Review*'s suggestion that the readers of poetry were mainly "young, half-educated women, sickly tradesmen, and enamoured apprentices"[3] was only a cheap sneer. Ballads and religious poems were popular among the literate poor — and nearly half of the poorest classes could read.[4] The middle classes, as well as consuming novels, read a great deal of poetry. Long periods of reading aloud to the family were a common way of passing domestic evenings and Sunday afternoons. Partly by way of cause of this, and partly by way of effect, poetry was usually intended to be understood immediately; dense imagery was avoided, and by and large poetry was easier to understand than the rather involved prose of the time. The custom of reading verse aloud, and the avoidance of dense imagery occasioned the belief even in the early nineteenth century that,

> neither language nor poetry are compressible beyond certain limits; and the poet, whose thoughts have been concentrated into a few pages, cannot be expected to have given a very full or interesting image of life in his compositions.[5]
>
> There must be bulk, variety and grandeur of design to constitute a first rate poet.... One great magnificent *whole* must be accomplished before we can pronounce upon the *maker* to be the σ Ποιητης. Pope himself never earned this title by a work of any magnitude but his Homer, and that being a translation only constitutes him an accomplished versifier.[6]

Even in the best educated bourgeois or armigerous family circle, no more than a quarter of its members would be proficient in the classical languages, and it is doubtful whether the hearth-side circle of the average gentleman farmer, surgeon or merchant would contain any classicists at all. To such an audience, Augustan poetry, with its alien overtones and comparative tightness of expression, would have a limited appeal.

The chapter epigraphs chosen by Ann Radcliffe for her novel *The Mysteries of Udolpho* give a fair idea of what sort of authors such family reading circles preferred. Of her fifty-seven epigraphs, twenty-two are from Shakespeare, nine from Thomson, six from Beattie, six from Milton, three from Collins, and three from Gray. She used only one epigraph from Pope, and none from Swift or Addison.

The proof of Shakespeare's popularity in the eighteenth century does not of course depend on Ann Radcliffe's taste in epigraphs. It was a century of growing bardolatry. As a character in Jane Austen's *Mansfield Park* was later to say, "Shakespeare one gets acquainted with without knowing how. It is part of an Englishman's constitution. His thoughts and beauties are so spread abroad that one touches them everywhere, one is intimate with him by instinct." Yet his reception as a poet was ambiguous. He was often referred to as The Bard; Dr Johnson and the versifying Earl of Carlisle[7] (among others) called him "The Poet of Nature", and Milton's reference in *L'Allegro*,

> sweetest Shakespeare, Fancy's child,
> Warble his native wood-notes wild

was endorsed by eighteenth-century pundits, and even copied, for example, by Joseph Warton in *The Enthusiast, or the Lover of Nature*:

> What are the lays of artful Addison,
> Coldly correct, to Shakespeare's warblings wild?
>
> (l. 169-70)

Yet generally it appeared that Shakespeare was regarded as a poet only because he wrote in verse. His prosodic technique was in no way appreciated and his imagery was so far discounted that not only were his sonnets, the nearest thing in Shakespeare to pure exercises in imagery, never printed separately, but they were on at least one occasion omitted from an edition of his complete works, with the result that the editor was congratulated for "forbearing to obtrude such crude efforts upon the public eye; for where is the utility of propagating compositions which no-one can endure to read?"[8] Samuel Rogers considered the song in *As You Like It*, "Blow, blow, thou winter wind", as "alone worth them all".[9] What Shakespeare was admired for was not his poetry, as such, but his psychological insight. He was regarded less as a marvellous poet than as a marvellous observer of human behaviour.[10] This attitude survived throughout the nineteenth century; a passage in Lord Holland's description of the assassination of the prime minister Spencer Perceval, in 1812, gives a striking demonstration of this mode of appreciating Shakespeare:

The consternation was great; the appearance of most present ghastly. I remember I wondered to myself whether my face was as much altered as those of the persons around me — a thought which proves (as what indeed does not?) the accuracy and truth of the observation of Shakespeare on our feelings.
>
> Look I so pale, Lord Dorset, as the rest?
>
> is the exclamation of one of his characters, on hearing in a large company of the violent death of the Duke of Clarence.[11]

Thus, in spite of his great popularity, and his influence on some strange by-ways of eighteenth-century literature, Shakespeare was not able to contribute to the main line of poetic development.

Milton attracted, if possible, an even more varied public, and unlike Shakespeare he was an influence on poetic style. His appeal was wider because it was not single but threefold. First, his early lyrics were the chief model for the school of Collins and the Wartons, who admired the imagery and feeling of these shorter poems. There was however some critical resistance to Milton's early work. These poems had been approved by Addison and borrowed from by Pope (in his *Eloisa to Abelard*)[12] but their Augustan successors found them uncongenial. In his Life of Milton, Johnson wrote of *Lycidas*, "whatever images it can supply are long ago exhausted, and its inherent improbability forces dissatisfaction on the mind". Of the sonnets he wrote, "of the best it can only be said, that they are not bad", and he devoted more space to explaining the subject of *L'Allegro* and *Il Penseroso* than he spared for commenting on their poetic quality. Evidently there was some truth in what Thomas Warton later wrote in his Preface to Milton's *Poems upon several Occasions*, published in 1785:

> It was late in the present century, before they attained their just measure of esteem and popularity. Wit and rhyme, sentiment and satire, polished numbers, sparkling couplets, and pointed periods, having so long kept undisturbed possession in our poetry, would not easily give way to fiction and fancy, to picturesque description and romantic imagery.

But Milton was also the author of an accepted classic, *Paradise Lost*. No less than 105 editions of this work were published in the eighteenth century,[13] and its merit was a critical commonplace. Even the somewhat hostile Johnson admitted that the poem, "considered with respect to design, may claim the first place, and with respect to performance the second, among the productions of the human mind".[14] The style of *Paradise Lost* was a major influence on two of the best-selling poets of the period, Thomson and Young.

Thirdly, Milton was regarded as a religious poet. The theological ambiguities of *Paradise Lost* escaped the untutored mind, and the poem was regarded as quasi-ecclesiastical, not profane, and was therefore considered suitable Sunday reading in pious lower middle-class and working-class households. This was most important for Milton's impact on English culture, for in many literate households Sunday was the only day of the week when there was much time for books, so that *Paradise Lost* shared a special place with the Bible, *Pilgrim's Progress* and one or two other religious poems. In the 1780s, Ann Yearsley, the poetical Bristol milk-woman, was "well acquainted" with *Paradise Lost* and *Night Thoughts* (also a quasi-divine poem) but was unaware that Milton and Young had written anything else. She had read some Shakespeare and *Eloisa to Abelard*, and had even seen a translation of the *Georgics*, but she had never even heard of Thomson, Dryden and Spenser.[15] Ann Yearsley may be taken as a good example of how a religious subject matter assisted the circulation of Milton's poetry. The interest of the less educated was in fact so exclusively in the subject matter that there was a market for two different prose translations of *Paradise Lost*. Catering for the same taste were the thirty or more editions of Mary Collyer's execrable prose rendering of Gessner's *The Death of Abel*. Of this work, *The Quarterly Review* was afterwards to write,

> No book of foreign growth has ever become so popular in England as the Death of Abel. Those publishers whose market lies among that portion of the people who are below what is called the public, but form a far more numerous class, include it regularly among their "sacred classics"; it has been repeatedly printed at country presses, with worn types and on coarse paper; and it is found at country fairs, and in the little shops of remote towns almost as certainly as the Pilgrim's Progress and Robinson Crusoe..... Untutored intellects are pleased with its frothy sentiment and its florid language.

And it extended these remarks to cover *Paradise Lost* as well.[16] Yet the enormous circulation of Milton's epic among the lower classes does not seem to have caused it to be less respected by those of superior culture.

After Shakespeare and Milton the most popular poetry of the century was written during the century, and being contemporary, naturally had an even greater impact on literary fashion.

The earliest and perhaps most popular of these epoch-making works was James Thomson's *The Seasons*, the first part of which, "Winter", appeared in 1726, two years before Pope's *Dunciad* and seven before his *Essay on Man*. *The Seasons* deviated from the Pope-Dryden school in both style and subject matter. It was written in blank verse; though the influence of *Paradise Lost* can be seen in the peculiarities of word-order, latinism and compound epithets, the harmony and rhythm of Milton's poem was apparently beyond Thomson's power, so that his verse has a quality of laxness and unhurriedness and depends for its impact not simply on the power of individual words, which seem to have little weight, but on their cumulative effect.[17] In this respect *The Seasons* differs as much from the contemporary works of Pope as it does from *Paradise Lost*. This blandness and want of vigour in the use of language was matched by a lack of specificity in the poem's attempts to evoke rural scenery:

> Gradual sinks the breeze
> Into a perfect calm; that not a breath
> Is heard to quiver through the closing woods,
> Or rustling turn the many twinkling leaves
> Of aspen tall. The uncurling floods, diffus'd
> In glassy breadth, seem through delusive lapse
> Forgetful of their course. 'Tis silence all,
> And pleasing expectation.
> ("Spring", l. 155 foll.)

Although, as mentioned earlier, Thomson was regarded as the unrivalled expert in the detailed representation of nature, he was actually a prime example of that lack of particular vision which, it was argued in my Introduction, was characteristic of his age. "Closing woods", "twinkling leaves" — both these attempts at evocation totally fail to suggest the intended visual image to the reader. Thomson indeed lacked any gift for particular observation. In the Argument to the second part of *The Seasons*, "Summer", he remarked that, "the face of nature in this season is almost uniform" — hardly the opinion of a close student of the countryside. Yet it was natural description which was the theme of Thomson's poem.

Thomson had the good fortune to publish *The Seasons* at a time when various forms of art were being focused on nature and the countryside. The lead in this fashion had been taken by painting. During the previous two or three decades the works of Claude Lorraine and Poussin had been rising in the esteem of English gentlemen of taste, and *The Seasons* may be regarded as an attempt to do in verse what Claude Lorraine and Poussin had previously done in painting. It was Claude and Poussin who established for Thomson and his successors the rules of landscape composition and ordering. It was later pointed out that

> The Greek Poets... did not *describe* the scenery of nature in a picturesque manner, because they were not accustomed to *see* it with a painter's eye. Undoubtedly they were not blind to all the beauties of such scenes, but those beauties were not heightened to them, as they are to us, by comparison with painting — with those models of *improved* and *selected* nature, which it is the business of the landscape-painter to exhibit. They had no THOMSONS, because they had no CLAUDES.[18]

Even before Thomson, no less a poet than Pope had demonstrated the influence of landscape artists in his *Windsor Forest* (1713):

> Here waving Groves a chequer'd Scene display,
> And part admit, and part exclude the Day;
> As some coy Nymph her Lover's warm Address
> Nor quite indulges, nor can quite repress.
> There, interspers'd in Lawns and opening Glades,
> Thin Trees arise that shun each other's Shades.
> Here in full Light the russet Plains extend;
> There wrapt in Clouds the blueish Hills ascend.
> (l. 17 foll.)

One can almost sense Pope pointing out each meticulous feature on a canvas carefully displayed on an easel. Thomson was usually less deliberate, though in a later poem (*The Castle of Indolence*) he paid tribute to the painters to whom he owed so much:

> Sometimes the pencil, in cool airy halls,
> Bade the gay bloom of vernal landskips rise,
> Or Autumn's varied shades imbrown the walls:
> Now the black tempest strikes the astonished eyes;
> Now down the steep the flashing torrent flies;
> The trembling sun now plays o'er ocean blue,
> And now rude mountains frown amid the skies;
> Whate'er Lorrain light-touched with softening hue,
> Or savage Rosa dashed, or learned Poussin drew.
> (Canto 1, stanza 38)

One of Thomson's most important borrowings from Claude and Poussin was the idea of using genre figures to set off the landscape. The neatly dressed rustics disporting themselves in the foreground of Claude's and Poussin's pictures had their counterpart in the heroes and heroines of the brief narrative episodes which occur every now and then in *The Seasons*, such as the story of Damon and Musidora in "Summer". Similar figures had earlier formed the subject of Ambrose Philips's *Pastorals* of 1709 and of Allan Ramsay's stage pastoral *The Gentle Shepherd* (1725) of which twenty-three editions had been published by 1740; later the same types appeared in *The Progress of Love* (1732) by George Lyttelton, afterwards Lord Lyttelton, and in Shenstone's *A Pastoral Ballad* (1755). Wordsworth later (in 1815, in his *Essay Supplementary to the Preface*) claimed of Thomson's poem that the stories were among the places where "any well-used copy of the 'Seasons'... generally opens of itself", and it was argued that "the thunderstorm would not have been half so interesting without the tale of the two lovers; nor the harvest-scene, without that of Palemon and Lavinia; nor the driving snows, without the exquisite picture of a man perishing among them."[19] Just as the genre figures in landscape painting were intended to appeal to the viewer's sympathetic attention, so the human episodes in *The Seasons* had a crucial function in engaging the reader's sense of involvement.

Yet Thomson's use of episodes was not exclusively derived from French landscape painting; he also had a classical source. Thomson was of course influenced in his treatment of the theme of nature by the *Georgics* of Virgil,[20] but extended narrative episodes of the type employed in *The Seasons* were entirely absent in the *Georgics*. Thomson adopted the episode, not from Latin poetry, but from Latin rhetoric. In Latin rhetoric there is a commonplace device called *exemplum* where an example is cited in order to make a point.[21] A particularly good instance of *exemplum* is in Dr Johnson's famous letter to the Earl of Chesterfield in 1755:

> Seven years, my Lord, have now past, since I waited in your outward rooms, or was repulsed from your door; during which time I have been pushing on my work through difficulties, of which it is useless to complain, and have brought it, at last, to the verge of publication, without one act of assistance, one word of encouragement, or one smile of favour. Such treatment I did not expect, for I never had a Patron before.
>
> The Shepherd in Virgil grew at last acquainted with Love, and found him a native of the Rocks.
>
> Is not a Patron, my Lord, one who looks with unconcern on a man struggling for life in the water, and, when he has reached

ground, encumbers him with help? The notice which you have been pleased to take of my labours, had it been early, had been kind etc. etc.

Here, as in *The Seasons*, the *exemplum* is merely a flourish of emphasis, clarifying nothing, though perhaps casting a certain colour over the context.

Thomson was actually much less classically orientated than Johnson, but his exploitation of a device of classical rhetoric was characteristic of his work. Despite its apparent divergence from the neo-classicism of the Pope school of poetry, *The Seasons* was thoroughly neo-classical in spirit. Nature was portrayed as very much part of a man-centred order of things: productive, providing opportunities for recreation, occasionally dangerous but generally exploitable. Even the interest in nature to which Thomson appealed was in keeping with classical tradition, for the vogue of nature stemmed from a fashion of disparaging town life, along lines pointed out seventeen centuries previously by Horace (who was himself influenced by the already long-established Epicurean ideal of retirement from the fretful business of the world). Tired of the town, people dreamt of leading fuller, more civilized lives in rural seclusion. There already existed a considerable body of English poetry on this theme when Thomson began writing.[22] Even so urban a poet as Pope could write (in *Ode on Solitude*):

> Happy the man, whose wish and care
> A few paternal acres bound,
> Content to breathe his native air
>   In his own ground.
>
> Whose herds with milk, whose fields with bread,
> Whose flocks supply him with attire;
> Whose trees in summer yield him shade,
>   In winter fire.

Yet the countryside was appreciated not for itself but for its relationship to man, and especially for its relationship to *urban* man. This was a period in which there was a growing awareness of the extent to which towns, especially London, dominated the political, economic, intellectual and social life of what was still largely a rural society. The corollary of this was a novel self-consciousness about the relative position of town and country, and precisely because it was the town which was the focus of cultural life, this self-consciousness manifested itself in an essentially town-based fascination for the countryside. As indicated by the passage from Pope's *Windsor Forest* quoted above, Thomson was not the first poet to reflect this preoccupation and in the same year as *The Seasons* began to appear there was published another, much shorter, poem by John Dyer entitled *Grongar Hill*, which exhibited exactly the same attitude towards the country. Thomson's importance was not that he was the first to write about nature, but that he was the first to write a *book-length* poem *entirely* devoted to natural description.

The Seasons fell in so perfectly with contemporary taste that it achieved enormous popularity. It was an immense influence on other writers of the day, and was still regarded as a model during the early nineteenth century. It was also remarkable for the catholicity of its appeal. *The Edinburgh Review* said in 1811 that Thomson "has always been popular with a much wider circle of readers than either Pope or Addison",[23] and this wide readership included on the one hand Burns and John Clare, two lower-class poets who were greatly influenced by Thomson's work, and on the other hand university graduates such as Gisborne and Hurdis and the antiquarian Dibdin.[24] William Hazlitt was fond of recounting how Coleridge once found "a little worn-out copy" of *The Seasons* in the parlour of a remote Somersetshire inn and exclaimed, "*That* is true fame!"[25] and at the time of this incident Thomson's works were still being frequently reprinted, as well as being available in any number of editions in second-hand bookstalls up and down the country.

Yet for all *The Seasons*' influence, it was without rival in public esteem only during the first few years of its vogue, and whereas Thomson owed his success to an implicit endorsement of neo-classical values, the school of poets who began to share his ascendancy during the 1740s built their appeal on the exploitation of aspects of life which the Augustan self-image of the day tried to suppress. From the 1740s onwards readers apparently began to desire literature that was increasingly bizarre, melodramatic and emotional. The generally accepted view of the relationship of this taste to the social climate of the times was expressed by Kenneth Clark many years ago:

> When life is fierce and uncertain the imagination craves for classical repose. But as society becomes tranquil, the imagination is starved of action, and the immensely secure society of the eighteenth century indulged in day-dreams of incredible violence.[26]

Alas, "the immensely secure society of the eighteenth century" is a phenomenon unknown to history. It was a society frequently threatened by invasions from abroad and conspiracies at home, a society hardened by public executions (including the occasional burning at the stake of women),[27] the random torture of animals, heavy drinking, highway robbery, destructive riots, and death from disease both endemic and epidemic. These things had existed in the seventeenth and sixteenth centuries, but now they were so to speak thrown into relief by the increased material prosperity of a large part of the population, and the extension of a commercial and industrial system which more and more required internal stability in order to function. It was precisely because life was more fierce and uncertain than the people of the eighteenth century thought proper that they loved the classic repose which has subsequently been thought to typify the age. Because of its very turmoils they constructed out of their own insecurities a self-image of classical order, while at the same time frequently relapsing into the "day-dreams of incredible violence" natural to an uncouth society.

The first notable instance of the revulsion against classical values was the emergence of the "graveyard genre" about fifteen years after the appearance of the first part of *The Seasons*. Of course there had been an enduring tradition of melancholy in English poetry, stretching back through Milton. Thomas Parnell's *A Night-Piece on Death*, one of the most characteristic examples of eighteenth-century melancholy, was written at least as early as the 1710s, and in 1728 Thomson's college friend David Mallet published *The Excursion* which contained a long reflective passage inspired by

> a Place of Tombs,
> Waste, desolate, where *Ruin* dreary dwells,
> Brooding o'er sightless Sculls, and crumbling Bones.
> Ghastful *He* sits, and eyes with stedfast Glare
> The Column grey with Moss, the falling Bust,
> The Time-shook Arch, the monumental Stone,
> Impair'd, effac'd, and hastening into Dust,
> Unfaithful to their Charge of flattering Fame.

But it was only with the Rev. Dr Edward Young's *Night Thoughts* (1742) and the Rev. Robert Blair's *The Grave* (1743) that poetry about death and graveyards achieved really large-scale popularity.

Like *The Seasons*, *Night Thoughts* was written in blank verse loosely modelled on Milton's. This was especially apparent with regard to the use of compound epithets, words borrowed from Latin, and interchangeable parts of speech, though many of the poem's lines had an inappropriate aphoristic neatness, for Young was actually more accustomed to writing couplets, at which he had achieved a mastery little inferior to Pope's; and this perhaps explains the curious jerkiness of his blank verse which prevents its being mistaken for Milton. At the same time the poem was very different from the work of Thomson or any of Young's other contemporaries in its enthusiastic obscurity and its deliberate echoes of seventeenth-century language:

> While o'er my limbs *Sleep*'s soft dominion spread,
> What, tho' my soul phantastic Measures trod,
> O'er Fairy Fields; or mourn'd along the gloom
> Of pathless Woods; or down the craggy Steep
> Hurl'd headlong, swam with pain the mantled Pool;
> Or scal'd the Cliff, or danc'd on hollow Winds,
> With antic Shapes, wild Natives of the Brain?
> (Bk. 1, l. 91 foll.)

"Craggy" and "steep" are words used by both Milton and Shakespeare; "mantled pool" was a borrowing from Shakespeare's *The Tempest*, "antic shapes" was taken from Richard Carpenter's *Experience, Historie, and Divinitie*; even "pathless woods" may be an echo of "wild pathless woods" in William Dampier's *A New Voyage round the World*.[28] These second-hand phrases were employed to evoke a world of violent transition, half-tones and mystery. Rather more original in its vocabulary, though similar in its effect and intention, was *The Grave*, by the Scots minister Robert Blair, which appeared in 1743:

> The sickly Taper
> By glimmering thro' thy low-brow'd misty Vaults,
> (Furr'd round with mouldy Damps, and ropy Slime,)
> Lets fall a supernumerary Horror,
> And only serves to make thy Night more irksome.
> (1743 edn., p. 4)

The appeal of this kind of subject matter was shown by the popular success of the Rev. James Hervey's *Meditations among the Tombs* (1746) which was a sort of prose poem, of which Coleridge later wrote:

> the bloated style and peculiar rhythm ... is poetic only on account of its utter unfitness for prose, and might as appropriately be called prosaic, from its utter unfitness for poetry.[29]

By the end of the century there had been over thirty editions of

Hervey's *Meditations*, as well as a blank-verse paraphrase by Thomas Newcomb. But the most enduring of the graveyard genre was of course Gray's *Elegy written in a Country Churchyard* (1751) which, in spite of its title, seems rather to have been written in a well-stocked library, for it contains borrowings from Young, Blair, Shenstone, Parnell, Thomson, Thomas Warton, Collins and Milton,[30] a circumstance which indicates how self-consciously literary graveyard poetry could be.

Because of their subject matter — death and melancholy reflections on death — these graveyard poems, and Gray's *Elegy* especially, achieved a deceptively personal note. Closer examination shows, however, that they too had the lack of specificity which was so characteristic of Augustan verse. Even Blair's *The Grave*, for all its simplicity and directness, was about a general subject, not one particular grave, but *any* grave: that this is so is made clear from the very beginning, for the poem's epigraph from the Book of Job designates the grave as "The House appointed for all living". The details dwelt on in the poem were all routine, predictable details, of common applicability. Similarly in Hervey's *Meditations among the Tombs* the evocation is generalized:

> A BEAM or two finds its way through the Grates, and reflects a feeble Glimmer from the Nails of the *Coffins*. So many of those sad Spectacles, half concealed in Shades, half seen dimly lit by the baleful Twilight, add a deeper Horror to these gloomy Caverns.
>
> (1746 edn, p. 50.)

Gray's *Elegy* too is only seemingly a description of a single moment of awareness in one particular churchyard. In its earlier forms it was even less concerned with specific personal experience; at least the references to "some village Hampden", Cromwell and Milton locate the referential scheme in England, but in the earlier Eton manuscripts the allusions were to "a Village Cato", "a mute inglorious Tully" and a "Caesar, guiltless of his Country's Blood". At one time Gray may have intended to make the poem more general still; after his death the following lines were alleged to have been written by him as part of the *Elegy*:

> Some rural Lais with all conquering charms,
> Perhaps now moulders in the grassy bourne,
> Some Helen, vain to set the fields in arms,
> Some Emma dead of gentle love forlorn.[31]

This stanza, especially the last line, is far from bearing the unmistakable stamp of Gray's talent; but it really does appear from a rereading of the *Elegy* that there has been some excision (not recorded in any manuscript) between

> Their Lot forbad: nor circumscrib'd alone
> Their growing Virtues, but their Crimes confin'd;
> Forbad to wade through Slaughter to a Throne,
> And shut the Gates of Mercy on Mankind,

and

> The struggling Pangs of conscious Truth to hide,
> To quench the Blushes of ingenuous Shame,
> Or heap the Shrine of Luxury and Pride
> With Incense kindled at the Muse's Flame.

The references to "Pangs", "Blushes", "ingenuous Shame" and "Luxury" in this second stanza seem to refer to women whereas the previous stanza and those preceding it are definitely about masculine activities, and it may well have been the case that Gray originally intended to follow up his survey of male criminality with an equally extended account of female vice, of which the "Some rural Lais" stanza was a part and for which the "struggling pangs of conscious truth" stanza was intended to provide a conclusion. Had he proceeded with any such plan, the *Elegy* would have appeared very much less personal than it is in its surviving form.

Gray was at his most Augustan in his careful work of revising the *Elegy* till it achieved its deceptively individual tone, which has enabled the poem to survive where Blair and Young are largely forgotten. Yet in Gray's own century his popularity was equalled by Blair's and exceeded by Young's. Samuel Rogers recalled of the generation after Young's death, "I knew more than one lady who had a copy of it [*Night Thoughts*] in which particular passages were marked for her by some popular preacher."[32] We have already encountered the milkwoman-poetess of Bristol whose acquaintance with *Night Thoughts* was equalled only by her familiarity with *Paradise Lost*. Wordsworth quoted Young in *Tintern Abbey* — a rare distinction for any but Spenser and Milton in the Wordsworth canon — and a tribute of a different kind was paid by one William White who was hanged in 1795 for shooting a girl who had rejected his love and who quoted extensively from *Night Thoughts* in his final speech from the scaffold.[33]

It is possible to separate four strains in the poetry of the graveyard genre, viz. morbid imagination, melancholy, reflection, and love of melodramatic, mood-fixing surroundings such as Gray's "Ivy-mantled Tow'r" and "those rugged Elms, that Yew-Tree's Shade" and Hervey's *"antient Pile*, reared by Hands, that, Ages ago, were moulderèd into Dust".[34] These graveyard characteristics are to be found even, on occasion, in Pope, as in his *Eloisa to Abelard*:

> These moss-grown domes with spiry turrets crown'd,
> Where awful arches make a noon-day night,
> And the dim windows shed a solemn light;

and

> Black Melancholy sits, and round her throws
> A death-like silence, and a dread repose.
> (ll. 142-4, 165-6.)

But such elements only really became prominent in the 1740s. It was during that decade too that gothic follies first began to be built by country gentlemen with a taste for graveyard *frissons* and for reminders of the past, and especially reminders of the medieval monastic order the despoliation of which two centuries earlier had in many cases laid the foundations of their ancestral wealth.[35] The cult of the gothic past was later to replace graveyard poetry as the main expression of the reaction against rationalism and classicism, but in the 1740s they were merely equal symptoms of cultural restlessness. Not that Augustanism evaporated overnight; one of the popular successes of the 1740s was *The Pleasures of Imagination*, published in 1744 by a twenty-two-year-old Newcastle doctor, Mark Akenside. This long blank-verse poem was a variation on Thomson's *The Seasons*, but with rather more philosophizing and less natural description, and the philosophy, derived from Shaftesbury and Addison, belonged to a generation before Thomson.[36] Yet rather more indicative of the mood of the period was the work of Collins and the brothers Warton, which began to appear from 1744 onward.

To some extent these works were a sub-division of the contemporary graveyard genre. Thomas Warton's *The Pleasures of Melancholy* (1747), for example, could be said to be a graveyard poem with the difference that, instead of inspiring edifying thoughts, the tombs generated an almost necrophiliac ecstasy:

> 'Mid hollow charnel let me watch the flame
> Of taper dim, shedding a livid glare
> O'er the wan heaps; while airy voices talk

> Along the glimm'ring walls; or ghostly shape
> At distance seen, invites with beck'ning hand
> My lonesome steps, thro' the far-winding vaults
>
>   Thus Eloise, whose mind
> Had languish'd to the pangs of melting love,
> More genuine transport found, as on some tomb
> Reclin'd, she watched the tapers of the dead;
> Or thro' the pillar'd iles, amid pale shrines
> Of imag'd saints, and intermingled graves,
> Mus'd a veil'd votaress.

Thomas Warton's elder brother Joseph struck a similar note in parts of his *An Ode to Fancy* (1746):

> Let us with silent footsteps go
> To charnels and the house of woe;
> To Gothic churches, vaults, and tombs,
> Where each sad night some virgin comes,
> With throbbing breast and faded cheek,
> Her promised bridegroom's urn to seek.

But Collins and the Wartons went much further than Young and Blair, and their range was much wider. They took all areas of imagination, fancy and subjective experience as their territory. They wrote odes to Evening, to Superstition, to Solitude, to the Approach of Summer. Joseph Warton's *The Enthusiast, or the Lover of Nature* (written 1740, published 1744) pioneered a far more emotionally-charged and extravagant attitude to nature than was to be found in Thomson:

> Yet let me choose some pine-topt precipice
> Abrupt and shaggy, whence a foamy stream,
> Like Anio, tumbling roars; or some black heath,
> Where straggling stands the mournful juniper,
> Or yew-tree scath'd, while in clear prospect round,
> From the grove's bosom spires emerge, and smoke
> In bluish wreaths ascends, ripe harvests wave,
> Low, lonely cottages, and ruin'd tops
> Of Gothic battlements appear, and streams
> Beneath the sun-beams twinkle.
>   (*The Enthusiast*, 1. 29 foll.)

Yet they showed the classical-mindedness of their age in that they did not proceed without an accepted and respected model. The Wartons even went so far as to attribute some of their own poems to their father, a respectable (and safely deceased) minor poet of the previous generation, and rewrote some of his genuine poems in order to make a precedent for their own practice;[37] but it was above all Milton whom they took as their guide and authority: not, however, the Milton of *Paradise Lost* (though the verse of *The Pleasures of Melancholy* and to a lesser extent that of *The Enthusiast* was influenced by *Paradise Lost*) but rather the Milton of *Il Penseroso* and *L'Allegro*:

> Tell me the path, sweet wand'rer, tell,
> To thy unknown sequester'd cell,
> Where woodbines cluster round the door,
> Where shells and moss o'er lay the floor,
> And on whose top an hawthorn blows,
> Amid whose thickly-woven boughs
> Some nightingale still builds her nest,
> Each evening warbling thee to rest:
> There lay me by the haunted stream,
> Rapt in some wild, poetic dream,
> In converse while methinks I rove
> With Spenser through a fairy grove;
> 'Till suddenly awak'd, I hear
> Strange whisper'd music in my ear,
> And my glad soul in bliss is drown'd
> By the sweetly-soothing sound!
> (J. Warton, *Ode to Fancy*, l. 33 foll.)

Like Milton, their images from nature tended to be general and inclusive rather than referring to some specific unique individual experience: "some pine-topt precipice", "some black heath", "some nightingale". The "foamy stream" was not actually the Anio, merely "Like Anio". They evoked not an unrepeatable moment of awareness but rather a mood which all their readers might experience; their appeal was not to each of their readers' sense of his own uniqueness, but rather to their shared fund of memories and perceptions. By taking Milton as their model, the Wartons merely turned their back on one form of neo-classicism in order to revive another form.

The Wartons took the lead in a whole new fashion of imitating early Milton. According to R. D. Havens, only seventeen poems published between 1700 and 1735 can be regarded as imitations of *L'Allegro* and *Il Penseroso*, or as showing the influence of these two poems. Then between 1736 and 1740 eleven such poems were published, between 1741 and 1745 sixteen, and in 1746 alone sixteen poems imitating or influenced by Milton's octosyllabics.[38] This was only one aspect of a general phase of experimentation in freer prosodic forms, taking Milton as inspiration. Thomas Warton claimed later that "the school of Milton rose in emulation of the school of

Pope".³⁹ Among those who followed in the footsteps of Collins and the Wartons were William Shenstone and Christopher Smart. Both Shenstone's *A Pastoral Ode* and Smart's extraordinary *A Song to David* (1763) used the same stanza form as Collins's *Ode to Pity* and *Ode, to A Lady on the Death of Colonel Ross in the Action of Fontenoy*.

The Wartons backed up the example of their poetry by a systematic critical offensive, inaugurated by Joseph Warton's Advertisement to his *Odes on Various Subjects* (1746). Warton wrote that he

> is in some pain lest certain austere critics should think these too fanciful and descriptive. But he is convinced that the fashion of moralizing in verse has been carried too far. ...

"Moralizing in verse" could apply equally to Pope, to Young, or to Thomson. To rival these accepted Masters, the Wartons had recourse to earlier periods of English poetry. As well as imitating Milton, they referred frequently to Shakespeare and Spenser. Milton and Shakespeare were, so to speak, the common property of all eighteenth-century writers, but Spenser remained a minority taste. Shenstone had published a sentimental poem entitled *The School-Mistress*, professedly "In Imitation Of Spenser" in 1737; in the Advertisement to the revised edition of 1742 he stated:

> What particulars in Spenser were imagined most proper for the Author's imitation on this occasion, are his language, his simplicity, his manner of description, and a peculiar tenderness of sentiment remarkable throughout his works.

The precocious Akenside used Spenserians in his *The Virtuoso*, written in 1737 when he was sixteen. Gilbert West brought out *A Canto of The Fairy Queen. Written by Spenser. Never before Published* in 1739, and a few years later Richard Owen Cambridge began work on his *Archimage; A Poem, Written In Imitation Of Spencer*, which however was not printed till 1803. In 1748 no less a person than James Thomson published a lengthy poem in Spenserians, *The Castle of Indolence*, and *Thales*, supposedly an imitation of Spenser written over forty years previously, was published for the first time in 1751.⁴⁰ Thomas Warton attempted to introduce Spenser to an even wider readership with his *Observations on the Fairy Queen of Spenser* in 1754 but eight years later he was still able to refer to Spenser as an "admired but neglected poet",⁴¹ and there were only three editions of *The Faerie Queene* during the whole of the eighteenth century, one of which took sixteen and another eighteen years to sell out.[42] The poetical works of Thomas Warton and his brother Joseph abounded however in allusions to and echoes of Spenser, and Thomas's *Observations* could be said to have conferred a certain weight and dignity on his and his brother's poetical experiments. Far more important, however, as a literary manifesto was the first volume of Joseph Warton's *An Essay on the Writings and Genius of Pope*, which appeared in 1756.

Warton's *Essay* was respectfully received and was twice reprinted and the twenty-six-year delay before the appearance of the second volume is something of a mystery.[43] The keynote of his argument was that, "The Sublime and the Pathetic are the two chief nerves of all genuine poesy", and he asked "What is there very Sublime or very Pathetic in POPE?"[44] He thought Pope's *Windsor Forest, The Rape of the Lock* and *Eloisa to Abelard* would be remembered by posterity, rather than his satires, "For WIT and SATIRE are transitory and perishable, but NATURE and PASSION are eternal".[45] His selection of *Windsor Forest* and *Eloisa to Abelard* influenced other students of Pope; the second poem, indeed, had many points of similarity to the work of Warton and his younger brother, and the *Essay* may be viewed as an attempt to pull down Pope's main achievement, while recruiting his minor work to the Wartonian cause.

Another aspect of the Wartons' reassessment of the past was their resurrection of the sonnet after nearly eighty years of neglect. Though the real pioneer was one Thomas Edwards, who published thirteen sonnets in the 1748 edition of Dodsley's *Miscellany*, it was Thomas Warton, with Milton as his inspiration, who did most to revive its popularity. The sonnet was the ultimate contrast to the long, discursive blank-verse essays of Thomson, Young and Akenside; melody, conciseness and thematic unity were virtues more required by a poem of fourteen lines than by a philosophic disquisition in three, four or nine books, and if the Wartons could not claim the commercial success of their more long-winded rivals, they could at least point to a much more respectable literary pedigree, stretching back beyond Milton, and also to an increasing number of dilettanti imitators. The loyalty to antique models which was one of the Wartons' proudest boasts was ridiculed by Johnson, in his lines on Thomas Warton's poems, c. 1777:

> Phrase that Time hath flung away,
> Uncouth Words in Disarray:

> Trickt in Antique Ruff and Bonnet,
> Ode and Elegy and Sonnet.

But it became increasingly apparent, after the middle of the century, that the Wartons' interest in the past placed them in the mainstream of cultural fashion.

It was in the 1760s that the vogue of the past really established itself. Macpherson's supposed translation of the ancient Gaelic epic bard Ossian appeared in 1762. Richard Hurd's *Letters on Chivalry and Romance*, which argued that medieval romances ought to be judged by the standards of their own time, appeared in the same year; despite the academic nature of this treatise it went through six editions by 1788. Horace Walpole's fantasy *The Castle of Otranto*, the first gothic horror novel, was published in 1764. Chatterton's brief career of forging medieval verse came in this decade, which also saw Thomas Warton labouring at his massive and never to be completed *History of English Poetry* (the first volume of which appeared in 1774). In 1767 Richard Jago published *Edge-Hill*; superficially this was yet another contemplative descriptive poem of a type which Denham had pioneered with his *Cooper's Hill* as long ago as 1642 and which had been growing in popularity ever since the 1720s, but Jago made an important innovation by introducing long historical disquisitions and battle scenes which started a fashion for poems blending history with natural description:

> Now Death, with hasty Stride, stalks o'er the Field;
> Grimly exulting in the bloody Fray.
> Now on the crested Helm, or burnish'd Shield,
> He stamps new Horrors; now the levell'd Sword
> Tempers with keener Rage; with Iron-Hoof,
> Now tramples on th'expiring Ranks; or gores
> The foaming Steed against th' opposing Spear.
>
> (1767 edn., p. 155.)

Also in 1767 appeared William Mickle's *The Concubine*, which in its fifth edition ten years later was retitled *Sir Martyn, a poem in the manner of Spenser*. Whereas Shenstone's earlier "Imitation of Spenser", *The School-Mistress*, had merely aimed at copying the spirit and rhythms of *The Faerie Queene*, Mickle's pseudo-antiquarianism extended even to imitating the syntax and orthography of the sixteenth century, though his mode of delineating landscape for example was unrepentingly Augustan:

> In yonder dale does wonne a gentle Knight —

> Fleet as he spake still rose the imagerie
> Of all he told depeinten to the sight;
> It was, I weet, a goodlie baronie:
> Beneath a greene-clad hill, right faire to see,
> The castle in the sunny vale ystood;
> All round the east grew many a sheltering tree,
> And on the west a dimpling silver flood
> Ran through the gardins trim, then crept into the wood
> *(The Concubine*, pt. 1, stanza 13)

Perhaps the most significant event of the decade however was the appearance in 1765 of *Reliques of Ancient English Poetry*, edited by the Rev. Thomas Percy, afterwards Bishop of Dromore. Wordsworth was to confess his debt to this ballad anthology fifty years later (in his *Essay Supplementary to the Preface*, 1815);

> I do not think there is an able writer in verse of the present day who would not be proud to acknowledge his obligation to the *Reliques*; I know that it is so with my friends; and, for myself, I am happy in this occasion to make a public avowal of my own.

Southey expressed himself even more forcibly, referring to the publication of the *Reliques* as "the great literary epocha of the present reign, which will prove to English poetry what the discovery of the pandects did to jurisprudence".[46] In fact ballads and ballad imitations had enjoyed some popularity long before Percy; Lady Wardlaw's imitation *Hardyknute* had appeared as long ago as 1719 and David Mallet had had some success with his *William and Margaret*, published in 1724:

> 'Twas at the silent Midnight-Hour
> When All were fast asleep;
> In glided MARGARET'S grimly Ghost,
> And stood at WILLIAM'S Feet.

Possibly, however, the ballad had suffered from being associated with the doggerel or prose narratives published as chapbooks, which were still a major component of the reading of the poorest classes. These narratives (Robin Hood, Guy of Warwick, Valentine and Orson *et cetera*) would have been known to most sophisticated readers, but were regarded as suitable only for children or the more ignorant among the lower classes.[47] What Percy did was to rescue the ballad from being lumped together with chapbook literature, and it was only after the publication of his *Reliques* that the ballad became fully acknowledged as being in the mainstream of the English poetic tradition.

In part this general fascination for the past resulted from both writers and readers projecting on to a romanticized antiquity all the sensationalism and fantasizing which their imaginations craved and which had been denied a proper cultural expression in terms of their own day and age. But it was also crucially linked to the growing awareness that society was undergoing a fundamental social and economic transformation. As society more and more moved away from its past, into a new social and economic era, so it was more and more able to see its past as something separate, distinct and rather remarkable. This novel awareness of how much the past differed from the present had been developed first of all in France by the Philosophes. Though it has been argued that there is a distinctly English tradition of thinking about progress and change, of whom the central figure was Edmund Law,[48] the first widely understood exponents of the idea of history in the English language were in fact four Scottish savants who were chiefly influenced by French thinking: William Robertson, whose *View of the Progress of Society In Europe* appeared in 1769; John Millar, whose *Observations Concerning the Distinction of Ranks in Society* came out in 1711; Gilbert Stuart whose *View of Society in Europe in its Progress from Rudeness to Refinement* was published in 1788, and James Dunbar, whose *Essay on the History of Mankind in Rude and Cultivated Ages* appeared in 1780. Awareness of the process of change inevitably generated a growing interest in what had been lost. From Dyer's *The Ruins of Rome* (1740) onwards, English writers began more and more to celebrate the irrevocable pastness of the past.[49] Edward Gibbon's planning his *Decline and Fall of the Roman Empire* as he sat "musing amidst the ruins of the Capitol, while the bare-footed fryars were singing vespers in the Temple of Jupiter",[50] was typical; perception of the finality and completeness of change was one of the most effective stimuli to the mid-eighteenth-century imagination.

The principal literary manifestation of this interest in the past was the gothic horror novel, which became an established genre in the 1770s. These novels owed much to the poetry of the day. The characteristic settings for example were borrowed from poetry: a comparatively early example of the gothic novel, Clara Reeve's best-seller of 1777, *The Old English Baron* (entitled in its first edition *The Champion of Virtue, a Gothic Story*), was almost classically restrained in its language, whereas both Egerton Brydges's *Mary de Clifford* and Ann Radcliffe's

The Mysteries of Udolpho in the 1790s were lavish of florid verbiage and gothic and rural picturesque settings which owed an evident debt to Thomson and Young:

> the ramparts were silent and solitary. Their lonely appearance, together with the gloom of the lowering sky, assisted the musings of her mind, and threw over it a kind of melancholy tranquillity, such as she often loved to indulge. She turned to observe a fine effect of the sun, as his rays, suddenly streaming from behind a heavy cloud, lighted up the west towers of the castle....[51]

The connection between poetry and the gothic horror novel was also indicated by the deep love of poetry which characterized the gothic horror heroine and hero. Ann Radcliffe's characters quoted Thomson and wrote verse; and in Egerton Brydges's *Mary de Clifford* the juvenile leads almost never ceased composing poetry.

Another consequence of the social changes of the period was the emergence of the cult of sentimentality and the associated cult of benevolence. The intellectual antecedents of these cults can be traced back to the writings of latitudinarian Anglican clergy in the late seventeenth century.[52] In the eighteenth century the Earl of Shaftesbury, Francis Hutcheson (*Inquiry into the Original of our Ideas of Beauty and Virtue*, 1725), David Hume (*An Enquiry Concerning the Principle of Morals*, 1751) and Adam Smith (*Theory of Moral Sentiments*, 1759) had given progressively more explicit intellectual justification to the idea that spontaneous emotional responses to people and circumstances were the best and most genuine guide to conduct and that the promptings of the heart, rather than disciplined and repressed, should be encouraged and indulged.[53] Yet of course it was not the eloquence of Hutcheson, Hume and Adam Smith which established these ideas as generally accepted rules of conduct; rather it was the increasing material prosperity, comfort and security of the middle classes, and their increasing awareness of the grim squalor in which people of other classes and other countries lived, which caused benevolence to be established as a fashionable idea, and it was the increasingly leisured and tranquil lives of middle-class women which encouraged them to seek in excesses of sensibility a substitute for the stimulus of the real problems which their lives lacked. Not that sensibility was an all-female craze; men were expected to indulge their spontaneous griefs and joys as readily as women, and three classics of sentimentalism, Goldsmith's *The Vicar of Wakefield* (1766), Sterne's *The Sentimental*

Journey (1768) and Mackenzie's *The Man of Feeling* (1771) — which Burns described as "a book I prize next to the Bible"[54] — were all by men.

The cult of benevolence and sensibility, and to an extent the contemporary interest in change and the past, contributed to the success of two of the most characteristic poems of the 1770s, Goldsmith's *The Deserted Village* (1770) and James Beattie's *The Minstrel* (1771).

The Deserted Village has been preserved from oblivion by its mellifluence and by the common assumption that it is a typical example of late Augustan verse. Its mellifluence is undeniable, but as for its versification it was not so much typical as a harbinger of reaction. Since the first quarter of the eighteenth century the couplet had been in decline. In Steele's *Poetical Miscellanies* of 1714, eleven-thirteenths of the poems were in couplets; in the first three volumes of Dodsley's *A Collection Of Poems* in 1748, only just over a half were in couplets, and in the last three volumes 1755-8, only a quarter.[55] Poets like Johnson and Churchill who remained faithful to the couplet were exceptions, and largely confined themselves to the writing of verse satires. Goldsmith disliked the new styles of versification, however, and in his dedication to an earlier poem, *The Traveller*, he had written:

> What criticisms have we not heard of late in favour of blank verse, and Pindaric odes, choruses, anapests and iambics, alliterative care and happy negligence! Every absurdity has now a champion to defend it.

The success of *The Deserted Village* was a major factor in the reaction against the innovations, or restorations, which Goldsmith deplored. The poem was also important for its attitude to its subject matter. It applied nostalgia for the past to one of the more notable evils of contemporary society, social change in the countryside, but the manner in which it did so was calculated to reassure rather than to disturb Goldsmith's readers. The peasantry whom Goldsmith described from the smoggy comfort of central London were tame and contented:

> And all the village train, from labour free
> Led up their sports beneath the spreading tree,
> While many a pastime circled in the shade
> The young contending as the old survey'd.
> (l. 17 foll.)

No absentee landlord or mortgage broker needed to worry for

the security of his distant farms, when there was such a village preacher and such a village schoolmaster as Goldsmith portrayed on the spot to uphold the sanctity of the law. The fact that the village was described in the past tense, having been depopulated by an improving proprietor, merely added a touch of pleasing melancholy to the poem. It *has* been argued that *The Deserted Village* was really a passionate indictment of social progress, contrasting the happy and productive life of the village community in former days with the unhappiness and sterility brought about by the new era,[56] but in fact the comfortably nostalgic tone of the poem leads the reader away from genuine hostility to the changes described; the poem is surely less an indictment of contemporary society than an attempt to forestall and disarm criticism of it.

James Beattie's *The Minstrel* was more ambitious and more aspiring. The poem described the education of a young country boy in lonely communion with nature, "from the first dawning of fancy and reason till that period at which he may be supposed capable of appearing in the world as a MINSTREL", as it is put in the Preface. Thus, although weak and over-idealized, *The Minstrel* anticipated Wordsworth's *The Prelude* in its theme of the poet's education; indeed Dorothy Wordsworth was later to write that Beattie's protagonist, Edwin, the minstrel, resembled her brother William when in his late teens.[57] The action was set in "a rude age", that is, the medieval period, but the usual gothic stage properties were mostly lacking. The social aspect was scarcely more stressed than the historical: the reader was told,

> Fret not yourselves, ye silken sons of pride,
> That a poor Wanderer should inspire my strain,

for after all, "poor Edwin was no vulgar boy" (Pt. 1, stanzas 4 and 16). Class, like history, was neglected in favour of philosophizing and natural description. An interesting feature of *The Minstrel* was its prosody. It was written in Spenserians, or rather in a nine-line stanza with Spenser's rhyme scheme but with more end-stopped lines, so that the rhythm was considerably more forced and mechanical than Spenser's fluid gallop, though still considerably less laboured than in Thomson's *The Castle of Indolence*. Byron, who did not read Spenser till after he had written most of his *Childe Harold's Pilgrimage*, copied the stanza of *Childe Harold's Pilgrimage* from Beattie and quoted Beattie's opinion of the stanza in his Preface; and where their mood coincides the resemblance between Beattie and Byron is very striking:

> Let Vanity adorn the marble tomb
> With trophies, rhymes, and scrutcheons of renown,
> In the deep dungeon of some Gothick dome,
> Where night and desolation ever frown.
> Mine be the breezy hill that skirts the down;
> Where a green grassy turf is all I crave,
> With here and there a violet bestrown,
> Fast by a brook, or fountain's murmuring wave;
> And many an evening sun shine sweetly on my grave.
> *(The Minstrel*, Pt. 2, stanza 17)

Equally the resemblance to the egalitarian, death-the-leveller philosophy of graveyard poetry is very evident. Beattie's poem was eventually to inspire more than one real "poor villager": the stocking-weaver poet Robert Millhouse, the shoemaker poets John Struthers and Charles Crocker,[58] and most notably, John Clare whose *The Village Minstrel* published in 1821 was an earthier and less stately attempt at a similar theme, written in the same Spenserian measure.

With Goldsmith and especially Beattie we find ourselves a world away from the preoccupations of the 1720s. The wordy arcadianism of Thomson has been refined and much more controlledly focused; the social values implied or referred to may not be substantially different but there are resonances of experiences and preoccupations — the themes of melancholy and youthful aspiration, the antiquarianism, the sentimentalism, the striving towards the frontiers of the individual psyche — which are quite foreign to the 1720s. By the 1770s in fact poetry was considerably closer to the moral world of what was subsequently labelled Romanticism. The years 1720 to 1770 may not have been years of literary triumph, but they had certainly been years of literary change.

2
The 1780s

> Whatever relation ... of cause and impulse Percy's collection of Ballads may bear to the most *popular* poems of the present day; yet in a more sustained and elevated style, of the then living poets, Bowles and Cowper were, to the best of my knowledge, the first who combined natural thoughts with natural diction; the first who reconciled the heart with the head.
>
> (Coleridge, *Biographia Literaria* (2 vols., 1817), vol. 1, pp. 24-5; Everyman edition (1956) p. 13)

The decade during which Wordsworth, Southey and Coleridge were in their teens saw the publication of no dramatic poetic manifesto, saw no revolution in taste, no concerted reaction against the productions of the previous seventy years. Six new poets made their public reputation in this decade, of whom Cowper and Burns have achieved a permanent place in the huge pantheon of memorable minor poets; Hayley, Pratt, Merry and Bowles, their contemporaries, wrote works which are now dead beyond revival. Yet it was during the 1780s, and especially through the medium of the work of these six poets that the limits of the literary controversies of the next thirty years were marked out.

The two most notable poems of the early years of the decade were *Sympathy*, a didactic poem by Samuel Jackson Pratt and *The Triumphs of Temper*, an allegory by William Hayley (who is better known to posterity as the patron of Blake and as the first biographer of Cowper). *Sympathy* went through six editions in 1781 and 1782, and five more in the next twenty-five years; *The Triumphs of Temper*, though it sold less well at first, nevertheless reached an eleventh edition by 1801. *Sympathy* was perhaps the most widely-read *poetical* treatment of the theme of universal benevolence discussed in the last chapter; though it contained passages of sentimental rhapsodizing —

> Hail, lovely griefs, in tender mercy giv'n!

> And hail, ye tears, like dew-drops fresh from heav'n!
> Hail, balmy breath of unaffected sighs,
> More sweet than airs that breathe from eastern skies!

for the most part it was a laboured exposition of the doctrines of mutual dependence:

> This then is clear, while human kind exist,
> The social principle must still subsist,
> In strict dependency of one on all,
> As run the binding links from great to small.

A similar banality of thought and language was evident in Hayley:

> The Mind's soft Guardian, tho' as yet unsung,
> Inspires with harmony the female tongue,
> And gives, improving every tender grace,
> The smile of angels to a mortal face;
> Her powers I sing; and scenes of mental strife,
> Which form the maiden for th' accomplished wife;
> Where the sweet victress sees, with sparkling eyes,
> Love her reward, and Happiness her prize.
> Daughters of Beauty, who the song inspire,
> To your enchanting notes attune my lyre!
>   (*The Triumphs of Temper*, l. 1 foll.)

These two poems were of some historical importance, for two reasons. First they demonstrated and confirmed *The Deserted Village*'s success in reviving the heroic couplet. And secondly they embodied and served to propagate a particular view of poetry. These two points require some brief discussion.

After the 1720s longer poems (with the exception of verse satires) tended to be written in blank verse: *The Seasons, The Grave, Night Thoughts, The Pleasures of Imagination*, even Richard Glover's epic *Leonidas*. In the final quarter of the century however the couplet returned to favour. *The Triumphs Of Temper, Sympathy*, Crabbe's *The Village*, Rogers's *The Pleasures of Memory,* Darwin's *The Botanical Garden,* Campbell's *The Pleasures of Hope*, even Wordsworth's early *An Evening Walk* and *Descriptive Sketches,* all employed the couplet. Cowper's *The Task* and the poems inspired by it were as exceptional for their use of blank verse in the 1780s and 1790s as they would have been if written in rhyme thirty years earlier, and such blank verse poems as were published often had prefaces making reference to the fact that blank verse was no longer popular. "It is become a fashion to think that poetry, and blank verse, are inconsistent," complained William Hayward Roberts, as early as 1774.[1] "I was ... well aware, that by choosing to write in blank verse, I should not court popularity, because I perceived it was growing much out of vogue", wrote William Mason in 1781.[2] Counter-attacks, such as Cowper's claim in 1782 that Pope

> Made poetry a mere mechanic art;
> And ev'ry warbler had his tune by heart
> *(Table Talk*, ll. 656-7)

were rare, though they foreshadowed the most frequent criticism of couplet verse in the 1800s.

The revival of the couplet was partly a matter of simple reaction. Poetasters had become dissatisfied with the huge, cumbersome verse paragraphs, formless thoughts and flaccid emphasis of the Thomson school; once blank verse had established itself as the norm for longer poems, alert writers were bound to become sensitive to the rival possibilities of other prosodic forms. But more important was the fact that the heroic couplet had distinct advantages over blank verse, especially for versifiers deficient in poetic and intellectual power. The rhyme could make up for the absence of thought and rhythm, and even though, in the hands of any but the most masterly rhymer, its employment enforced an attenuation and limitation of the free flow of ideas, this disadvantage was compensated for by the way its jinglingly musical sound caused the reader to pay more attention to the rhymes than to the actual meaning of the words. The difficulty of saying anything was made up for by it being unnecessary to say as much as in blank verse; consequently it was an ideal form for poets who had little to say.

Richard Payne Knight's *The Progress of Civil Society*, which was not published till 1796 but which was sufficiently typical of the couplet revival, contained an explanation of the advantages which versifiers found in the heroic couplets:

> Oft too, the rhyme, with neat and pointed grace,
> Fixes attention to the proper place;
> Directs with truer aim the shafts of wit,
> And marks, with emphasis, the spot to hit,
> Bids it to sentiment its edge impart,
> And guides the gleams of fancy to the heart.
> (Bk 3, l. 525 foll.)

In a footnote to these lines, Knight quoted the dictum of Samuel Johnson that in blank verse, "language suffered more distortion to keep it out of prose, than any inconvenience or limitation to be apprehended from the shackles and circumspection of rhyme". This comment, published in Boswell's biography of Johnson in 1791,[3] was probably familiar to Johnson's circle of acquaintances at an earlier date. Johnson himself had written two lengthy rhyming couplet poems during the first half of his life, *London* (1738) and *The Vanity of Human Wishes* (1749) and he was at pains to demonstrate his dislike of blank verse in his *Lives of the English Poets* (1779-81). In his Life of Milton, blank verse was criticized as tiresome; in his Life of Akenside it was said to be diffuse; of Shenstone's *Love and Honour* he wrote: "I wish it well enough to wish it were in rhyme." Johnson obviously had much influence on contemporary opinion, and in this instance the impact of his views was greatly reinforced by the example of his friend Goldsmith, whose achievement in *The Traveller* and *The Deserted Village* gave an irresistible recommendation to the couplet. Indeed it was surely the example of Goldsmith rather than the *obiter dicta* of Johnson which ensured that the general conditions favouring the revival of the heroic couplet would take effect, and it was the tone of Goldsmith rather than of Pope or Dryden or even of Johnson which predominated during the revival.

The main difference between the couplet of the earlier part of the century and the couplet of Goldsmith was that the latter lacked the trenchancy and tension of the former. It has been argued that the establishment in mid-century of the view that human nature was on the whole good, by replacing the previously accepted view that people were naturally bad, selfish, and vicious — the view which had provided the basis for Augustan satire — did away with the occasion for the cruel mordancy and pessimistic suspiciousness of Augustan couplet verse.[4] Certainly it is true that Goldsmith's couplet was not a vehicle of criticism, as Pope's had been. The second line of Goldsmith's couplets embodied not a stinging antithesis or a bitter emphasis as is so frequently the case in Pope, but merely a reassurance; the tautness of invective had given way to a bland discursiveness. Yet in fact Goldsmith's contemporaries wrote as much satire as the earlier generation had done; and on the whole their satire had the same relaxed tone as Goldsmith's arcadian descriptions, as for example in this description of the prime minister William Pitt viewing his back-bench supporters:

> Mild and more mild he sees each placid row
> Of Country Gentlemen with rapture glow;
> He sees convuls'd with sympathetic throbs,

> Apprentice Peers and deputy Nabobs!
> Nor Rum Contractors think his speech too long,
> While words, like treacle, trickle from his Tongue!
> (Joseph Richardson, French Laurence et al. *The Rolliad*,
> 1. 364 foll.)

I mentioned earlier that *Sympathy* and *The Triumphs of Temper* were also important as embodying and propagating a certain concept of poetry. What this concept was may be demonstrated by an excerpt from Hayley's Preface to *The Triumphs of Temper*:

> It seems to be a kind of duty incumbent on those who devote themselves to Poetry, to raise, if possible, the dignity of a declining Art, by making it as beneficial to Life and Manners as the limits of Composition, and the character of modern Times will allow... a Poem, intended to promote the cultivation of good-humour, may still, perhaps, be fortunate enough to prove of some little service to society in general; or, if this idea may be thought too chimerical and romantic by sober Reason, it is at least one of those pleasing and innocent delusions, in which a poetical Enthusisat may be safely indulged.

His reference to "a declining Art", his coy description of himself as "a poetical Enthusiast", and his pretence of fearing that his excessively modest objectives "may be thought too chimerical and romantic by sober Reason", hardly suggest a man driven by inner forces to set his vision of reality down on paper. In fact he seems to have regarded poetry as merely a prettier, though perhaps more trivial, form of prose, particularly distinguished by being in verse. Some people may choose to consider this view as merely the extreme form of tendencies inherent in all eighteenth-century poetry; and indeed the popularity of Hayley and Pratt in the 1780s does suggest that their idea of poetry was readily accepted.

A similar tentative and uncommitted view of poetry was perhaps evident in the opening passages of another of the most popular longer poems of the decade, William Cowper's *The Task* (1785):

> I sing the SOFA. I who lately sang
> Truth, Hope, and Charity, and touch'd with awe
> The solemn chords, and with a trembling hand,
> Escap'd with pain from that advent'rous flight,
> Now seek repose upon an humbler theme;

In fact, however, this was a poem of a quite different calibre from *Sympathy* and *The Triumphs of Temper*. As well as being a much more serious work, it was much more original: more than any other poem it may be regarded as standing at the crossroads between post-Augustanism and Romanticism. Cowper was not only a direct influence on Wordsworth and Coleridge during their youth, he was also one of the creators of the standards used in judging poetry during their most creative period. At the same time he was to some extent in the tradition of Thomson, and Thomas Campbell for one was fond of speaking of Thomson and Cowper in the same breath.[5] Yet though both *The Task* and *The Seasons* were blank verse poems about nature, they differed in their diction and in their attitude to their subject matter. With regard to diction, Cowper avoided the over-ornate Miltonic style of Thomson, and came to be regarded as the pioneer of natural diction (see page 87). He drew prose and poetry together not, as did Hayley and Pratt, by versifying essentially prosaic ideas about supposedly poetic subjects, but by finding poetry in straightforward language and commonplace situations. But the transitional nature of his work comes out most strongly in his attitude to his subject matter. John Wilson, a poet and critic of the next generation, pinpointed Cowper's advance on earlier descriptive verse when he wrote,

> Cowper paints trees — Thomson woods. Thomson paints, in a few wondrous lines, rivers from source to sea, like the mighty Burrampooter*— Cowper, in many no very wondrous lines, brightens up one bend of a stream, or awakens our fancy to the murmur of some single waterfall.[6]

Cowper was the first poet of his age to revel in specific details, single particular moments in single particular places. Yet this specific vision was quite different from that of, say, Wordsworth a generation later. Whereas Wordsworth could be said to participate imaginatively in an experience, employing all his five senses and something more besides, Cowper's participation, despite his acknowledgement that "There is in souls a sympathy with sounds" (*The Task*, Bk. 6, l. 1), was almost always confined to the visual:

> admiration, feeding at the eye,
> And still unsated, dwelt upon the scene.
> .... with what pleasure have we just discern'd
> The distant plough slow moving, and beside
> His lab'ring team, that swerv'd not from the track,

---

* Burrampooter was the then customary spelling of Brahmaputra.

> The sturdy swain diminish'd to a boy!
> Here Ouse, slow winding through the level plain
> Of spacious meads with cattle sprinkled o'er,
> Conducts the eye along the sinuous course
> Delighted.
>
> (*The Task*, Bk 1, ll. 157 foll.)

The straightness and speed of the plough's course, the foreshortening of the ploughman's figure, the winding of the river, the openness of the plain and the spacing of the cattle dotted over it have all been exactly gauged, and marked down for ever, as if on a photograph. It is all intensely visual. Cowper is to an extent always a part of what he describes, in a way earlier poets were not; Thomson may have passed among natural scenes, but he had afterwards retreated to a distance, to select and edit what he intended to describe, whereas Cowper was always very much on the spot, but only as a person *seeing*, not in any other sense experiencing what he observed. When Cowper turned from description to moralizing — and moralizing was an important ingredient of *The Task* — his pronouncements were as detached and generalized as those of any earlier Augustan poet. Even in his shorter poem *The Cast-Away*, which is often regarded as his most deeply personal work, Cowper demonstrated his inability to escape from the general except through the medium of visual description; it is not the individual, but the community of experience which is stressed:

> I therefore purpose not, or dream,
>   Descanting on his fate,
> To give the melancholy theme
>   A more enduring date
> But misery still delights to trace
>   Its semblance in another's case.

And in places he achieved a distanced, lapidary tone worthy of Gray:

> No poet wept him: but the page
>   Of narrative sincere,
> That tells his name, his worth, his age,
>   Is wet with Anson's tear:
> And tears by bards or heroes shed
>   Alike immortalize the dead.

In *The Cast-Away* Cowper compares himself to a seaman washed overboard and left to drown alone, but it does not seem that he had any one particular seaman in mind, or any single incident;

the reference quoted above to Commodore Anson, leader of the epic voyage round the Horn in 1741 during which a number of seamen were drowned (not just one), is the only specific detail in the poem, and in the opening stanza the seaman is merely characterized as "such a destined wretch as I". The poem is not a parallel between the actual experience of one particular seaman, and the actual experience of William Cowper, it is merely an extended general simile.

Cowper's work was well received by the public and it was inevitable that *The Task* should inspire some imitators. The Rev. William Crowe, an eccentric country parson and Public Orator of the University of Oxford (whither he used to walk periodically from his parish in Wiltshire), published his *Lewesdon Hill* in 1788. "Hill poems" had been appearing in a steady flow during the 1780s, mostly at the level of "Hail verdant LANSDOWNE! health restoring hill!" or "Hail honour'd Mount! inspirer of my lays."[7] Crowe avoided the clichés and in places evoked a stark sombreness in his descriptions that looked forward to Wordsworth rather than back to Cowper:

> Up to thy summit, LEWESDON, to the brow
> Of yon proud rising, where the lonely thorn
> Bends from the rude South-east, with top cut sheer
> By his keen breath, along the narrow track,
> Up which the scanty-pastured sheep ascend
> Up to the furze-clad summit, let me climb
>
> (*Lewesdon Hill*, ll. 1 foll.)

But the Rev. James Hurdis's *The Village Curate*, also published in 1788, was more reminiscent of Thomson in its vocabulary and conception despite the attempt to copy Cowper's attention to specific scenes:

> Beyond the Brook
> Where the high coppice intercepts it not,
> Or social elms, or with his ample waist
> The venerable oak, up the steep side
> Of yon aspiring hill full opposite,
> Luxuriant pasture spreads before his eye
> Eternal verdure; save that here and there
> A spot of deeper green shows where the swain
> Expects a nobler harvest, or high poles
> Mark the retreat of the scarce-budded hop,
> To be hereafter eminently fair,
> And hide the naked staff that train'd him up
> With golden flow'rs
>
> (1788 edn., pp. 3-4)

and other passages were merely Pratt dressed as Cowper:

> I love to see
> How hardly some their frugal morsel earn;
> It gives my own a zest, and serves to damp
> The longing appetite of discontent.
>
> (p. 77)

Complementary to the Cowperesque rediscovery of the countryside was the work of Burns whose dialect poems appeared in 1786 and were printed in London, Belfast, Dublin, New York and Philadelphia, as well as in Scotland. Burns was himself an unsuccessful tenant farmer and his literary fame contributed to the public's taking a closer interest in the real lives of countryfolk. Burns's best poetry, though dealing with the type of people he lived among, owed much to an earlier Scots dialect tradition: *The Cotter's Saturday Night* and *Hallowe'en* were inspired by Robert Fergusson's *The Farmer's Ingle* and *Hallow Fair*, and despite his lack of formal education, Burns was fully conscious of his relationship to an earlier literary tradition, as is shown by some of his poems such as his *Address to the Shade of Thomson* and by his letters; but for his contemporaries he seemed an example of almost miraculous gifts manifesting themselves without any of the fostering help of birth or position, and after Burns it was never really possible for readers to see ignorant peasants in quite the idealized and unnatural light in which Thomson had portrayed them.

Differing no less than Cowper and Burns from the Hayley-Pratt school, though very unlike the unaffected directness of either, was the Della Cruscan group. In 1785 a coterie of expatriate English in Florence published some poems in a volume entitled *The Florence Miscellany*. Their doyen, Robert Merry, shortly afterwards returned to England and began publishing verse — mainly love lyrics — in a periodical called *The World*, run by a Major Edward Topham and an eccentric priest named Charles Este. *The World* specialized in accounts of "elopements, divorces and suicides tricked out in all the elegancies of Mr Topham's phraseology"[8] and it also published the correspondence of two of the leading prize fighters of the day, Humphries and Mendoza; but despite this unpromising vehicle for publicity, the poetry of Merry and his friends gained considerable attention. In 1788 some of their verses were published in volume form as *The Poetry of "The World"* and this collection was reprinted five times in the next four years under the title of *The British Album*. Merry had adopted the pseudonym *Della Crusca* in 1788[9] and the name was used to identify the whole group of which he was leader.

The chief characteristics of Della Cruscan verse were its imprecise and excessive use of emotive words and its exaggerated sensibility. Arguably these are also characteristic of much nineteenth-century verse, but they are rare in eighteenth-century poetry. Eighteenth-century sentimentality made use of stereotyped catchphrases which often conveyed an impression of deadness but sometimes led to a moderation of expression that in itself carried conviction, as in Gray's *Elegy*. It was with the Della Cruscans that the fashion of emotional hyperbole set in. Yet, for all the Italian influence evident in their work,[10] the Della Cruscans had a respectable English pedigree. Their work was a development — almost a travesty — of the Warton-Collins school. Like Collins and the Wartons, they went back to the early Milton, but produced strange echoes:

> Phillis shall jocund beat the ground
> Her locks with ivy chaplets bound.[11]

Indeed the early eighteenth-century poem closest to the Della Cruscan style was Thomas Warton's *The Pleasures of Melancholy*, though as copies of this were fairly rare, it is possible that the Della Cruscans never saw it.

Very often, Merry and his friends seemed to be desperately trying to play around with clichés, frantically trying to reform and recoin them, in order to squeeze out of them the last drop of spurious emotion. Thus, in *The Interview*, Merry despairingly exulted over his true love's husband:

> He never bathed him in the night-shade's dew,
> Nor drank the pois'nous meteors as they flew,
> Nor told the rending story to the moon,
> Link'd with the demons of her direst noon;
> He never smiled Distraction's ills to share,
> Nor gained the exalted glory of despair.

Even in his more reflective moods, Merry's abuse of epithets was perverse, thus, in *The Wreath of Liberty*:

> Summer tints begemmed the scene,
> And silky ocean slept in glossy green,
> And gauzy zephyrs, flutt'ring o'er the plain,
> On twilight's bosom drop their filmy rain.

It is difficult to tell whether it is noon or evening, whether the sun is shining or whether it is raining, whether the scene is inland, or on the high seas. The same primacy of sound and "feel" over literal sense was found in the work of "Sylvester Otway",* but with an even more extreme use of alliteration:

> Now sad reverse! I glide no gladsome rill,
>   But wind thro' wild'ring waste my weary way —
> Thro' wild'ring waste, th' abode of Winter Chill,
>   And Night, griefs-brooding Night! with gloomy wing alway.
>
> And O! the sad, sad silence of my bank!
>   Unbroke, save by the wasted wail of woe
> Weak wand'ring down the weeping willows dank,
>   That drooping drink the bitter brook below.
>
> *(Poems* (1789), p. 27.)

These ill-conceived attempts to introduce the diction of frenzy and passion into poetry inspired William Gifford, a nobleman's tutor, former shoemaker and future review editor, to attack the Della Cruscans in a bad-tempered and unamusing satire, *The Baviad* in 1792. That *The British Album* was not reprinted after 1792 was however only partly due to Gifford's abuse; six editions had certainly exhausted the demand for the Della Cruscan's rather feeble verse. And though, as a result of Gifford's strictures, the term Della Cruscan passed into critical vocabulary during the next twenty years as a term of condemnation (just as "namby-pamby" had done earlier in the century as a result of Henry Carey's *Namby-Pamby* which had parodied Ambrose Philips's verses to children) nevertheless the Della Cruscan influence survived. Some of Coleridge's earlier poems such as *The Rose* were Della Cruscan:

> As late each flower that sweetest blows
> I pluck'd, the Garden's pride!
> Within the petals of a Rose
> A sleeping Love I spied.
>
> Around his brows a beamy wreath
> Of many a lucent hue;
> All purple glow'd his cheek, beneath,
> Inebriate with dew.
>
> I softly seiz'd the unguarded Power,
> Nor scared his balmy rest:

---

* "Sylvester Otway's" real name was John Oswald. He was a Hindu and a vegetarian; later he was a supporter of the French Revolution and commanded a battalion of the French Republican army in the campaign against the Vendéans in 1793. He was killed by a cannon ball at the head of his troops in the Battle of Ponts-de-Cée; it is alleged that his two young sons, both drummer boys in his regiment, were killed at the same instant by grape-shot.

> And placed him, caged within the flower,
> On spotless Sara's breast.

Southey was sufficiently impressed by the style to parody it in *The Love Elegies of Abel Shufflebottom*; Montgomery was an unconfessed disciple; Leigh Hunt, though he grew up in the post-Gifford era, was also influenced, and through him, Keats; and Shelley was at least accused of adopting their manner.[12]

The emotional extravagances of the Della Cruscans were not unique in the 1780s; another instance of the same revulsion against calm and rationality was the vogue of German Romanticism. The earliest examples of German Romanticism to be translated into English, Gessner's *Death of Abel* and Klopstock's *Messiah*, appealed mainly to unsophisticated, religiously orientated readers, but in 1779 Goethe's *Die Leiden des jungen Werthers* appeared in English as *The Sorrows of Werter*. This work had a profound effect on young people's ideas about love and self-sacrifice. There were fourteen editions of *Werter* by 1815, but this probably gives an insufficient idea of the book's popularity in adolescent, sentimental circles. Various poetasters were inspired to write odes to Werter and so forth, which were published in daily papers. (Two odes to Werter were among the very small quantity of supposedly serious verse published by *The Daily Universal Register*, forerunner of *The Times*, in 1785.) Edward Taylor's poem *Werter to Charlotte* appeared in 1784, and *The Sorrows of Werter*, rendered into verse by Amolia Pickering, came out in 1788. Frederick Reynolds, then at the very beginning of his career as a writer of sentimental drama, turned the novel into a play in 1785: his script was turned down by three London theatres, but after successful runs in Bath and Bristol it was put on at Covent Garden and was a smash hit. (During the opening night at Bristol the youthful and overwrought playwright sat next to a gentlemen who, during the course of the performance, observed his agitation and said sympathetically, "Wretched sad stuff, Sir; and if you will begin to hiss I will join you with all my heart and soul.")

But the violent emotionalism of the young Goethe and his adaptors, and of the Della Cruscans, was not the only mode of self-expression to be favoured by younger readers. In 1789 William Lisle Bowles's *Fourteen Sonnets* appeared. Though his was not the most widely read collection of sonnets of the period — Charlotte Smith's *Elegaic Sonnets and Other Essays* had gone through four editions 1784-6 and remained marginally more popular — Bowles's particular brand of nostalgia and his technical proficiency established him as an important influence on the rising generation. Wordsworth, for example, was much struck, as he later recalled:

> When Bowles's Sonnets first appeared — a thin 4to pamphlet, entitled *Fourteen Sonnets,* — I bought them in a walk through London with my dear brother, who was afterwards drowned at sea. I read them as we went along; and to the great annoyance of my brother, I stopped in a niche of London Bridge to finish the pamphlet.[13]

On the publication of the third edition of the sonnets, Southey and his friend Robert Lovell called on Bowles's printer at Bath and, as Bowles later recalled, "spoke in high commendation of my volume, and... expressed a desire to have some poems printed in the same type and form".[14] Coleridge too was attracted by Bowles's poetry, and wrote a sonnet to him, "My heart has thank'd thee, Bowles! for those soft strains". Gilfillan, with his belief that the Wordsworth-Southey-Coleridge generation represented a dramatic break with the poetical school of the previous decades, attempted to set up Bowles as the earliest of the Romantic poets, the herald of the Romantic revolution. But if one rejects the notion of a dramatic break in the year 1798 in favour of the concept of gradually accelerating transition, Bowles shrinks to his true stature. His work made only a small advance on earlier poetry such as Thomas Warton's sonnet *To the River Lodon* (1777), and his importance was that he appeared at just the right time to focus attention on the potentialities of the sentimental, simply-expressed short poem:

> Itchen! when I behold thy banks again,
> Thy crumbling margin and thy silver breast,
> On which the selfsame tints still seem to rest,
> Why feels my heart a shivering sense of pain!
> Is it, that many a summer's day has past
> Since, in life's morn, I carolled on thy side!
> Is it, that oft since then my heart has sighed,
> As Youth and Hope's delusive gleams flew fast!
> Is it, that those who gathered on thy shore,
> Companions of my youth, now meet no more!
> Whate'er the cause, upon thy banks I bend,
> Sorrowing, yet feel such solace in my heart,
> As at the meeting of some long-lost friend,
> From whom in happier hours, we wept to part.

This banal nostalgia came as a breath of fresh air in a poetical climate dominated by the prose-minded verse of Hayley and Pratt and the unintelligible ravings of Della Crusca. Bowles's poems fitted in with the contemporary interest in the countryside, but they added an additional ingredient of personal melancholy and of emotional interaction with nature. Coleridge later wrote that in Bowles's best sonnets, "moral Sentiments, Affections, or Feelings, are deduced from, and associated with, the scenery of Nature".[15] Though he lacked the visual immediacy of Cowper, the sense he conveyed of personal involvement with nature was at least as vivid, for by projecting inner feelings on to external objects, he came nearer than Cowper to succeeding in converting rural scenes into a kind of vocabulary to express the language of the soul.

Bowles and Cowper were to be a major influence on Wordsworth and Coleridge during the following decade, but there was also to be a School of Merry, and a School of Hayley and Pratt flourishing during the 1790s and 1800s and much of the controversy of those years was to involve the principles embodied in their poetry. By the turn of the decade, the literary battleground had already been marked out, even though it was to be nearly another ten years before the real protagonists came forward.

3
The Age of Lyrical Ballads

> Truly, if a Thomas Campbell arose in our present era, and tried to make his way uphill as a Glasgow student with his "Pleasures of Hope" or "Gertrude of Wyoming", it is very doubtful whether our own age would allow him any encouragement. But thirty-five years ago the phasis of literary affairs was excessively different.
>
> (R. P. Gillies, *Memoirs of a Literary Veteran* (3 vols., 1851), vol. 3, p. 183)

By and large the 1790s, for all their reputation as a cultural turning point, merely saw the carrying forward of literary traditions already established during previous decades. These years saw, for example, the confirmation in popular taste of Burns and Cowper, especially the latter. Burns, who had now become on excise officer, published some new poems in 1793, three years before he died aged only thirty-seven; Cowper died in 1800; but even before their deaths their work was regarded as classic. Moreover at least one imitation of Cowper became a best-seller: the Rev. Thomas Gisborne's *Walks in the Forest*, which went through nine editions between 1794 and 1814. The two most important new poets of the early 1790s were not however in the Cowper tradition, but looked back to even earlier models.

Erasmus Darwin's *The Botanical Garden* came out in 1791 and was quickly reprinted twice. Darwin was a physician who composed his rhymes in his coach while travelling between patients, but he was also a scientist and *The Botanical Garden* gained notice as much because it was a scientific treatise as because it was an original poem. There was a considerable tradition in the eighteenth century of didactic poetry of this sort, though the notion of writing a biology text-book in rhyme struck some of Darwin's readers as laughable, hence *The Anti-Jacobin Review*'s parody *The Loves of the Triangles*:

> Let playful Pendules quick vibration feel;
> While silent Cyclois rests upon her wheel;
> Let Hydrostatics, simpering as they go,
> Lead the light naiads in fantastic toe.
> (Bk. 1, l. 13 foll.)

which is perhaps less ridiculous than the original:

> Sweet blooms GENISTA in the myrtle shade,
> And *ten* fond brothers woo the haughty maid.
> *Two* knights before thy fragrant altars bend,
> Adored MELISSA! and *two* squires attend. . . .
> (*The Botanical Garden*, Part 2, canto 1, l. 57 foll.)

Nevertheless, Darwin had an imitator, Frances Arabella Rowden, whose *A Poetical Introduction to the Study of Botany* came out in 1801.

Darwin's chief advance on earlier didactic poetry was his conscious exploitation of *recherché* terms and scientific names for the sonorous effect — a technique used earlier, and much more successfully of course, by Milton in passages of *Paradise Lost*. The influence of Milton may also be traced in Darwin's syntax, through the disguise of rhyming couplets:

> The dread Gymnotus with ethereal fire —
> Onward his course with waving tail he helms,
> And mimic lightings scare the watery realms.
> So, when with bustling plumes the Bird of JOVE
> Vindictive leaves the argent fields above,
> Borne on broad wings the guilty world he awes,
> And grasps the lightning in his shining claws.
> (*The Botanical Garden*, Part 1, canto 1, l. 202 foll.)

Darwin's style certainly contributed to the progressive movement away from Augustan simplicity and directness and he was frequently criticized for his obscurity; Byron for example later called him "That mighty master of unmeaning rhyme"[1] and Thomas James Mathias, who achieved some celebrity at this period with *The Pursuits of Literature*, a poem consisting almost entirely of footnotes, complained of his "pettinesses, glittering words, points, conceits and forced thoughts".[2] For a time however, Darwin was taken as a model by some poetasters, and even Coleridge imitated him, in passages of his *The Destiny of Nations*.[3]

Even more influential was *The Pleasures of Memory* which came out in 1792. Its author, Samuel Rogers, a dissenting banker from Stoke Newington who was trying desperately to establish himself as a cultured litterateur, had been born in

1764. His first published work was an *Ode to Superstition*, modelled on Collins and Joseph Warton, which sold twenty copies in four years.[4]

> Hence to the realms of Night, dire Demon, hence!
> Thy chain of adamant can bind
> That little world, the human mind,
> And sink its noblest powers to impotence.

The Pleasures of Memory, which took nine years to perfect[5] made up for this earlier failure by being "instantly popular, especially among the ladies"[6] and selling six editions 1792-4 and thirteen more 1795-1815. The title was obviously suggested by Akenside's *The Pleasures of Imagination* or by Thomas Warton's *The Pleasures of Melancholy*, but whereas these two poems were in blank verse Rogers used heroic couplets reminiscent of Goldsmith's, and indeed he was proud to be spoken of as "a child of Goldsmith".[7] But *The Pleasures of Memory* made an important advance on Goldsmith's *The Deserted Village* in that the description of change and decay in a locality was made a mode of illuminating change and loss in oneself. Rogers's ostensible personal involvement in the scenes he described may thus be seen as foreshadowing Wordsworth, but the comparison between Rogers and Wordsworth cannot be taken too far. There were one or two striking ideas in *The Pleasures of Memory*, for example.

> What softened views thy magic glass reveals,
> When o'er the landscape Time's meek twilight steals
> (Pt. 1, l. 91-2)

but in general the poem was deficient in power and the various poetic clichés of the day were strung together thick and fast. The peasants who "flocked to hear the minstrel play" and with "games and carols closed the busy day" are followed within only a half a dozen lines by

> yon old Mansion frowning thro' the trees
> Whose hollow turret wooes the whistling breeze ...
> That casement, arched with ivy's brownest shade ...
> The mouldering gateway ... the grass-grown court ...
> (Pt. 1, l. 13-15, 17)

Graveyard wisdom was supplied by the village sexton who,

> Oft as he turned the greensward with his spade
> ... lectured every youth that round him played,
> And calmly pointing where our fathers lay
> Roused us to rival each, the hero of his day.
> (Pt. 1, l. 142-8)

The debt to Goldsmith was not confined to the style:

> The School's lone porch, with reverend mosses grey,
> Just tells the pensive pilgrim where it lay.
> Mute is the bell that rung at peep of dawn,
> Quickening my truant-feet across the lawn;
> Unheard the shout that rents the noontide air,
> When the slow dial gave a pause to care.
> (Pt. 1, l. 97-102)

And there was more than a hint of Johnson:

> Survey the globe, each ruder realm explore;
> From Reason's faintest ray to Newton soar
> (Pt. 1, l. 185-6)

Rogers's poem suggested at least the title for Thomas Dermody's brief essay in Spenserians, *The Pleasures of Poesy*, and it gave Merry the idea of trying to cash in with *The Pains of Memory*. Rogers also of course inspired Campbell's *The Pleasures of Hope* and the whole host of other *Pleasures* which appeared in the early nineteenth century. These I shall discuss later in the chapter. Rogers's influence outside the *Pleasures* genre is less easy to trace as his style was virtually that of Goldsmith. Goldsmith indeed was still regarded as an appropriate model. Not only was Rogers proud to be called "the child of Goldsmith", *The Annual Review* complimented Pratt by saying his *Cottage Pictures, or the Poor* "sometimes reminds us of Goldsmith".[8] The Rev. Richard Wallis's *The Happy Village* (1805) was deliberately intended as a counterpart to *The Deserted Village*:

> Teach me a rising village to describe,
> Give me but Pow'r to modulate my lay
> As GOLDSMITH sung of one in deep Decay.
> (1802 edn., p. 5)

After 1792 however one should perhaps speak of a "school of Rogers and Goldsmith" rather than merely of a "school of Goldsmith". Thus in his *Malvern* (1798) the Rev. Luke Booker invoked both "Soft Muse of Auburn!" (i.e. Goldsmith) and

> ... thou Muse! not less plaintive nor less sweet,
> Who MEMORY's PLEASURES lately did rehearse
> On village green.
> (1798 edn., p. 1)

Among those who were certainly directly influenced by Rogers was Robert Southey, whose *The Retrospect*, written at

Oxford in 1794, contained passages indistinguishable from *The Pleasures of Memory*:

> Yet still will Memory's busy eye retrace
> Each little vestige of the well known place;
> Each wonted haunt and scene of youthful joy,
> Where merriment has cheer'd the careless boy.

The Retrospect was probably the best of Southey's first collection of poems, which was published towards the end of 1794 along with some pieces by his friend Robert Lovell. The whole volume was a medley of echoes — not just of Rogers, but of Gray, the Wartons and Merry as well.

The Monthly Review responded somewhat coolly: "We particularly object to a certain woe-begone and debilitating affectation of fine-feeling,"[9] but *The British Critic* was enthusiastic:

> In the present state of poetry, the volume here announced deserves, and we hope will receive, particular attention; it will at least have our praise to help it on its way, and this from a principle of gratitude; it has produced a gratification we do not very often experience.[10]

Southey's second collection in 1797 showed a significant advance on his first, though some of his poems "were written in earlier youth" and were of the same species as in the previous volume. Perhaps the two most interesting pieces were *The Soldier's Wife* and *The Widow*. Both poems were about destitute women; they were, in effect, episodes of lower-class life, of the sort employed by Thomson in *The Seasons*, converted into free standing vignettes,[11] though they also owed something to the ballad tradition in their emphasis on action and speech rather than description. Southey also included in his 1797 volume a couple of pseudo-ballads on more traditional topics and there can be no doubt that he was conscious of the stylistic parallel between his own sketches of modern life and folk narratives of the sort collected by Percy. At the same time, *The Soldier's Wife* and *The Widow* provide an interesting parallel to the work of Wordsworth in *Lyrical Ballads*.

Lyrical Ballads, mainly by Wordsworth but with some contributions by Southey's close friend Samuel Taylor Coleridge, appeared in 1798. So many arguments and counter-arguments surround this work that it requires some extended examination. The distinctive features of *Lyrical Ballads* were made notorious by the *Preface* written by Wordsworth for the 1800 edition.

By drawing attention to the accompanying poems, the *Preface* invited critics to attack those poems; Wordsworth was understood to have drawn up a new poetic system for himself; the *Preface* announced this system, but it was the poems which were supposed to put the new system into practice and it was the poems rather than the *Preface* which were attacked. But it is clear that it was *because* of the *Preface* that Wordsworth's poems were attacked; *The Edinburgh Review*, which took every opportunity to denigrate and misrepresent Wordsworth, gave special emphasis to "the devotion with which he has sacrificed so many precious gifts at the shrine of those paltry idols which he has set up for himself among his lakes and his mountains"[12] and even the relatively sympathetic Rev. Francis Wrangham considered that Wordsworth, "has shewn a perverse preference for the maintenance and exemplification of a system to the yielding to the nobler and more genial current of his natural feelings".[13] Later however Coleridge's hint in his *Biographia Literaria* that the poems should be examined separately from the *Preface* became the foundation of an orthodoxy favourable to Wordsworth, which prevailed right up until World War I. Victorian and Edwardian critics, while extolling Wordsworth's poems, either dismissed the *Preface* as misleading or even worthless (e.g. C. H. Herford, W. J. Courthope, George Saintsbury) or else did not mention it separately at all (e.g. Margaret Oliphant and C. E. Vaughan).[14] One of the last of the "Coleridge school" was M. L. Barstow who in 1917 wrote, on the subject of Wordsworth's idea of using the language of the lower classes of society, "the famous Preface is little more than a somewhat unwilling and frankly inadequate attempt to explain this same experiment."[15]

By 1917 however a more authoritative voice had already put forward a novel and more persuasive view, G. M. Harper, whose *William Wordsworth, His Life, Works and Influence* had appeared in the previous year, wrote of the *Preface*:

> In this he advanced what almost amounts to a systematic theory of poetic art.... It is an exposition of the fundamental laws of association as applied in poetry. It announces not only Wordsworth's theory of poetic diction, though that would be a notable performance, for Wordsworth's theory of poetic diction has given a fresh texture to nearly all English poetry for the last hundred years; but it heralds one of the most splendid triumphs of democracy....[16]

Harper went on to emphasize the importance of Wordsworth's concepts of feeling and active sympathy, at more length than can be quoted here. But he is worth re-reading. As well as the first, he was also the most convincing of the exponents of the view that the *Preface* had an importance transcending that of the poems it prefaced.

Since Harper, the importance of the *Preface* has been generally accepted, but there are two major schools of thought. One school, less intellectually ambitious, merely supposes that the *Preface* and the poems were the two complementary sections of a unified poetic manifesto that allegedly revolutionized English literature, the idea being that Wordsworth personally and individually caused "Romanticism". This view is a development of the much older and scarcely more tenable view, discussed in my introduction, that there was an essential discontinuity between eighteenth-century and Romantic poetry. Thus Needleman and Otis wrote: "Its publication may for convenience be said to inaugurate the renaissance of modern English poetry; it is the Magna Charta, officially ushering in the Romantic Period."[17] More recently in 1966 Margaret Drabble merely restated this at great length, ignoring several decades of scholarly interest in "pre-Romantics" like Gray and Cowper:

> very few people who are not close students of the whole course of English literature realise what a great original and revolutionary Wordsworth in fact was, and there is really not much point in reading the *Lyrical Ballads* and the *Preface* without some notion of the extreme novelty of Wordsworth's position. His true greatness is seen best in contrast with the poetic barrenness out of which he suddenly, amazingly appeared. . . .
> In politics, in religion, and in his emotional life he was unorthodox and original. But it is in his literary views that his originality is most powerful and important. There were plenty of other radicals and anarchists in England, but on the subject of poetry Wordsworth (with the backing of Coleridge) stood alone. In this field he was a lone pioneer. The date of the publication of the *Lyrical Ballads* (1798) is one of the most important single dates in the history of English literature, for it marks the end of an age, and the beginning of a new one.[18]

The other school of thought is closer to Harper, in emphasizing the importance of the *Preface* at the expense of the poems — a view which is quite the reverse of the pre-Harper orthodoxy. The happy discovery that while *Lyrical Ballads* were not Wordsworth's only, or even his best poems, the introductory essays attached to them were his only major critical writings, has inspired much ingenuity. Thus W. J. B. Owen sees the

Preface as an attempt to define a "new rhetoric" or a "permanent rhetoric" as "a means of aligning poetry with nature, of giving it, as far as possible, a form as 'steady' and as 'perennial' as that of the mountain",[19] and J. Scoggins argues that Wordsworth's purpose was to show "that man is not limited to intercourse with facts impressed upon the passive senses and combined mechanically in the associative faculty of understanding, but is an inmate of an active universe which his own imagination partly creates."[20]

Yet reading the *Preface* in this way as a kind of manifesto introductory to the entire Wordsworth canon is surely at least as misleading as earlier orthodoxies. The *Preface* undeniably contains many striking dicta on theoretical criticism but it was not written as a collection of dicta; it was written to amplify its opening comments on how *Lyrical Ballads* were published

> as an experiment, which, I hoped, might be of some use to ascertain, how far, by fitting to metrical arrangement a selection of the real language of men in a state of vivid sensation, that sort of pleasure and that quantity of pleasure may be imparted, which a Poet may rationally endeavour to impart.

The investigation of how "that sort of pleasure and that quantity of pleasure may be imparted" led Wordsworth into many interesting statements, but they were only a secondary part of his purpose. The main business was the "experiment". Coleridge too referred to *Lyrical Ballads* as an "experiment". Now an experiment is not a definitive statement: it will be indicative of some but not necessarily all of the experimenter's interests and priorities; and so it was with Wordsworth's poems in *Lyrical Ballads*. As Coleridge pointed out, "in these poems it is impossible not to perceive that the natural *tendency* of the poet's mind is to great objects and elevated conceptions";[21] that is, the poems contained hints of Wordsworth's true *forte*, but they were not a definitive statement of it. Wordsworth himself later, in *Essay Supplementary to the Preface*, referred to his longer blank-verse poetry as "the work to which they are subsidiary".

An experiment not only gives a partial view of the experimenter, it also adopts a partial, limited and selective view of the thing experimented on, in this case poetry. A partial limited and selective view of Wordsworth's opinions of eighteenth-century poetry is precisely what there is in his *Preface*. He was anxious to forestall "a numerous class of critics...

[who] would establish a canon of criticism which the Reader will conclude he must utterly reject if he is to be pleased with these volumes". In order to illustrate this anticipatory counter-argument, he picked on Gray, not as the exemplar of eighteenth-century taste in general — for Gray was certainly not that — but as a particularly extreme example of the kind of poet with whom he feared unfavourable comparison. Even Samuel Johnson in *The Lives of the Poets* had pointed out that "Gray thought his language more poetical as it was more remote from common use: finding in Dryden *honey redolent of Spring*, an expression that reaches the utmost limits of our language, Gray drove it a little more beyond apprehension, by making *gales* to be *redolent of joy and youth*." Johnson would therefore have accepted, without serious qualification, Wordsworth's key statement that Gray

> was at the head of those who, by their reasonings, have attempted to widen the space of separation betwixt Prose and Metrical composition, and was more than any other man curiously elaborate in the structure of his own poetic diction.

In other words Wordsworth picked on Gray as exemplifying, in an extreme degree, a tendency in eighteenth-century poetry which in *Lyrical Ballads* was consciously guarded against. In the Appendix to the 1802 edition, Wordsworth extended his argument by showing how even "so chaste a writer as Cowper" was led astray by the prevailing fashion; he quoted two stanzas from Cowper, one of which he condemned, and one of which he entirely commended. The point Wordsworth was making was not that he was the first to have written inartificial poetry, but that he was the first deliberately and systematically to avoid an artificial poetic diction. He nowhere states that the chief characteristic of earlier poets was the falseness of their diction and, though he cites passages of Gray and Cowper in which plain words express the meaning more powerfully than the over elaborate phrases which accompany them, he nowhere states that artificial diction must in every instance be unpoetical. All he was trying to do was justify a particular experiment, not attempting to launch a revolution.

Though it was unusual in its length and the number of important issues it raised, the *Preface* was not the only poetical manifesto of its day, and compared to other prefaces it was relatively mild in tone. Coleridge, in the second edition of his *Poems* (1797) countered the criticism of his obscurity by sneering, a living writer is yet sub judice; and if we cannot follow his conceptions or enter into his feeling, it is perhaps more consoling to our pride to consider him as lost beneath, than as soaring above, us.

(Preface, p. xviii)

And in the same year Southey asserted in the Advertisement to his *Poems*:

> I now think the Ode the most worthless species of composition, as well as the most difficult, and should never again attempt it.... The sonnets were written first, or I would have adopted a different title, and avoided the shackle of rhyme, and the confinement to fourteen lines.

This revolt against prevailing taste was expressed even more forcibly in Southey's and Coleridge's conversation:

> Southey told me that he had read Spenser through about *thirty* times, and that he could not read Pope through *once*.[22]

> [Coleridge] spoke with contempt of Gray and with intolerance of Pope. He did not like the versification of the latter.[23]

Wordsworth on the other hand used such terms of sweeping condemnation only in speaking of his contemporaries. He proudly claimed on one occasion that he could repeat several thousand lines of Pope from memory,[24] and in criticizing Dryden he added a great deal of praise:

> I admire his talents and Genius greatly, but his is not a poetical Genius: the only qualities I can find in Dryden that are *essentially* poetical are a certain ardour and impetuosity of mind with an excellent ear: it may seem strange that I do not add to this, great command of language: *that* he certainly has and of such language also as it is most desirable that a Poet should possess, or rather should not be without; but it is not language that is in the high sense of the word poetical, being neither of the imagination or the passions... there is not a single image from Nature in the whole body of his works; and in his translation from Vergil whenever Vergil can be fairly said to have his *eye* upon his object, Dryden always spoils the passage.[25]

In fact neither in writing nor in speech did Wordsworth do anything in the way of leading a polemical assault on eighteenth-century poetry; as will be seen, if anyone did that, it was Southey.

Like the *Preface*, the poems in *Lyrical Ballads* were much less of a break with tradition than is generally supposed.[26] Though Wordsworth warned, "The majority of the following poems are to be considered as experiments" (*Lyrical Ballads*, Advertisement, 1798), more than half of his contribution to the 1798 volume showed no significant deviation in style or language from current poetic fashion; and as R. D. Mayo has shown, Wordsworth's subject matter was equally unoriginal.[27] There were other contemporary poems entitled *The Beggar Girl* and *The Idiot*, and *The British Critic* even observed in 1800 that Bloomfield's poem *The Mad Girl* had "a trite subject".[28] Indeed, Thomas Russell had written a pseudo-ballad on a similar topic, entitled *The Maniac*, a decade earlier. *Lyrical Ballads* was in fact a contribution, and not a very early one, to the vogue of poetry about the poor which will be discussed in the next chapter. The narrative format of most of the poems, equally, was of a sort already popularized by Burns and Southey. At best, *Lyrical Ballads* could claim to be topical rather than innovatory, and *Lines written a few miles above Tintern Abbey*, a chain of reflections occasioned by a return to one of the poet's former haunts, was not even topical, looking back to Bowles (compare Wordsworth's "Once again/Do I behold those steep and lofty cliffs" with Bowles's "Itchen! when I behold thy banks again") and to the philosophical poetry of Akenside. It was in this poem that Wordsworth underlined his debt to the eighteenth century by incorporating a quotation from Young's *Night Thoughts*.*

Wordsworth himself was proud to confess what he owed to his predecessors, later writing in *The Prelude* (Book 8, ll. 510, 514-17):

> But when that first poetic Faculty ...
> Began to have some promptings to put on
> A visible shape, and to the works of art,
> The notions and the images of books
> Did knowingly conform itself,

and to dispute the novelty of his subject matter or technique is not to question his greatness as a poet. The essence of his genius does not lie in innovation, any more than Shakespeare's does, but rather in what he did with existing forms. Coleridge summed up what was special in Wordsworth's poetry when he wrote of

> the fine balance of truth in observing, with the imaginative

---

* *Tintern Abbey*, l. 106-7, "both what they half create/And what perceive"; cf. *Night Thoughts*, Night 6, line 424, "And half create the wondrous world they see". Wordsworth acknowledged the borrowing in a footnote.

faculty in modifying, the objects observed; and above all the original gift of spreading the tone, the *atmosphere*, and with it the depth and height of the ideal world around forms, incidents, and situations, of which, for the common view, custom had bedimmed all the lustre, had dried up the sparkle and the dew drops.[29]

Wordsworth in fact not only saw more precisely, with more particularity, than any earlier poet, but he also discovered more significance in what he saw. That was his innovation; yet it was not something that could be done by formula, and when his imagination flagged, what he wrote was not immeasurably better than the work of his contemporaries.

With regard to subject and execution the most original poem in *Lyrical Ballads* was not by Wordsworth at all but by Coleridge: *The Rime of the Ancient Mariner*. Though this poem was generally disliked by critics, and was amusingly parodied but never seriously imitated, yet it was no less symptomatic of the times than were Wordsworth's poems. Uniquely complex in its theme and structure, *The Rime* was no less remarkable as one of the first of the large number of long, melodramatic ballad-style narrative poems of the period. Coleridge was perhaps the first of his contemporaries to become aware that there was a reading public who wanted something more stimulating than the nostalgia of Rogers or the make-pretend righteous indignation of Southey.

Commercially *Lyrical Ballads* was a failure. Both Wordsworth and Coleridge were already known to a small public before 1798, Wordsworth for his *An Evening Walk* and *Descriptive Sketches*, both published in 1793, and Coleridge for two collections of rather derivative poems brought out in 1796 and 1797, and *Lyrical Ballads* brought them to begin with very little additional fame. Some of the first edition of 500 copies of *Lyrical Ballads* were remaindered, and Longmans returned the copyright *gratis* as being worthless. Further editions in 1800 and 1802 satisfied what demand there was; while at the same period Bloomfield and Campbell were selling thousands. *The Annual Register*, the yearly survey of current affairs, reprinted *Tintern Abbey* in 1803; this shows at least that there was some public interest in Wordsworth, though the thirteen other poems by other authors printed in the same edition of *The Annual Register* were of such various merit that Wordsworth's inclusion can scarcely be taken as recognition of his talent, and in 1818 Hazlitt claimed that he was little known to the public except through garbled extracts of his poems printed in reviews. It was *The Edinburgh Review*'s constant sniping as much as anything that kept Wordsworth's name before the public, for the sales of his poetry were certainly insufficient to establish a popular reputation. There was some point to Hartley Coleridge's skit written *circa* 1820:

> He lived amidst th' untrodden ways
> To Rydal Mount that lead
> A bard whom there was none to praise
> And very few to read.[30]

Wordsworth impressed Crabb Robinson, John Wilson and de Quincey, but amongst those whose opinions carried weight he found no favour. Even Southey reviewed him harshly in *The Monthly Review*, and in private he wrote of Wordsworth's poems, "some I shall re-read, upon the same principle that led me through Trissino,* whenever I am afraid of writing like a child or an old woman".[31] (Though he did borrow from *Lyrical Ballads* in some of his own poems,[32] and he later admitted that *The Brothers* and *Michael* were "excellent, I have never been so much affected, and so *well*, as by some passages there".)[33] Though the critical cant of the day subsequently associated the two men (along with Coleridge) in the so-called "Lake School", Southey was never anything like as intimate with Wordsworth as he had once been with Coleridge, and years later he confessed, "he highly disapproved both of Mr Wordsworth's theories and of his practice".[34] This was only partly because even as early as 1798 he was moving away from the fashionable "social realism" of his earlier work and moving on to more exotic styles and subjects;[35] Southey seems to have thrown himself into books as a refuge from the strenuous emotions of real life; his own poems were always ingeniously contrived but passionless, and he seems to have recognized in Wordsworth's poems a commitment and freshness which he was not capable of and which he seems to have found oddly disquieting. Judging by Francis Jeffrey's criticisms in *The Edinburgh Review* and the later remarks of numerous other writers, Southey's attitude of incomprehension and distaste was quite widely shared.

A contrast to, and commentary upon, the comparative failure of *Lyrical Ballads* was the success of *The Pleasures of Hope*, published in 1799, by Thomas Campbell, an impoverished twenty-one-year-old Glaswegian who, unable to settle on any

---

* Gian Giorgio Trissino, 1478-1550, poet and dramatist, was author of the unreadable epic *L'Italia Liberata dai Goti*.

career, was trying to scrape a living by private tutoring and miscellaneous writing.

Campbell was later described as "a rival to Rogers, but with more vigour, terseness and splendour".[36] Campbell's title, his discursive framework, and his use of the heroic couplet all pointed to comparison with Rogers, and William Beattie, his biographer, eventually dedicated his three-volume *Life and Letters of Thomas Campbell* (1849) to Rogers with the following words:

> When the tomb had closed upon Goldsmith — when, for a season, the oracles of Poetry were almost dumb; it was your happy destiny to break the silence, to revive the spirit, and introduce a new era of polished song. Your "Pleasures of Memory" found Thomas Campbell — a youthful but ardent votary — in the "lonely Hebrides"; it struck his heart with inspiring impulse, and quickened all his noblest inspirations. It was the magic key that unlocked the fountain of his genius; its sparkling waters gushed forth in the "Pleasures of Hope", and from that hour — a priest and Brother of the sacred choir — a child of precocious but permanent fame, he found an honoured station beside his classic prototype.

Yet Rogers himself never became a friend of Campbell's (for all that they had many acquaintances in common) and confessed, "His *Pleasures of Hope* is no great favourite with me".[37] In many respects the two men's poems were extremely different. It is true that they both struck the same note of sentimentality; in fact *The Pleasures of Hope* owed much of its appeal to the numerous pathetic pen sketches it contained such as the description of the returned traveller who

> Meets at each step a friend's familiar face,
> And flies at last to Helen's long embrace;
> Wipes from her cheek the rapture-speaking tear,
> And clasps, with many a sigh, his children dear!
> While, long neglected, but at length caress'd,
> His faithful dog salutes the smiling guest,
> Points to the master's eyes (where'er they roam)
> His wistful face, and whines a welcome home
> (Pt. 1, l. 81 foll.)

or the destitute wayfarer:

> Yon friendless man, at whose dejected eye
> Th' unfeeling proud one looks — and passes by;
> Condemned on Penury's barren path to roam,
> Scorn'd by the world, and left without a home —

> Ev'n he, at evening, should he chance to stray
> Down by the hamlet's hawthorn scented way,
> Where, round the cot's romantic glade, are seen
> The blossom'd bean-field, and the sloping green,
> Leans o'er its humble gate, and thinks the while —
> Oh! that for me some home like this would smile,
> Some hamlet shade, to yield my sickly form,
> Health in the breeze, and shelter in the storm. . . .
>
> (Pt. 1, l. 299 foll.)

Since the day of Thomson such vignettes had been a common feature of eighteenth-century poetry, but Campbell excelled in them, in his precision of detail and controlled sentiment. (It is interesting to note that genre painting, the pictorial representation of exactly the same type of scenes, was becoming increasingly fashionable at this period, and that it was another Scot, David Wilkie, who over the next dozen years was to establish himself as the leading practitioner in this field.) Yet the precise depiction of intimate scenes was only one ingredient of *The Pleasures of Hope's* success. Among the more popular passages were those dealing with the subject of National Liberty:

> Oh! bloodiest picture in the book of Time,
> Sarmatia fell, unwept, without a crime;
> Found not a generous friend, a pitying foe,
> Strength in her arms, nor mercy in her woe!
> Dropt from her nerveless grasp the shatter'd spear,
> Clos'd her bright eye, and curb'd her high career; —
> Hope, for a season, bade the world farewell,
> And Freedom shriek'd — as KOSCIUSKO fell! *
>
> (Pt. 1, l. 375 foll.)

Later Byron and Thomas Moore were to write in a similar vein, but it is curious that, only ten years after the commencement of the French Revolution, and within months of the Irish rebellion of 1798, Liberty was already sufficiently uncontroversial to be acceptable as part of a best-selling poet's stock in trade. But perhaps even more significant was the generally frenzied, hyperbolical, almost Della Cruscan tone of Campbell's poem, frequent concatenation of sonorous words and striking images, as in the final lines of Part 2:

> Eternal Hope! when yonder spheres sublime
> Peal'd their first notes to sound the march of Time,

---

* Tadeusz Kościuszko (1746-1817) led the resistance to the partition of Poland (Campbell's "Sarmatia") in 1794. In 1799 he was living in retirement near Paris.

> Thy joyous youth began — but not to fade —
> When all the sister planets have decay'd;
> When wrapt in fire the realms of ether glow,
> And Heaven's last thunder shakes the world below;
> Thou, undismayed, shalt o'er the ruins smile,
> And light thy torch at Nature's funeral pile.

Rant of this kind, appealing more to the ear than to the mind, was far removed from the characteristic language of the eighteenth century, and there was some truth in the claim later made that: "The *Pleasures of Hope* may be considered the connecting link between the past and the present school of poetry. It is written in the metre and manner of the first, and with the glow, animation and energy of the other."[38]

Campbell succeeded in writing one or two especially neat lines in *The Pleasures of Hope*:

> 'Tis distance lends enchantment to the view
> And robes the mountain in its azure hue.
> (Pt. 1, l. 7-8)

but he seems to have found his predecessors in contemplative verse, from Young to Rogers, somewhat dull.[39] He also avoided the commonplace subjectivity of viewpoint which was one of the hallmarks of the Goldsmith-Rogers school, and indeed few poets of his generation were less subjective than Campbell: he was later to remark ruefully, when penning a few reminiscences for the use of his biographer, "no man — unless he be a poet of the Lake school — thinks himself a hero".[40]

Significantly enough Campbell thought Thomas Penrose's *The Field of Battle* "one of the very finest poems in the English language":

> The field, so late the hero's pride,
> Was now with various carnage spread;
> And floated with a crimson tide,
> That drench'd the dying and the dead.

This deservedly little-known poem describes how Maria paddled, or perhaps one should say waded, through this superabundance of blood in search of her husband Edgar:

> Her ghastly hope was well nigh fled —
> When late pale Edgar's form she found,
> Half bury'd with the hostile dead,
> And bor'd with many a grisly wound.
>
> She knew — she sank — the night-bird scream'd
> — The moon withdrew her troubled light,

And left the fair — though fall'n she seem'd
To worse than death — and deepest night.

One of Campbell's earliest works, *The Wounded Hussar*, had a very similar subject, and it appears that it was this sort of emotional hyperbole and over-emphasis of language which was what Campbell regarded as the very essence of poetry. The Della Cruscans had also believed this, of course, but the much greater success of *The Pleasures of Hope* helped establish this view in the minds of a much larger public.

Campbell's fellow Romantic poets however were almost unanimous in disliking his work. Southey thought "his Pleasures of Hope are neither sense nor English. Something there is in him but not much".[41] Coleridge said that he "obviously had no fixed design, but when a thought (of course, not a very original one) came into his head, he put it down in couplets, and afterwards strung the *disjecta membra* (not *poetae*) together. Some of the best things in it were borrowed."[42] Wordsworth said:

> Campbell's *Pleasures of Hope* has been strangely over-rated: its fine words and sounding lines please the generality of readers, who never stop to ask themselves the meaning of a passage. The lines,—
> "Where Andes, giant of the western wave
> With meteor-standard to the winds unfurl'd
> Looks from his throne of clouds o'er half the world"
> are sheer nonsense,— nothing more than poetical indigestion. What has a giant to do with a star? What is a meteor standard? — but it is useless to inquire what such stuff means.[43]

Dorothy Wordsworth wrote of another of Campbell's poems, his battle lyric *Hohenlinden*: "if it is not nonsense ... there is very little sense in it, and ... the author neither understood nor looked steadily at his subject. I believe he is not capable of this last effort of mind if I may judge from the huddling nonsense of the Pleasures of Hope."[44]

For Wordsworth and his sister, authenticity, truth to nature, was the vital precondition for the exercise of poetic imagination. Wordsworth looked at things with a fresh eye and a fresh mind, in order to nourish a fresh imagination and he sought to express his insight in a language which was basically as straightforward and syntactically orthodox as that of Pope; Campbell on the other hand merely looked at words and phrases with a fresh eye, rather in the way the Della Cruscans seem to have done, and his imagination was sufficient only for playing around with word sounds. As a result his sentences were often meaningless strings of phrases, and there was a fundamental confusion in even his most successful images, thus, in the final stanzas of *Hohenlinden*,

> Few, few, shall part where many meet!
> The snow shall be their winding sheet,
> And every turf beneath their feet
> Shall be a soldier's sepulchre,

the notion of single turfs being in themselves man-sized sepulchres was ludicrous, as Rogers and Wordsworth once pointed out.[45] It was typical of Campbell that during the one battle he did witness (the Battle of Ratisbon, not the more famous Battle of Hohenlinden) he observed two details, preserved only in his conversation, that are more striking than any contained in his poem: he heard the French army singing "one of their national hymns" before the battle, and later in the day he saw the French cavalry entering Ratisbon fresh from the battle field, the troopers wiping their bloody sabres on the manes of their horses.[46] He probably found these telling incidents unversifiable.

That Rogers, Wordsworth and Coleridge bothered to condemn Campbell was partly due to the latter's success with the public. *The Pleasures of Hope* ran through ten editions between 1799 and 1815 and inspired extravagant praise:

> There was never anything like him — he is the very spirit of Parnassus.... He will surpass everything, ancient or modern — your Pindars, your Drydens, and your Grays. I expect nothing short of a Scotch Milton, a Shakespeare, or something more than either![47]

In retrospect, Campbell's poem may appear merely a travesty of the tone and diction of Byron and Shelley, but it appeared while they were still children, and it was in part a product, in part a creator of the public taste which Byron later exploited. This is the historical importance of *The Pleasures of Hope*: it was the first commercially successful long poem written in a "romantic" style; it showed the reading public what they wanted from poetry, and it showed other men of letters what the public wanted.

The Pleasures of Hope, in combination with Rogers's *The Pleasures of Memory*, also exerted influence in quite the opposite direction by adding new prestige to the already firmly established genre of philosophical, discursive verse which in many ways was more characteristic of the eighteenth century than of the Romantic period. The first thirty years of the nineteenth century, which saw so much innovation, also saw an unparalleled torrent of imitations. Some, like *Clifton Grove*, by the fifteen-year-old Henry Kirke White (1803), were perfectly respectable attempts to transfer the mood and texture of Rogers and Goldsmith to a new setting, but the period's fondness for imitations also showed itself in John Jeffrey's *The Pleasures of Retirement* (1800), David Carey's Spenserian *The Pleasures of Nature* (1803), P. L. Courtier's *The Pleasures of Solitude* (two editions 1803), John Stewart's *The Pleasures of Love* (two editions 1806), Frances Arabella Rowden's *The Pleasures of Friendship* (1810 reprinted 1811 and 1818), Charles Verral's *The Pleasures of Possession; or, the Enjoyment of the Present Moment, contrasted with those of Hope and Memory* (1810), Anna Jane Vardill's *The Pleasures of Human Life* (1812); *The Pleasures of Life* (1818); *The Pleasures of Home* (1818, republished in 1825), *The Pleasures of Sympathy* (1822), *The Pleasures of Fancy* (1822); *The Pleasures of Society* (1824) and, the last of the flood, L. E. Evans's *The Pleasures of Benevolence* (1830). (Perhaps one should also mention F. Newnham's *The Pleasures of Anarchy*, a dramatic sermon in five acts, published in 1809 and reprinted in 1815 and 1829.) After glancing through these numerous productions one is almost bound to conclude that the worst Augustan reflective verse was written during the Romantic period, which possibly helps explain the difficulty Wordsworth had in establishing his reputation, and the respect accorded to the critical pronouncements of *The Edinburgh Review* and *The Quarterly Review*.

Nevertheless, a new poetic idiom was emerging. It had its roots, certainly, in the work of earlier writers, but its overall effect and import were different and novel. But it was the idiom of Campbell rather than of Wordsworth, and if during the 1790s there was a year of revolution in poetry — a supposition not to be readily admitted — it was 1799, the year of Campbell, not 1798, the year of *Lyrical Ballads*. Wordsworth's poetry is remembered because it speaks out beyond his own time; Campbell's is forgotten because it is too entirely in the idiom of his own day. And it was because Campbell was so attuned to the idiom of his day that his poetry had more influence than *Lyrical Ballads* in pushing forward the development of the new style of poetry.

4
The Great Age of Rural Poetry

> ... it is impossible to read the productions of Burns, along with his history, without forming a higher idea of the intelligence, taste and accomplishment of the peasantry than most of those in the higher rank are disposed to entertain.
>
> (*The Edinburgh Review*, vol. 13 (1809), p. 275)

For all his success, Campbell was not the country's best-selling poet in the opening years of the nineteenth century, nor even its best-selling *living* poet. Of the dead, Burns and Thomson were still the most popular. In the case of Thomson, considering that his poetry had been constantly reprinted since the 1720s, and considering that there was a highly active trade in second-hand books, even the publication of no less than *five* separate editions of his works in 1802 can give a poor idea of how popular he was. Of the living poets, the best-seller was a kind of disciple of Thomson and Burns, and of Goldsmith: Robert Bloomfield, author of *The Farmer's Boy*.

Though so very similar to its eighteenth-century prototypes, *The Farmer's Boy* probably would not have been so much of a success if it had appeared any earlier than 1800, and in order to understand why this should be so it is necessary to go back a couple of decades, to the 1780s.

During the eighteenth century there had been an increasing interest in the picturesque aspects of the countryside. Thomson's of course was the earliest name to be associated with this interest, but later in the century there was a movement away from the view Thomson had popularized, the view that the countryside was to be seen principally as the source of food and other items needed by man, and the location of simple human values in their purest form. Increasingly people began to esteem the countryside more in proportion as it was more remote from any human concern whatsoever. Thomson's was a peopled, man-centred nature; there arose a fashionable preoccupation with an empty, lonely, inhuman and unhumanized nature.[1] The Warton-Collins school of poetry contributed to this development with their odes to Solitude, though even here their imaginary countryside was not entirely empty of people:

> But when Phosphor brings the dawn,
> By her dappled coursers drawn,
> Again you to the wild retreat,
> And the early huntsman meet,
> Where, as you pensive pace along,
> You catch the distant shepherd's song. . . .
> (J. Grainger, *Ode on Solitude*, 1755)

In later evocations of the wilderness even the huntsman and the shepherd were missing. More and more as the century progressed, unspoilt countryside in underpopulated areas like Wales and the Lake District exerted their spell over the imagination of the reading public; West's guide to the Lakes sold seven editions between 1778 and 1799, and the Rev. William Gilpin achieved an almost equal success with his *Observations on the River Wye, and several parts of South Wales*.

At the same time there was a certain interest in the people whose lives were most inextricably bound up with the countryside, the rural poor. In a society still largely paternalistic, this interest was partly a matter of social expediency, though there was also a prevailing intellectual curiosity about natural man and the effects of civilization. By the 1780s, concern for the rural poor was as much an established tradition as the not altogether compatible fashion for admiring nature uncontaminated by human presence. Pratt discussed the rural poor in *Sympathy*; Cowper, in Book Four of *The Task*, gave a long disquisition on rural poverty, the excessive number of country ale-houses, and the desertion of the countryside by the rich, and the Rev. George Crabbe, in his poem *The Village*, set out to

> paint the cot,
> As truth will paint it, and as bards will not.
> (Bk. 1, l. 53-4)

At times Crabbe expressed himself more starkly than almost any other eighteenth-century poet:

> yon house that holds the parish poor
> Whose walls of mud scarce bear the broken door,
> There, where the putrid vapours, flagging, play,

> And the dull wheel hums doleful through the day; —
> There children dwell who know no parents' care;
> Parents, who know no children's love, dwell there!
> Heart-broken matrons on their joyless bed,
> Forsaken wives, and mothers never wed.
> (Bk. 1, l. 299 foll.)

But Crabbe's general thesis was accepted, and poems in a similar, if weaker, vein, appeared in the daily papers:

> There, plung'd in woe, the artist unemploy'd
> Weeps o'er his wretched family's despair;
> His every stay, his every hope destroy'd
> And naught now left but hunger, cold and care.[2]

Burns's dialect poems which belong to the same period struck a more cheerful note, but he too, in his own life as well as in his writings, engaged the public's sympathy for poor country folk.

Poetry about the rural poor had its counterpart in painting. From the 1780s onwards artists like Richard Westall and Julius Caesar Ibbetson were beginning to specialize in depicting the rural poor going about their daily tasks.

This new sympathy for the rural poor was one of those self-generated cultural fashions so familiar to us in the twentieth century — such as the preoccupation with the "environment" in the early 1970s. There was no direct link with socio-economic developments. At the beginning of the 1780s the War of American Independence had resulted in increased salt, malt and land taxes which affected even the poorest households, and the war also caused the usual disruption in areas dependent on overseas trade. A sharp fall in the price of wheat in 1779-80 must have been an embarrassment to farmers operating on a narrow profit margin, though it was directly beneficial to poor families. All through the war, taken as a whole, and during the years that followed, wheat prices rose very little above the average for previous decades, and meat prices showed a slight overall decline,[3] so that whatever other difficulties were caused by the war, the poor were probably not worse off with regard to basic living standards than in previous decades. On the other hand, if the poor were no worse off in the 1780s than they had ever been, other sections of society were becoming richer from the profits of trade and manufactures, for this was the period of the so-called industrial revolution; and as the middle and upper classes became more affluent, so their notions of how human beings should live became more gracious. As a result there was an increase of social consciousness among the property-owning classes. Whereas only one new philanthropic society or institution was established in England in the 1760s, and only three in the 1770s, the 1780s saw the establishment of eleven, and the 1790s of eighteen.[4] The 1780s' establishments included The Society for the Abolition of the Slave Trade, the Benevolent, or Strangers' Friend Society, The Society of Universal Good Will, The Society for the Relief of Poor, Pious Clergymen, of the Established Church, Residing in the Country, and the Society for Carrying into Effect his Majesty's Proclamation Against Vice and Immorality. In the long run it was the missionary projects abroad, the educational and penal reforms and the agitation against the slave trade, which were the most positive achievement of the new philanthropy, but an increased concern for the English poor was also a consequence. And, at a time when the vast majority of the population lived in the country or in smaller towns, and industrial areas were still few and remote, the poor was generally taken to consist only of the rural poor.

It is indeed remarkable that the new social awareness largely overlooked the consequences of the most vital socio-economic development of the period, even though it was precisely that development which contributed most to the material security of the socially aware classes. While the rural poor maintained their *status quo*, the urban poor were increasing in numbers and degradation. Vice, ignorance, squalor, disease, starvation, horrifyingly evident in some rural areas, were magnified by overcrowding and industrial hazards in the slums which grew up in Manchester and Birmingham and other manufacturing cities during the later eighteenth century. Yet public comment on these new conditions was unusual, and aroused little public interest.[5] It was not till the cholera epidemic and movement for social reform in the 1830s that the full awfulness of the city slums became generally known.

During the 1790s the interest in the rural poor was maintained, and Southey and Wordsworth became practitioners in what was by now a well established tradition of poetry about impoverished countryfolk. The outbreak of war with revolutionary France in 1793 and a series of bad harvests did in fact bring on a period of genuine crisis. Widespread rural destitution led to the spread of the Speenhamland System, whereby low wages were supplemented from the Poor Rate. In some areas this necessitated such heavy rates that the middle classes found the poor an embarrassing drain on their pockets; and this made poverty all the more topical as a subject. In 1795 there were food riots in several parts of the country. Both the parliamentary opposition and the numerous provincial reform societies which had sprung up after 1792 stressed the poverty and want of the labouring classes, and as the war went on, and harvests continued uncertain, the subject of rural destitution showed no sign of losing its topicality. This cannot however be adduced as a proof of a connection between social conditions and poetry, as the poetical fashion undoubtedly ante-dated the social crisis in time.

To a great extent the vogue of the picturesque stemmed from the same social changes which generated the philanthropic movement. It may be indeed that the interest in *unspoilt* countryside represented an unconscious attempt to deny the existence of rural poverty; it may be that the vogue of the picturesque was sustained by uneasiness concerning change in the countryside and died away when the public finally came to terms with the new economic order which had been gaining ground during the previous two or three generations. But the growth of towns and the extension of transport facilities — both the inevitable accompaniments of the economic changes of the period — were certainly major factors in the emergence of the cult of the picturesque. Both the growth of towns and the revolution in transportation can be seen as forms of penetration by the urban environment into the countryside. In 1700 most English towns had not yet grown beyond their medieval street plans; only London had a population of over 35,000 while only Norwich and Bristol had populations over 20,000 and only York, Exeter, Yarmouth and Newcastle populations over 10,000, whereas by 1820 there were besides London six towns with over 50,000 inhabitants, nine more with over 25,000 and forty-five with over 10,000.[6] These towns were linked with increasing efficiency not only by canals (used mainly for heavy transport) but also by improved roads. Whereas between 1663 and 1750 there were only 146 Acts of Parliament to establish turnpikes, between 1751 and 1772 alone there were 389.[7] Perhaps the real boom in road transport did not come till the improvements in road building and coach design in the 1820s and 1830s (though for example the London-Manchester stage-coach journey was reduced from four days in 1754 to two days in 1784[8]), but sufficient was achieved to make the leisured public increasingly aware of the physical extent of their own country, and increasingly able to traverse it with relative ease and convenience. Samuel Johnson blamed turnpike roads for opening up and integrating the provinces:

Every place communicating with every other. Before these were cheap places, and dear places. Now all refuges destroyed for elegant or genteel poverty. Want of such a last hope to support men in their struggle through life, however seldom it might be resorted to. Disunion of families by furnishing a market to each man's abilities, and destroying the dependence of one man on another.[9]

But the extent to which the new turnpike roads also gave scope to the curiosity of increasing numbers of leisured people was no less important. Inevitably this interest in the rural picturesque sustained an interest in the poetry of rural description. The growing towns were almost never seen as objects of interest: Wordsworth's sonnet "Earth has not anything to show more fair" (composed 1802) and Joanna Baillie's *London*, which belongs to the same period —

> It is a goodly sight through the clear air,
> From Hampstead's heathy height to see at once
> England's vast capital in fair expanse,
> Towers, belfries, lengthen'd streets, and structures fair,

were rare exceptions, coming comparatively late in the day, and even then the subject of *London* suggested to Joanna Baillie

> Thoughts, mingled, melancholy, undefined,
> Of restless, reckless man, and years gone by,
> And Time fast wending to Eternity.

More typical was the tone of altogether undiluted hostility with which Joseph Cottle, in his underrated *Malvern Hills* (1798) wrote of countrymen who went to towns to

> be immured,
> From morn's first dawn till evening far is spent
> In dust, and stench, and pestilence!
> (ll. 533-5)

or the nostalgic regret of Southey (*To a Friend Settled in the Country*):

> Richard, the lot which fate to thee has given,
> I not unenvying shall recall to mind,
> In that foul town, by other fate confined,
> Where never running brook, nor verdant field,
> Nor yonder wide circumference of heaven,
> Sweet solace to the wearied soul can yield.

Much of the poetry of rural description looked back to the conventions of the Augustan period. Thus the Rev. Luke

Booker's *Malvern* often revived the tone of Akenside, with post-Gilpin modifications:

> From scenery so luxuriant to depart
> Loath is the Muse, tho' tempted now to plume
> Her wing for range more ample.— Cambria's Heights,
> Where the bright sun declines, burst on the view,
> All forms assuming, bold — abrupt — grotesque....
> (1798 edn., p. 16)

Frequently historical discourses were introduced, after the fashion of Jago, as in Thomas Maurice's *Richmond Hill*:

> There Chivalry unsheath'd her shining blade,
> And tournaments their warlike pomp display'd;
> The dauntless champion, marshall'd for the fight,
> The beauteous damsel charm'd th'admiring sight,
> The martial sports, that pleased a barbarous age
> Fired the bold youth, and fanned his native rage.
> (1807 edn., pp. 59-60)

The subordination of the countryside to the preoccupations of the civilized visitor was still emphasized. Thus Richard Wallis wrote in *The Happy Village*:

> Sweet Contemplation and a Mind at Ease,
> Will make the slightest touch of Nature please;
> But if absorb'd in Sorrow's cheerless Gloom,
> Lost are her brightest tints, and fairest Bloom;
> Yet kind Religion can restore the taste
> For woodland Fragrance, and the daisy'd Waste.
> (1802 edn., p. 12)

This interest in the picturesque was reintegrated with philanthropic tradition by Robert Bloomfield. Bloomfield was a ladies' shoemaker in his mid-thirties, but he had had some experience of working on the land as a boy, and this was distilled into his poem *The Farmer's Boy*, which was published in 1800 under the auspices of his discoverer, Capell Lofft, and broke all records for new poetry by selling 26,000 copies in three years.[10] Appearing in a period of agricultural crisis, *The Farmer's Boy* demanded attention because it was not merely *about* that crucial class, the rural poor, but was actually *by* one of that class; and it won its enormous popularity because it was, in fact, sheer escapism — escapism written with the authority of a former participant — telling the reader only those things which he had hoped were true, but in which he had begun to lose faith. Since, while he was actually writing the poem, Bloomfield was working in an overcrowded attic workshop in the London slums, he was probably inspired by the same need for escapism as his readers. The farmer's boy of his title was in spirits "Light as the lark that carol'd o'er his head", "genuine transport" glowed in his bosom, and moral guidance was supplied by the life of agriculture which displayed

> in every part
> A moral lesson to the sensual heart.

The home of this happy peasant was located thus:

> Where noble Grafton spreads his rich domains,
> Round *Euston's* water'd vale, and sloping plains,
> Where woods and groves in solemn grandeur rise,
> Where the kite brooding, unmolested flies,
> The woodcock and the painted pheasant race,
> And skulking foxes destined for the chase;
> ("Spring" l. 37 foll.)

The little shoemaker's vogue was tremendous. The Duke of Grafton, delighted at the discovery of "a real untaught genius starting from our neighbourhood", settled an annuity on him and found him a job in the Seal Office.[11] The King's second son, the Duke of York, sent ten guineas and "a handsome complimentary letter".[12] Julius Caesar Ibbetson, a rising genre painter was inspired by *The Farmer's Boy* to paint *The Farmyard*, with which he hoped to cash in on Bloomfield's success. The first edition of Bloomfield's second book, *Rural Tales*, was fixed at an unprecedented 7,000 copies, 5,000 duodecimo, 1,500 octavo and 500 quarto, so great seemed the probable demand.[13] Yet poetically, Bloomfield's success was barren. "Originality, on themes so hackneyed as pastoral delights, is invaluable, and we have it here, free from all taint of affectation, pure and unadulterate," wrote one reader;[14] but few practising poets seemed to agree. Southey penned a favourable notice for *The Critical Review*; there were a number of imitations; one, by William Holloway, entitled *The Peasants Fate*, another by Joseph Holland, with the suitably laborious title *An Appendix to the Season of Spring, in the Rural Poem of Bloomfield's "Farmer's Boy"*, and a third by David Service, also a poetical shoemaker, who had formerly been a herd boy "on the North banks of the Clyde", and whose *The Caledonian Herd-Boy* (Yarmouth 1802) caught Bloomfield's style perfectly:

> Now the trees blossom, and the meadows smile,
> And chanting birds the fleeting hours beguile;

> The growing corn of many-tinted hue
> Is gemm'd by night's all fertilizing dew;
> The ewes and lambkins dance along the plain
> Transported with the spring's return again;
> The mountains clothe themselves in robes of green
> And rise triumphant, 'midst the joyful scene:
> *(The Caledonian Herd-Boy* (1802 edn.) l. 3 foll.)

Yet many other contemporary writers seem to have had a very poor opinion of Bloomfield. Mary Russell Mitford referred to him as "that feeble verse-spinner",[15] Charles Lamb complained that Bloomfield made him "sick";[16] other writers totally ignored Bloomfield's very existence.

Bloomfield's popularity was short-lived, for the poetic vogue of the rural poor was virtually over by 1805. Pratt's *Cottage Pictures, or the Poor* (three editions 1801-03) and Bloomfield's *Rural Tales* (four editions 1801-05) seem to have almost smothered the public appetite. *Rural Tales* consisted of ballads, verse tales, songs (including one, *pace* Wordsworth, about "Lucy"). These were more deliberately artless than *The Farmer's Boy*:

> Dear boy, throw that icicle down,
> And sweep this deep snow from the door:
> Old Winter comes on with a frown;
> A terrible frown for the poor.
> In a season so rude and forlorn,
> How can age, how can infancy bear
> The silent neglect and the scorn
> Of those who have plenty to spare?
> ("Winter's Song", stanza 1)

Perhaps they were also less effective; after the four large editions of these poems were sold off, Bloomfield relapsed into comparative poverty and obscurity.

Bloomfield had achieved his success despite the fact that his poetry was already old-fashioned in 1800. In particular, his sentimentality was the bland, slightly self-conscious sentimentality of the 1770s and 1780s, very different from the rhetorical fervour which Campbell had popularized with *The Pleasures of Hope*. More in tune with the public's growing appetite for passion and pathos was James Grahame's *The Sabbath*. Though the principal influence on *The Sabbath* was Cowper's *The Task*, and though the poem's religious subject partly explains its popularity — it went through seven editions between 1804 and 1812 — Grahame appealed skilfully to the market discovered by Campbell for touching genre sketches:

> O Scotland! much I love thy tranquil dales:
> But most on Sabbath eve, when low the sun
> Slants through the upland copse, 'tis my delight
> Wandering, and stopping oft, to hear the song
> Of kindred praise arise from humble roofs;
> Or, when the simple service ends, to hear
> The uplifted latch, and mark the gray-hair'd man,
> The father and the priest, walk forth alone
> Into his garden-plot, or little field,
> To commune with his God in secret prayer —

and for melodrama:

> There on the heathless moss outstretch'd he broods
> O'er all his ever-changing plans of death:
> The time, place, means, sweep like a stormy rack,
> In fleet succession o'er his clouded soul; —
> The poniard — and the opium draught, that brings
> Death by degrees, but leaves an awful chasm
> Between the act and consequence, — and the flash
> Sulphureous, fraught with instantaneous death; —
> The ruin'd tower perched on some jutting rock etc.

Grahame's *British Georgics* (an imitation, this time, of Thomson) was published in 1809 but "did not obtain the same degree of popular favour",[17] largely because it did not strive to make the same appeal to its readers' emotions.

The public appetite for comforting insipidities about the poor did not cease after the opening years of the century. In 1810, for example, the Rev. Legh Richmond published a sentimental novel entitled *The Dairyman's Daughter* about a poor, evangelical-minded country girl who overcomes various trials and tribulations before dying of consumption. There were numerous 20,000 volume editions of this work, so that by 1829 there were calculated to be no less than two million copies in circulation.[18] But *The Dairyman's Daughter* was in prose; after about 1805 readers seemed increasingly to regard poetry as more appropriate for different kinds of subject. Poems about the poor continued to be written, such as *The Peasant's Death*, published 1806, by John Struthers, yet another farmhand-become-shoemaker, but the public interest in such poems seemed to have evaporated. Bloomfield had owed some of his success to the fact that within a few months of the first publication of *The Farmer's Boy* food shortages and grain riots had made his subject especially topical, but the poor did not cease to be poor after 1801 merely because they had ceased rioting; nor, when the rioting resumed in 1811, was there any revival in interest in poems about the poor. As a poetic subject they had simply ceased to be fashionable. This was well understood by the Rev. George Crabbe, whose *The Village* (1783) had been a seminal work of the rural poverty genre. *The Parish Register*, which Crabbe began writing in 1802 and published in 1807, was the last descriptive poem about the rural poor to be even a modest success, and Crabbe's later works, *The Borough* (1810), *Tales* (1812) and *Tales of the Hall* (1819), were about increasingly more genteel subjects. It was to be well over a decade before John Clare was able to repeat Bloomfield's success and establish himself as the authentic peasant minstrel of his generation; and even then his celebrity was only a fraction of what Bloomfield's had been, and his appeal was much less to the reading public's need to reassure itself about the lower classes.

The main literary significance of the vogue of the rural poor was its contribution — rather a faltering one — to a process of democratization of poetry and its subject matter. There was a movement away from the upper-class élitism of the best early eighteenth-century poetry. Partly because they came later, Burns, Cowper, Crabbe, even Pratt and Bloomfield, went further along the route opened up by Thomson and Beattie. Cowper in particular was viewed as a pioneer:

> The great merit of the writer appears to us to consist in the boldness and originality of his composition, and in the fortunate audacity with which he has carried the dominion of poetry into regions that had been considered as inaccessible to her ambition. The gradual refinement of taste had, for nearly a century, been weakening the vigour of original genius. Our poets had become timid and fastidious, and circumscribed themselves both in the choice and management of models, who were thought to have exhausted all the legitimate resources of the art. Cowper was one of the first who crossed the enchanted circle.... In disdaining to follow the footsteps of others, he has frequently mistaken the way, and has been exasperated, by their blunders, to rush into an opposite extreme... we can scarcely read a single page with attention, without being offended at some coarseness or lowness of expression, or disappointed by some "most lame and impotent conclusion".... [19]

Yet the posthumous acceptance of Burns and Cowper in no way assisted their poetic heirs. *The Edinburgh Review* was particularly careful to distinguish between, and contrast, the rural classics and "the Lake School" of Wordsworth and Southey, extolling the one by denigrating and misrepresenting the other:

> Those gentlemen [Wordsworth and Southey] are outrageous for simplicity; and we beg leave to recommend to them the simplicity of Burns. He has copied the spoken language of passion and affection, with infinitely more fidelity than they have ever done.... Let them contrast their own fantastical personages of hysterical schoolmasters and sententious leech gatherers, with the authentic rustics of Burns's Cotter's Saturday Night, and his inimitable songs, and reflect on the different reception which these personifications have met with from the public. Though they will not be reclaimed from their puny affectations by the example of their learned predecessors, they may, perhaps, submit to be admonished by a self-taught and illiterate poet, who drew from Nature far more directly than they can do, and produced something so much liker the admired copies of the masters whom they have abjured.[20]*

They heyday of Burns's and Cowper's reputation was indeed the nadir of the fame of Wordsworth.

The vogue of the picturesque lasted a few years longer than that of the poor (perhaps because it had a more direct appeal to readers' appetite for emotional hyperbole) and it had a much more evident influence on the poetry which came afterwards. Thomas Campbell blamed the "inordinate preference of descriptive poetry" on Thomson and Cowper: "their successes and the extreme easiness of descriptive poetry, have raised up a lamentable school, which we regret to think the public taste has too much encouraged."[21] Yet to some extent the increasing taste for the melodramatic in poetry made the pictorial serenity of Thomson and Cowper unfashionable; *The Edinburgh Review* even regretted, in Cowper's case, "those unfortunate circumstances, which doomed the eye of a real poet to rest on the flat and unmeaning pastures of Buckinghamshire".[22] More and

---

* Burns, in a letter to Dr Edward Moore, said that he possessed a copy of Pope's works as a youth, but that his *vade mecum* was then *A Select Collection of English Songs*. Later he read Thomson and Shenstone, adopting from them the Spenserian stanza he used in *The Cotter's Saturday Night*. The epigraph of this poem was from Gray, and it contained two quotations from Pope, so that it embodied more varied literary echoes (even though only three or four in number) than any of Wordsworth's mature work of comparable length. Burns's chief inspiration however was the dialect poetry of Robert Fergusson.

Wordsworth, incidentally, in a poem written in 1803 but not published till 1842, described Burns as "He...
> Whose light I hailed when first it shone,
>   And showed my youth
> How Verse may build a princely throne
>   On humble truth"
>
>   (*At the grave of Burns*)

more it appeared that simple description was not enough. The runaway success of Scott (discussed in the next chapter) with his strict subordination of description to narrative, showed what the poetry-reading public wanted. But the picturesque suffered not merely from a change of fashion, but also from a devastating satirical attack. The year of this attack, 1812, virtually marks the end of picturesque description as a separate verse genre.

The satire which "killed off" picturesque was William Combe's *The Tour of Doctor Syntax in Search of the Picturesque*. Dr Syntax, the hero, a poor schoolmaster, goes on a tour in order to write a tour-narrative, which he hopes he will be able to publish to supplement his meagre income. The poem combined a series of ludicrous adventures which befell him on the way, with a satire on the Gilpin school:

> Nature, dear Nature, is my goddess,
> Whether array'd in rustic bodice,
> Or when the nicest touch of Art
> Doth to her charms new charms impart:
> But still I, somehow, love her best,
> When she's in ruder mantle dress'd —
> I do not mean in shape grotesque,
> But when she's truly *picturesque*.
>
> (Canto 14)

Combe, who had been born as long ago as 1741, had had a varied career — schoolboy at Eton, lawyer, provincial playboy, soldier in both the French and British armies, waiter at Swansea, teacher of elocution, cook at Douai College. He had been a prolific writer, and had even attained the position of a pensioned government hack, but *Doctor Syntax* was his masterpiece. There were nine editions of it between 1812 and 1819, and at least twelve imitations by 1828.[23] The picturesque school found itself completely discredited; loco-descriptive poems did not cease to be written, but after 1812 they tended to be only the work of amateur poetasters, published by provincial booksellers, and none of them attained any popularity, unless one counts Lord Byron's *Childe Harolde's Pilgrimage* (the first two cantos of which appeared in 1812, and the last two in 1816 and 1818) which translated description and reflection to a Mediterranean setting, and supercharged them with a large injection of the author's laboured self-obsession. The emergence of the rival school of narrative poetry, and especially the phenomenal success of Scott's and Byron's metrical romances, may have been the underlying cause for the picturesque school's fall from favour, but it was certainly Combe who delivered the *coup de grâce*.

Of course, natural description did not disappear from poetry. But whereas the picturesque school had been concerned with evoking the fairly familiar British countryside, and derived much of its appeal from its portrayal of the predictable in a way that was both novel and reassuring, later poets, like Byron and Shelley, concentrated on the unfamiliar, the exotic, the disturbing, as a background for their unfamiliar, exotic narratives. And instead of the descriptions being detailed and evaluative and static, they became sketchy, suggestive, dynamic. Yet it would not be altogether just to see a dichotomy between the two approaches, for there is a kind of continuity of development between them. In the earlier eighteenth century, rounded hills such as were described by Thomson were considered picturesque. The more rugged peaks of the Lake District began to be admired in the 1770s, 1780s and 1790s, at the time that formal theories of the picturesque were being elaborated, and by the 1800s the Alps began to come into fashion. The popular taste, in fact, was for ever higher and more precipitous mountains, and this was reflected in the poetry of the day. Shelley, whose poetry embodied the most extreme elements of the taste of his age — so much so that he was too strong for the stomachs of most of his contemporaries — was fascinated by the highest of the Alps, Mont Blanc. He made it the starting point of one of his shorter poems (*Mont Blanc*, 1816) and in his Preface to *The Revolt of Islam* (1818) he claimed:

> I have been familiar from boyhood with mountains and lakes and the sea, and the solitude of forests: Danger which sports upon the brink of precipices, has been my play-mate. I have trodden the glaciers of the Alps, and lived under the eye of Mont Blanc.

The mountain also figures in his wife's novel, *Frankenstein*. Elsewhere in his poetry Shelley went to an even higher mountain range, the Caucasus: *

---

* Cf. the setting for *Prometheus Unbound* which begins in "A Ravine of Icy Rocks in the Indian Caucasus". The Indian Caucasus also figures in Book 1 of Bowles's *The Spirit of Discovery* (1804) and in his notes Bowles showed that he regarded the Hindu Kush as being an extension of the Caucasus range and that it was to the former mountain chain (actually a thousand miles east of the true Caucasus range, and even higher) that he applied the term Indian Caucasus; where Shelley located the mountain is not on record.

> At midnight
> The moon arose: and lo! the ethereal cliffs
> Of Caucasus, whose icy summits shone
> Among the stars like sunlight, and around
> Whose cavern'd base the whirlpools and the waves
> Bursting and eddying, irresistibly
> Rage and resound for ever....
> (*Alastor*, l. 351 foll.)

Poetry scenery, in fact, becoming progressively more dramatic, more and more supercharged with, and reflecting, human emotions. Poets had become habituated to natural description, and more and more began to employ it imaginatively in ways which would have been regarded as extraordinary by the picturesque writers of the eighteenth century. The picturesque in fact had not been so much repudiated, as absorbed and totally transformed.

PART TWO:
THE CRUCIAL YEARS

5
The Metrical Romance

> These are the themes that claim our plaudits now;
> These are the Bards to whom the Muse must bow;
> While MILTON, DRYDEN, POPE, alike forgot,
> Resign their hallowed Bays to WALTER SCOTT.
>
> (Byron, *English Bards, and Scotch Reviewers*, ll. 185-8)

Since the publication of Bishop Percy's *Reliques* the ballad had been gaining in popularity, and the vogue received further encouragement in the 1790s with the English discovery of the German poet Gottfried Augustus Bürger, whose gothic horror ballad *Lenore* appeared in English in five separate translations, by J. T. Stanley, William Spencer, Henry James Pye (the Poet Laureate) Walter Scott and William Taylor* — an unusual testimony to a foreign author's popularity. Walter Scott and William Taylor both also translated Bürger's *Der Wilde Jäger*. There were a number of attempts at original compositions in the same macabre vein, such as Nathan Drake's *The Spectre*, Southey's *Donica* and *St Patrick's Purgatory* and "Monk" Lewis's *Alonzo the Brave, and Fair Imogine*, and there was also a serious antiquarian interest in the ballad and associated poetic forms which led to the publication in 1802 of Scott's *The Minstrelsy of the Scottish Border* (in which most but not all of the poems were authentic folk ballads), James Sibbald's *Chronicles of Scottish Poetry; from the Thirteenth Century to the Union of the Crowns*, and Joseph Ritson's *Ancient English Metrical Romanceës*.

This ballad craze ran parallel to the fashion which was gaining ground for brief genre narratives of the sort written by Southey, and by Wordsworth in *Lyrical Ballads*. Despite their own interest in and debt to the ballad form, Southey and Wordsworth must be seen as working in a different tradition,

---

* There were also several versions in the nineteenth century, including one by Dante Gabriel Rossetti.

that of the Thomsonian episode converted into a short poem in its own right, but as with ballads, their poems about common folk involved in the ordinary incidents of contemporary life were essentially *narrative* poems; interest in description and reflection was giving way to a preference for dramatic story-lines.

The popularity of ballads was also of course connected with the vogue of gothic romance. They shared the same subject matter of star-crossed lovers and spectral hauntings, the same antique setting, and had the same dramatic appeal. Though the 1790s saw the popular success of Ann Radcliffe's chaste *The Mysteries of Udolpho*, there seems to have been during the same period an increasing demand for fiction of unprecedented sensationalism, lubricity and violence. M. G. Lewis's novel *The Monk* (1796) was perhaps the best example of this; it featured an abbot who is seduced by a girl disguised as a monk and who later plots with his paramour to deflower the heroine. The latter is eventually raped in a tomb:

> He stifled her cries with kisses, treated her with the rudeness of an unprincipled Barbarian, proceeded from freedom to freedom, and in the violence of his lustful delirium, wounded and bruised her tender limbs! Heedless of her tears, cries and entreaties, He gradually made himself Master of her person, and desisted not from his prey, till He had accomplished his crime and the dishonour of Antonia.
>
> (vol. 3, chap. 4)

In a novel published in 1804 one of the characters says,

> Novels now-a-days, unless they are excessively sentimental, don't sell. Romances are more in fashion; and these must have ghosts, mysteries, subterraneous caverns, suffering Matildas, heroic Fitzallans, villainous Osmonds, persecuted Reginalds; they must be lighted up with torches, be loaded with fragments of decayed and mouldering castles, haunted with male or female spectres, have their pages stained with the acts of cruel barons, and be interspersed with a little licentiousness; such as will provoke the passions of the younger part of the sexes.[1]

To a great extent the trappings of ancient castles and supernatural presences were merely a means to an end; the core of the appeal of such novels was their treatment of sex and violence. When it is realized that even so innocuous a work as *The Mysteries of Udolpho* derived its theme of the trapped and helpless maiden from Richardson's *Clarissa*, that classic of procrastinated rape and sado-masochism, the popularity of the gothic novel will be better understood. But the gothic novel also leaned heavily on the contemporary preoccupation with death, especially violent death. In part this preoccupation was also sexual in character,[2] but in part it went back to the tradition of melancholy which had flourished so notably in the graveyard poetry of the 1740s. By the 1800s the obsession with death was at its peak. Newspapers, especially local ones, were full of macabre details of fatal accidents and the like — "was soon after seized with a most violent hydrophobia, and expired on Tuesday sen'night, in indescribable agonies"; "his head being almost dashed to pieces"; "the villains beat his head in pieces in the presence of his wife"; "the wheel passing over his head killed him on the spot"; "he was killed on the spot, the upper part of the skull being beat in so, that the brains oozed out through the cavities."[3] Public hangings, in which criminals were killed by slow strangulation (the technique of the long drop, which ensures instant death, not being perfected till the reign of Queen Victoria) were invariably the resort of large crowds; in a mob which gathered to see two murderers hanged at the Old Bailey on 23 February 1807, no less than twenty-eight people were trampled to death, so great was the crush, and *The Annual Register*, reporting the incident, did not fail to mention that "The shrieks of the dying men, women, and children, were terrific beyond description".[4]* This anxiety to dwell on such subjects with leisurely delight was curiously exemplified by the diary of a "Lover of Literature" which contained observations such as:

> Our deep abhorrence of the crime of murder is the off-spring not of devotion, but of a cultivated and refined humanity — of a heart revolting at blood, the shrieks of terror, the convulsive agonies, the ghastliness, and all the horrors of sudden and violent death.[5]

It was probably no coincidence that England's first recorded sadistic mass-murderer, the perpetrator of the Ratcliffe Highway murders of 7 and 19 December 1811, belongs to this period; and it was surely characteristic of the times that the principal suspect in this case, having committed suicide in jail, was buried with a stake through his heart at a crossroads in the East End of London, in the presence of a huge crowd.

Among those who set themselves to cater for this general

---

* The Old Bailey disaster was not unique; in 1844 twelve people were crushed to death and five more fatally injured at a hanging outside the County Hall in Nottingham.

taste for the sensational was Coleridge. *The Rime of the Ancient Mariner* was a poem about death (and resurrection), and while he was writing it he was also working on *Christabel*, a poem about both death and sex. The eponymous heroine is a maidenly victim in the best gothic tradition. Her strange guest, Geraldine, though ostensibly female, seems to represent some kind of sexual threat, as is indicated by the emphasis on Christabel's physical vulnerability:

> Her gentle limbs did she undress,
> And lay down in her loveliness,
>
> (Pt. 1, l. 237-8)

and by the deliberate suggestiveness of such passages as

> A star hath set, a star has risen,
> O Geraldine! since arms of thine
> Have been the lovely lady's prison.
> O Geraldine! one hour was thine —
> Thou hadst thy will! [6]
>
> (Pt. 1, l. 302-6)

In no sense did this poem break new ground with regard to its subject matter. With regard to its format however, *Christabel* was of greater innovatory significance than any other poem Coleridge ever wrote.

Though the first part was written in 1797 and the second part in 1800, *Christabel* was not published till 1816. It was however recited to Walter Scott by John Stoddart, a friend of both Scott and Coleridge. Scott, a young lawyer with a budding reputation in Edinburgh literary circles, was acquainted with the longer medieval poems — he was at the time actually preparing an edition of one for publication — and *Christabel* made a profound impression on him, not because it could have appeared entirely novel to him, but because it seemed to him an excellent modern version of a kind of poem with which he was already familiar. Coleridge's poem helped him focus his attention on possibilities which must have already been shaping in his mind and it was after hearing Stoddart's recitation that he began to write his first full-length work, *The Lay of the Last Minstrel*. Coleridge himself later exonerated Scott of conscious plagiarism,[7] but the similarity of style in *Christabel* and *The Lay* became a commonplace of literary gossip in the Coleridge circle.[8] Someone even published a letter signed S.T.C. in *The London Courier* (15 September 1810), accusing Scott of plagiarism. In the 1830 edition of Scott's works, Scott bowed to public opinion by admittng Coleridge's influence and making "the acknowledgment due from the pupil to his master". Yet in fact this acknowledgement was unnecessary and unjustified. The versification of *Christabel* and *The Lay* seem to have been separately derived from medieval models, and that of *The Lay* is substantially different from Coleridge's.[9] And there was little similarity of subject matter; *Christabel* was a tale of enchantment and strange malevolent forces whereas *The Lay*, for all its atmosphere of spells and portents and fatalities, was a straightforward romance of chivalry. The theme and action and historical colouring were entirely Scott's own, or, if they were borrowed from anyone, it was from Goethe.[10] All that Scott owed to Coleridge was an idea; but it was one of the most seminal ideas of their generation.

Previously, narrative poems had either been fairly short and informal, i.e. ballads, or else excessively lengthy and conventionalized, i.e. epics. Since 1790 about a dozen attempts at epic poetry had been published in England, of which only Southey's *Joan of Arc*, Joseph Cottle's *Alfred* and Richard Cumberland's *Calvary* had had sufficient success to justify reprinting — *Calvary* probably because of the recommendation of its religious subject matter. Nevertheless this steady flow of unread epics (which was to continue till the 1820s) indicates that writers were aware of a market for narrative poetry;[11] only Blake, whose epics were more in the way of visionary works, can be said to have been uninfluenced by considerations of his probable market, and he was spoken of as "a decided madman", and his *Jerusalem* was described as "a perfectly mad poem".[12] The trouble with the epics was that they were too long, too difficult to read, too emotionally remote. Ballads on the other hand, though vivid and readable, were not long enough to "get one's teeth into", and they did not fit in with the current critical equation of bulk and merit (see pages 19 and 121 in this book). Ballads could be popular enough — as ballads — but they could never be accepted as great literature. What Scott achieved with *The Lay of the Last Minstrel* was the combination of the bulk — and the room for development of plot — of the epic, with the dash, readability and fervour of the ballads; and to this amalgam Scott added picturesque description and authentic evocation of the romantic past:

> Soon in his saddle sate he fast,
> And soon the steep descent he past,
> Soon cross'd the sounding barbican,
> And soon the Teviotside he won.
> Eastwood the wooded path he rode,

> Green hazels o'er his basnet nod;
> He pass'd the Peel of Goldiland,
> And cross'd old Borthwick's roaring strand;
> Dimly he viewed the Moat-hills mound,
> Where druid shades still flitted round,
> In Hawick twinkled many a light;
> Behind him soon they set in night;
> And soon he spurr'd his courser keen
> Beneath the tower of Hazeldean.
>
> (Canto 1, stanza 25)

It was a mixture which in the first decade of the nineteenth century could not have possibly failed to be popular.

Published in 1805, *The Lay* sold 21,300 copies in five years,[13] and was followed by the even more popular *Marmion* in 1808. In 1810 Scott's third verse romance, *The Lady of the Lake*, sold 20,300 copies in its first year alone, despite the exorbitant price of 42 shillings for the larger size editions, and the unusually large amount of blank paper surrounding the print.[14] Scott's sales were indeed so enormous that they represented not merely a tremendous commercial success, but a veritable revolution in public taste; people who had previously rarely looked at, or purchased, any poetry except perhaps Bloomfield's were evidently reading Scott's verse.

Naturally this popular success involved some power of influence on the public. *The Monthly Review* considered this influence to be a bad one, claiming that Scott's "carelessness in composition is, we conceive, making a rapid progress in barbarizing our language and corrupting our taste", and that he "has indeed largely contributed to humble and to corrupt our national taste in poetry".[15] There was surely some truth in this, for though an over-emphatic and slapdash style had been common enough since the Della Cruscans at least, it had never before received so much public admiration. Nor was Scott's influence transmitted by himself alone; he inspired numerous attempts to imitate his style, by Margaret Holford in *Wallace, or the Fight of Falkirk*, William Stewart Rose in *The Crusade of St Louis* and *St Edward the Martyr*, William Sotheby in *Constance de Castile*, James Hogg in *The Queen's Wake*, Margaret Harvey in *The Lay of the Minstrel's Daughter*, and the anonymous author of *The Crusaders, or the Minstrels of Acre* who, according to his Preface, "conceived that the wild harp, which Mr WALTER SCOTT has touched with so masterly a hand, might not only adapt itself to a diversity of subjects; but might even sound in unison with the sublime lyre of Scriptural

Prophecy". John Wilson Croker's *The Battle of Talavera*, which applied Scott's metre and language to the topical subject of Wellington's campaigns in the Peninsula, quickly went through eight editions; Scott's own *The Bridal of Triermain* was at first passed off as an anonymous imitation of himself, and was respectfully reviewed as such. Scott was also an important influence on the narrative poetry of Byron, who took overemphasis and slapdashedness to even greater lengths, but other poets, like the Rev. Robert Bland and Byron's friend Francis Hodgson, imitated Scott in his type of subject while adhering to more old-fashioned prosodic forms, such as regular heroic couplets in Bland's *Edwy and Elgiva* (1808) and Spenserians in Hodgson's *Sir Edgar* (1810). Nor was Scott's influence only on narrative. He contributed, by his success, to the demise of the descriptive and philosophical genres. It is no exaggeration to say that all the earlier moves towards a more direct, more impassioned, more humanly emotional style of poetry, from the Wartons and Collins to Wordsworth and Campbell, were consummated in and through the triumph of Walter Scott.

Both *Lyrical Ballads* and *The Pleasures of Hope* may be perhaps best understood as the culmination of a complex tradition which had been developing throughout the eighteenth century. The only discontinuity between *Lyrical Ballads* and other poetry of its time was the discontinuity between the poetic genius of Wordsworth and the smaller talent of his contemporaries. With Scott, though his place in a developing tradition is equally clear, there was a real break. A new audience had been discovered, new expectations awakened; much more than any poet since Young, Scott had tapped a market created by the psychological climate of the period, which had been scarcely touched before. What this psychological climate was I shall discuss in the next chapter, but the essential point is that Scott did not merely take a literary tradition a step further, he created a new one from his intuitive response to the cultural environment of his age.

By his contemporaries Scott was regarded as a very great poet indeed. Even the reviewers who objected to his style admitted his "genius and originality".[16] For an example of the enthusiasm engendered among the reading public, both then and later, it is worth quoting from Charlotte Brontë's *Jane Eyre* — written, be it remembered, by a woman who could recommend Milton, Shakespeare, Thomson, Goldsmith, Pope ("if you will, though I don't admire him"), Byron, Campbell, Wordsworth and Southey to her friend Ellen Nussey.[17] In chapter 6 of the third volume of *Jane Eyre* occurs the following passage:

> He laid on the table a new publication — a poem: one of those genuine productions so often vouchsafed to the fortunate public of those days — the golden age of modern literature. Alas! the readers of our era are less favoured. But courage! I will not pause either to accuse or repine. I know poetry is not dead, nor genius lost; nor has Mammon gained power over either, to bind or slay: they will both assert their existence, their presence, their liberty, and strength again one day. Powerful angels, safe in heaven! they smile when sordid souls triumph, and feeble ones weep over their destruction. Poetry destroyed? Genius banished? No! Mediocrity, no: do not let envy prompt you to the thought. No; they not only live, but reign, and redeem: and without their divine influence spread everywhere, you would be in hell — the hell of your own meanness.
>
> (Chap. 32 of one-volume eds.)

And, as was soon explained, the poem in question was *Marmion*.

Scott himself did not take his verse tales as seriously as this. "I can, with honest truth, exculpate myself from having been at any time a partisan of my own poetry," he wrote in 1830.[18] In many ways he was a conventional man of letters of the late eighteenth century, urbane, unimpassioned and scholarly. Although his earliest published works were translations from modern German and imitations of Border ballads, he was, more than anything else, an admirer of the Augustans; his favourite poet was Johnson but he also brought out an edition of Dryden which he hoped, vainly as it happened, would inaugurate a revival of interest in that poet.[19] He apparently had no strong views on the poetry of his contemporaries, and not only kept himself aloof from public literary controversies, but even maintained a neutral role in his private conversation. Partly this was because of his innate good nature, but it also suggests that he had no real interest in a living poetic tradition; a man who could be equally prompt in defending both Campbell and Wordsworth from adverse criticism could not have devoted much serious reflection to either of them.[20]

Scott's generosity of mind amidst the mutual jealousies and petty bickerings of the literary world did not save his poetry from the low opinion of Southey, Rogers, Coleridge and Wordsworth. Southey called *The Lay of the Last Minstrel* "a very amusing poem; it excites a novel-like interest, but you discover nothing on [?] after perusal".[21] Rogers damned him with faint praise: "On the whole, his *poetry* is too carelessly

written to suit my taste; but parts of it are very happy."²²
Coleridge had some shrewd criticisms:

> If I were called upon to form an opinion of Mr Scott's poetry, the first thing I should do would be to take away all his names of old castles, which rhyme very prettily, and read very picturesquely; then, I would remove out of the poem all the old armour and weapons, next I would exclude the mention of all nunneries, abbeys and priories, and I should then see what would be the residuum — how much poetry would remain.²³

Wordsworth, who was on friendly terms with Scott, and whose own *The White Doe of Rylstone*, though not exactly inspired by Scott, was written with a consciousness of his success with the metrical romance, had an even lower opinion. Though not in the habit of sneering at his friends behind their backs, "He assented to the observation 'that the secret of Scott's popularity is the vulgarity of his conceptions, which the million can at once comprehend,' "²⁴ and in a letter to Rogers he quoted the epigram,

> Tom writes, his Verses with huge speed,
> Faster than Printer's Boy can set 'en,
> Faster far than we can read,
> And only not so fast as we forget 'en.²⁵

But both Campbell and Lord Byron admired Scott, partly because they always admired what sold well, partly because they were critically naïve, but mainly because Scott genuinely struck a sympathetic chord in them.

Scott's influence on Byron was of particular importance, for Byron found in Scott not only the idea of the verse tale, but also the so-called Byronic hero. Late eighteenth-century novels contained notable examples of the Byronic type. Eino Railo, in *The Haunted Castle*, has traced such figures back to Shakespeare,²⁶ which is perhaps taking ancestor-hunting too far; but certainly Moore's Zeluco and Ann Radcliffe's Montoni had already made the reading public familiar with (to quote Railo, page 31):

> the lonely, stalwart, saturnine and black-browed man of beautiful countenance, whose spiritual life is in the grip of some secret influence, and who, by reason of his intelligence and strength of will and the volcanic nature of his passions, stands out from his surroundings as an independent individual.

Byron himself referred to the protagonist of *Childe Harold's Pilgrimage* as "perhaps a poetical Zeluco" (in his "Addition to the Preface" in the fourth and later editions). The character-type had even found its way into verse, for example in a fragment (not printed till 1833) by Henry Soame, a former Trinity College, Cambridge, undergraduate who had committed suicide in India in 1803 while serving as an officer in the 25th Light Dragoons:

> Sour'd, but untam'd, in disappointment's school,
> He look'd ordain'd to ruine or to rule;
> Through his dark cluster'd ringlets, here and there
> Shone ere its time a sorrow-silvered hair;
> On his pale cheek a bitter smile there sate,
> Which seem'd to mock the impotence of fate;
> Upon his haughty brow defiance lower'd;
> Despair was in his hollow eye embower'd: —
> Still, o'er the wild expression of his face
> Would beam, by starts, a momentary grace;
> Faint emanations of the God were seen
> To indicate the thing he should have been.

But it was Scott, in his *Marmion*, who popularized this species of humanity in poetry and who made him the hero rather than the interesting but subordinate villain. In his poems, Scott's characterization tends to be thin, and one has to read the whole of *Marmion* to capture its hero's true personality, such as it was, but a couple of passages show Scott's rendering of the proto-Byronic type:

> His eye-brow dark, and eye of fire,
> Shewed spirit proud, and prompt to ire;
> Yet lines of thought upon his cheek,
> Did deep design and counsel speak.
> (Canto 1, stanza 5)
> Marmion, whose steady heart and eye
> Ne'er changed in worst extremity;
> Marmion, whose soul could scarcely brook,
> Even from his king, a haughty look;
> Whose accent of command controuled,
> In camps, the boldest of the bold. . . .
> (Canto 3, stanza 14)

All that was left to Byron to add was the characteristic of secret remorse, and his own personal charisma which encouraged the public to believe that examples of the Byronic hero existed in real life, and that he himself was the finest of such specimens. This identification of Byron and the Byronic hero has survived into the second half of the twentieth century. That Byron denied the identification himself[27] is justly disregarded — he was not a man to utter serious truths, and especially not about himself, in spite of the innocent faith of one modern critic that "Byron never poses".[28] More relevant is the fact that anyone of any perspicacity who knew Byron personally found little in him of the Byronic hero, save only the physical apearance. Lady Caroline Lamb thought he was "mad, bad, and dangerous to know", but then she was herself a silly hysterical woman who was very much in love with him; Leigh Hunt and Edward Trelawny, who knew Byron much better and had much more experience of mankind, found him mean, vulgar, vain and not even particularly quick-witted; the bitterness with which both these men wrote of him after his death, which is in such contrast to the adulatory tone of their reminiscences of Shelley, testifies to their disappointment in Byron as a person.[29] It would seem that Byron and the Byronic hero were merely connected by wish-fulfilment — the wish-fulfilment of mean, vain, petty Lord Byron himself, who wanted to be thought incapable of small crimes yet giant enough to have perpetrated moral enormities; and the wish-fulfilment of a sensation-seeking public eager to believe that such exciting and remarkable people existed. Yet Byron was able to deceive most of his generation, which was so eager to be deceived, and the rumours and scandals connected with his name, running through High Society and percolating down to the genteel middle-class readers in the quiet side streets of remote country towns, lent an irresistible savour to his poetry. Thus, though he did not invent the Byronic hero, Byron certainly helped to establish it in the popular imagination. Yet even the extent to which he did this has perhaps been exaggerated. Scott's sales, though soon to be outdistanced by Byron's own, had been enormous in the half dozen years before Byron's reputation was established, and the Byronic hero was to be found in Scott too, not to mention in the novels of Ann Radcliffe and Dr Moore. Charlotte Brontë's Mr Rochester is often cited as the classic example of the Byronic type turning up in a strange guise, but such internal evidence as there is in *Jane Eyre* — specifically the passage quoted above — would suggest that it was Marmion who was Mr Rochester's closest literary ancestor. A revision of some other generally accepted Byronic genealogies might well be in order.

Between Scott's first triumph and Lord Byron's however, there elapsed half a dozen not unimportant years. All Scott's poems were set in medieval and early modern Scotland and the border country. This enabled him to incorporate authentic picturesque descriptions, but took no account of the public's increasing thirst for wilder, more alien landscapes than those north country uplands with which Scott was familiar. Even his closest imitators (other than Margaret Holford and later James Hogg) went overseas, to southern Europe and the near East, for the location of their action. But more influential than Scott's imitators was James Montgomery, whose *The Wanderer of Switzerland* (published in 1806) quickly went through three editions. This was not the first poem to be set in the Alps; Goldsmith's *The Traveller*, published in 1764, had merely taken the Alps as its starting point:

> Even now, where Alpine solitudes ascend,
> I sit me down a pensive hour to spend;
> And, placed on high above the storm's career,
> Look downward where an hundred realms appear;
> (l. 31-4)

but the Rev. Thomas Sedgwick Whalley had published a descriptive-reflective poem on *Mont Blanc*, in 1788; Wordsworth's *Descriptive Sketches*, also about the Alps, had come out five years later; Bowles's *The Sorrows of Switzerland*, which like *The Wanderer of Switzerland* dealt with the French invasion of the cantons, had appeared in 1801 and Coleridge's *Hymn Before Sun-Rise in the Vale of Chamouni* in 1802. Montgomery's *Wanderer* was however the first Alpine poem to make any popular impact. Thereafter soaring peaks and plunging cliffs became familiar settings for poems. As I have already suggested, it would appear that as the years passed the public taste craved for the ever more dramatic in scenery; where mere hills sufficed in the 1760s and 1770s, the more awe-inspiring panoramas of the Lake District had become preferred in the 1780s and 1790s — not merely by Wordsworth but even by his arch-critic Jeffrey.[30] After 1806 it was the turn of the Alps, the two most commercially successful Alpine poems being Byron's *Manfred* (1817) and Campbell's *Theodric* (1824).

Yet Montgomery was more than merely the popularizer of mountain scenery; he was an important analogue to Scott. *The Wanderer of Switzerland* had been commenced two years before *The Lay* was published;[31] and Montgomery, who knew little or nothing of medieval metrical romances, conceived his poem as being of ingredients quite different from those brought together by Scott. In his Preface he wrote:

> An heroic subject is celebrated in a lyric measure, on a dramatic plan. To unite with the majesty of epic song the fire,

rapidity and compression of the ode, and to give to both the grace and variety of earnest impassioned conversation, would be an enlargement of the boundaries of Parnassus. In such an adventure, success is consecrated by the boldness of the first attempt.

Nevertheless his impetuous, easy rhythm (catalectic trochaic tetrameters), impassioned tone and dramatic theme appealed to exactly the same taste that Scott exploited. Incidentally, Montgomery's vocabulary and simplicity was also reminiscent of *Lyrical Ballads*, though Montgomery himself later wrote of Wordsworth:

> I am sure the poetry of two men cannot differ much more widely than his does from mine. I hate his baldness and vulgarity of phrase, and I doubt not he equally detests the splendour and foppery of mine; but I feel the pulse of poetry beating through every vein of thought in all his compositions, even in his most pitiful, puerile, and affected pieces.[32]

Yet a hybrid of *The Lay of the Last Minstrel* and a "Lucy" poem might very well have resembled Montgomery's opening in *The Wanderer of Switzerland*:

> Shepherd: "Wanderer! whither dost thou roam?
> Weary Wanderer, old and grey!
> Wherefore hast thou left thine home
> In the sunset of thy day?"
>
> Wanderer: "In the sunset of my day,
> Stranger! I have lost my home:
> Weary, wandering, old and grey
> Therefore, therefore, do I roam."

Soon however (stanza 6) the verse entered a strain of hyperbole more reminiscent of Merry and Campbell:

> O'er thy mountains, sunk in blood,
> Are the waves of ruin hurl'd;
> Like the waters of the flood,
> Rolling round a buried world.

The Edinburgh Review claimed that it had supposed Montgomery to be "some slender youth of seventeen,* intoxicated with weak tea, and the praises of sentimental Ensigns",[33] and complained, "Whenever he does not whine, he must rant. The

---

* Montgomery was actually in his mid-thirties, had served two terms in prison for seditious libel, and had been established as a newspaper editor in Sheffield for over ten years.

scanty stream of his genius is never allowed to steal quietly along its channel; but is either poured out in melodious tears, or thrown up to heaven in all the frothy magnificence of tiny jets and artificial commotions."[34] But it was precisely this exaggeration of tone that the public now admired. And not only the public: Byron, who sneered at Scott in his *English Bards, and Scotch Reviewers,* praised *The Wanderer in Switzerland* in a footnote to that satire[35] and Southey considered Montgomery "undoubtedly a man of genius".[36]

Besides the medievalism of Scott and the mountainy melodramas of Montgomery, there was another variation of the verse romance. Scott's poems had their love interest, but the sentimental treatment of women was not a vital ingredient. Mary Tighe's *Psyche* (1805), an allegorical love story in Spenserians which was later to influence poets as dissimilar as Keats and Bernard Barton,[37] featured a suffering heroine, but it had been too ethereal and restrained to suit the taste of the day. The distinction of being the first to translate the exaggerated emotional sensibility already found in novels and love lyrics into the central theme of a best-selling long poem belonged to Thomas Campbell.

Campbell's *Gertrude of Wyoming* appeared in 1809. Though puffed by his crony Jeffrey in *The Edinburgh Review* it was not a great success with the critics, but the public had been eagerly waiting for a second major poem from the author of *The Pleasures of Hope. Gertrude of Wyoming* was very different from Campbell's earlier poem both in theme and treatment. Campbell's new heroine, Gertrude, was an "enthusiast for the woods" and an avid reader of Shakespeare; the poem described her life in the unspoilt wilds of America and her tragic death during a Red Indian attack. Campbell's adoption of the Spenserian stanza was not, perhaps, a great success:

> On Susquehana's side, fair Wyoming,
> Although the wild-flower on thy ruin'd wall
> And roofless homes a sad remembrance bring
> Of what thy gentle people did befall,
> Yet thou wert once the loveliest land of all
> That see the Atlantic wave their morn restore.
> Sweet land! may I thy lost delights recall,
> And paint thy Gertrude in her bowers of yore,
> Whose beauty was the love of Pennsylvania's shore.

This stanza form imposed a nervelessness and chasteness of language which rendered the poem too insipid to equal public expectations. One reader declared: "If I mistake not, in the year 1910, while *Gertrude of Wyoming* will continue to delight us, the very name of SCOTT, with his *Lay*, and his *Marmion*, and his *Lady*, will be shrouded in oblivion."[38] But this does not seem to have been the general impression, and compared to *The Lay of the Last Minstrel* and its sequels, *Gertrude of Wyoming* was only a modest success, taking sixteen years to reach its ninth edition.

Whereas Scott set his poems in areas that were thoroughly familiar to him, Campbell chose a back-drop so little known, not merely to himself but to everyone in Britain, that *The Modern Gazetteer* of 1810 could only say of Wyoming that it was "a name formerly given to a tract of country in Pennsylvania, on Susquehannah river, above Wilkesbarre. In this tract lies the scene of Mr Campbell's Poem of Gertrude of Wyoming."* Both the setting and the mood of the poem probably owed something to Chateaubriand's novel *Atala* (1801),[39] and Campbell was certainly not unique in recognizing the readership appeal of mingled exoticism and sentimentality, as was demonstrated by the appearance within the next three years of two more love romances set in far off places.

The first of these poems was *Christina*, written by Mary Russell Mitford and partially revised and added to by Coleridge.[40] This was a love story attached to the famous mutiny on *H.M.S. Bounty*. (A similar subject was later tackled by Byron in *The Island*. It was, incidentally, not till three years after the publication of *Christina* that the mystery then still surrounding the *Bounty* mutineers was cleared up by the chance discovery of the last survivor of the mutineers on Pitcairn Island.) Next year John Wilson's *The Isle of Palms* was published. This described the love of a ship-wrecked couple, but was mainly descriptive and philosophical, as very little happened in the way of action save that the woman produced a baby. John Wilson, who had written an admiring but expostulatory letter to Wordsworth in 1802, supposedly took the co-author of *Lyrical Ballads* as his model, though his language and theme were more lush than those of his hero:

> A Summer Night descends in balm
> On the orange-bloom, and stately Palm,

---

* Campbell's Wyoming was not the state of that name (then not yet established). Wyoming is quite a common place-name further east, from Ontario southwards to Virginia. Campbell's Wyoming was the Wyoming Valley, today a depressed coal mining area in north eastern Pennsylvania. Wyoming borough (population about 4,000) has a memorial to the Indian massacre referred to in the poem.

> Of that romantic steep,
> Where, silent as the silent hour,
> Mid the soft leaves of their Indian bower,
> Three happy spirits sleep.
> (*The Isle of Palms*, Canto 4, l. 1 foll.)

and the hypnotic lilt was unlike anything in Wordsworth. It is odd to think of these poems, which adumbrate the great escapist symbol of the twentieth century and which are so close to pre-war Hollywood in their spirit, as being, the one the stepchild of Coleridge, and the other the stepchild of Wordsworth.

In a very different idiom, but involving the same movement towards the development of a narrative format, were the verse tales of the Rev. George Crabbe. His descriptive verse essay *The Borough* (1810) contained a number of tales, of which "Peter Grimes" is the best known; it was followed in 1812 by his *Tales* which was simply an anthology of short verse narratives concerning ordinary English men and women in commonplace situations, such as "The Gentleman Farmer", " 'Squire Thomas; or, the Precipitate Choice" and "Advice; or, the 'Squire and the Priest". There seems however to have been only a limited demand for verse tales set in familiar places and dealing with familiar circumstances; Mary Russell Mitford's projected follow-up of *Christina*, a series of *Narrative Poems on the Female Character, in the various relations of life*, was discontinued after the appearance of the first volume in 1813, most probably because of lack of public response. Readers seemed to want more violent excitements.

Byron's first verse romance, *The Giaour*, which came out in February 1813, gave the readers all the violent excitement they wanted:

> Who thundering comes on blackest steed,
> With slackened bit and hoof of speed?
> Beneath the clattering iron's sound
> The caverned Echoes wake around
> In lash for lash, and bound for bound;
> The foam that streaks the courser's side
> Seems gathered from the Ocean's-tide:
> Though weary waves are sunk to rest,
> There's none within his rider's breast;
> And though to-morrow's tempest lower,
> 'Tis calmer than thy heart, young Giaour!
> (l. 180 foll.)

Byron was already well-known for his reflective, descriptive poem *Childe Harold's Pilgrimage*, the first two cantos of which had appeared the previous year, and *The Giaour* was an instant best-seller. It was followed in quick succession by *The Bride of Abydos* (1813), *The Corsair* (1814), *Lara* (1814), *The Siege of Corinth* (1816) and *Parasina* (1816).

Byron's popularity quickly eclipsed that of Scott. Possibly the fact that his poems were actually much shorter than Scott's helped; but it was also the case that the values virtually established by Scott were trebly confirmed by Byron. Imitation of eighteenth-century models became at last discredited. The new and the daring became respectable instead of the old and the time-honoured, and this was more through Byron's influence than anyone else's. He also improved on his immediate predecessors with various new departures in content. His favourite Greek and Levantine settings were his own idea. W. S. Rose had used the same locale slightly earlier, but had been ignored by the public; but through Byron the eastern Mediterranean became widely popular as a literary backdrop. His emphasis on character in his poems — though his characters had little variety among themselves — was also an idea of his which had been unsuccessfully attempted by earlier versifiers of lesser note, but which he alone succeeded in legitimizing.

Yet like Scott before him, Byron had no real intellectual commitment to the kind of poetry he wrote. The poets he admired most were the English Augustans. He thought Johnson's *Vanity of Human Wishes* "sublime . . . a grand poem — and so true".[41] Of Pope he wrote:

> I have always regarded him as the greatest name in our poetry. Depend upon it, the rest are barbarians. He is a Greek Temple, with a Gothic Cathedral on one hand, and a Turkish Mosque and all sorts of fantastic pagodas and conventicles about him. You may call Shakespeare and Milton pyramids if you please, but I prefer the Temple of Theseus or the Parthenon* to a mountain of burnt brick-work.[42]

Comparing the poetry of his own age to Augustan verse, he said,

> we are upon a wrong revolutionary poetical system, or systems, not worth a damn in itself, and from which none but Rogers and Crabbe are free; and . . . the present and next generations will

---

* Byron's true opinion of the Parthenon was recorded by Samuel Rogers (*Table Talk*, p. 237-8): "When he and Hobhouse were standing before the Parthenon, the latter said, 'Well, this is surely very grand!' Byron replied, 'Very like the Mansion-House!'"

finally be of this opinion. I am the more confirmed in this by having lately gone over some of our classics, particularly *Pope*, whom I tried in this way — I took Moore's poems and my own and some others, and went over them side by side with Pope's, and I was really astonished (I ought not to have been so) and mortified by the ineffable distance in point of sense, harmony, effect, and even *Imagination*, passion, and *Invention*, between the little Queen Anne's man, and us of the Lower Empire. Depend upon it, it is all Horace then, and Claudian now, among us.[43]

He admired Rogers for his resemblance to the Augustans. "I value him more as the last of the *best* school."[44] "His elegance is really wonderful — there is no such thing as a vulgar line in his book."[45] Even in later years, when he began to suspect that there was more to poetry than the avoidance of vulgarity, Byron continued to praise Rogers:

> "The Pleasures of Memory" is a very beautiful poem, harmonious, finished, and chaste; it contains not a single meretricious ornament. If Rogers has not fixed himself on the higher fields of Parnassus, he has, at least, cultivated a very pretty flower garden at its base.[46]

Though a keen reader, Byron never studied earlier writers as critically and systematically as Wordsworth, Coleridge, Southey or Scott did, and his opinion of the dead poets most influential on the literary developments of his own time was, to say the least, superficial. Shakespeare he considered "damned humbug".[47] He claimed he could not read Spenser, and when Leigh Hunt persuaded him to try, he reported, "I cannot see anything in him."[48] In his last letter to his half-sister Augusta Leigh he wrote, "I hate *reading* verse — and always did,"[49] and perhaps for once he was telling the truth. He preferred prose, and seemed to like poetry the more the closer it was to prose.

Byron initially sneered at Scott in his *English Bards, and Scotch Reviewers* but later christened him "the Monarch of Parnassus, and the most *English* of Bards",[50] and acknowledged that,

> Scott is certainly the most wonderful writer of the day. His novels are a new literature in themselves, and his poetry as good as any — if not better (only on an erroneous system) — and only ceased to be popular, because the vulgar learned were tired of hearing "Aristides called the Just" and Scott the Best, and ostracised him.[51]

His debt to Scott with regard to the Byronic hero archetype is suggested by some lines of his youthful satire, *English Bards, and Scotch Reviewers*:

> Next view in state, proud prancing on his roan,
> The golden-crested haughty Marmion,
> Now forging scrolls, now foremost in the fight,
> Not quite a Felon, yet but half a Knight,
> The gibbet or the field prepared to grace;
> A mighty mixture of the great and base.
> (l. 165 foll.)

though two lines later *Marmion* was described as "thy stale romance".

Though Byron wrote on a couple of occasions of the "erroneous system" followed by himself and Scott — that is, erroneous according to Augustan models — yet he was inconsistent enough to praise the verse of two notable propagandists of the new style of poetry. Of Leigh Hunt's *The Story of Rimini* (which was actually prefaced by a swingeing attack on the Augustans) he wrote, "Leigh Hunt's poem is a devilish good one — quaint, here and there, but with the substratum of originality, and with poetry about it, that will stand the test."[52] Coleridge's *Christabel* he thought was

> the wildest and finest I ever heard in that kind of composition ... [it] took a hold on my imagination which I shall never wish to shake off ... I do not know that even "Love" or the "Antient Mariner" are so impressive — and to me there are few things in our tongue beyond these two productions.[53]

He was in fact instrumental in persuading Coleridge finally to publish *Christabel* in 1816.

Byron also admired Southey's poetry, "though he wished the world to believe he despised it".[54] In *English Bards, and Scotch Reviewers*, at the outset of his career, and in *The Vision of Judgment* towards its end, he made Southey the target for his most vicious satire; yet privately he wrote of Southey's epic *Roderick the Last of the Goths* as "one of the finest poems he had ever read",[55] and in 1815 he remarked of recent publications, "Nobody but S****y has done anything worth a slice of bookseller's pudding, and *he* has not luck enough to be found out in doing a good thing."[56]

Concerning Wordsworth, Byron was never over-kind, even in private. "The lyrical ballads, jacobinical and puling with affectation of simplicity as they were, had undoubtedly a certain merit," he wrote;[57] but he did not think Wordsworth had fulfilled the promise shown in them. Yet it was Wordsworth whom

Byron plagiarized to a greater extent than any other poet, living or dead. The third canto of his reflective poem *Childe Harolde's Pilgrimage* was so Wordsworthian that no less than eight reviewers noted the "Lakist" influence.[58] Wordsworth himself thought the entire canto had been cribbed from *Tintern Abbey*, "and spoiled in the transmission".[59] Thomas Medwin actually challenged Byron on the matter; the poet answered in a characteristically offhand manner:

> Very possibly. Shelley, when I was in Switzerland, used to dose me with Wordsworth physic even to nausea; and I do remember then reading some things of his with pleasure. He had once a feeling of Nature which he carried almost to a deification of it: — that's why Shelley liked his poetry.[60]

Byron was well known to be a plagiarist — another of his more daring spoliations was in *Lara*, the story and many phrases of which derived from Harriet Lee's novel *The German's Tale*[61] — and this practice was of some importance in his poetic success. He knew what the public wanted; but it was not what he liked himself. He preferred Pope; the public preferred Scott. He had no taste for nature. (Rogers recorded a meeting with Byron in Italy: "We travelled some time together; and if there was any scenery particularly worth seeing, he generally contrived that we should pass through it in the dark."[62]) Yet he knew the public liked natural description. Plagiarism was the easiest way to disguise the gap between the public taste and his own. Byron's descriptions were either clichés or else borrowings from other writers which the public were too ill-read to recognize. Thus it was that Byron had an important role in popularizing some of the characteristics of Wordsworth's poetry.

It has been thought worthwhile to devote so much space to the poetic ideas of Byron, for it is impossible to understand early nineteenth-century taste without some detailed knowledge of the man of whom it could be written, even by a somewhat unfavourable critic, that his verse tales, "though hardly answering the expectation which he once excited — would have been, of themselves, sufficient to establish the renown of many scores of ordinary writers."[63] Byron was praised with almost unbelievable fervour by the hard-hearted Jeffrey.[64] Isaac d'Israeli, another leading critic, wrote of one of his poems: "There is no scene, no incident, nothing so marvellous in pathos and terror in Homer, or any bard of antiquity ... in a word I could not abstain from assuring you, that I never read any poem that exceeded in power this to me, extraordinary production."⁶⁵ His impact on the public was as great as that on the critics. Year by year from 1813 until his death in 1824 he was, in all but two years, easily the best-selling living poet. In four different years he outsold the combined works of the half dozen next most popular poets, living or dead (see Appendix). He was not yet thirty by the time there were more copies of his poems in circulation than had ever been published of Pope's, or Goldsmith's, or Gray's. Needless to say he inspired a host of imitators. *The Monthly Review* commented ruefully in 1821, "For the period of about six years of our critical labour, we found occasion to remark, concerning every alternate poem at least which came before us, that it was an imitation of (Sir) Walter Scott; and, for about the same period subsequently, we have had to observe that Lord Byron is the object of such copying."⁶⁶ One such imitation, *The Widow of Naïn*, written by Thomas Dale, an undergraduate at Corpus Christi College, Cambridge, was itself a considerable success and went through eight editions between 1819 and 1825.

The third most popular writer of metrical romance, after Byron and Scott, was Thomas Moore. Moore, a dapper little Irishman who had been, inexplicably, taken up by Byron as a kind of literary *alter ego*, had already made his reputation as a diner-out, song-writer, lyric poet and satirist when, in 1817, he brought out *Lalla Rookh*, a collection of four oriental verse tales. Leigh Hunt described *Lalla Rookh* as "the very perfection of Della Cruscan sentiment, and affected orientalism of style",⁶⁷ and Moore's language was indeed remarkable for its etiolated lushness. Several of his contemporaries, quite independently of each other, exercized their minds to find suitable metaphors to describe his diction. Byron said his poetry was like

> the Valley of Diamonds, where one is so dazzled by the sparkling on every side that one knows not where to fix, each gem beautiful in itself, but over-powering to the eye from their quantity ... [like] the fields in Italy, covered by such myriads of fire flies shining and glittering around, that if one attempts to seize one, another still more briliant attracts, and one is bewildered from too much brightness.⁶⁸

Wordsworth said:

> he is too lavish of brilliant ornament. His poems smell of the perfumer's and milliner's shops. He is not content with a ring and a bracelet, but he must have rings in the ears, rings on the nose — rings everywhere.⁶⁹

"Barry Cornwall" (Bryan Waller Procter) wrote:

Mr Moore's verses are... too saccharine, they want substance and relief. One may be smothered even with roses, and if the roses want their natural dew and freshness, the suffocation becomes unpleasant.[70]

To all of which Moore had no comeback, for as he engagingly confessed, "I have read very little poetry of any kind."[71] His lushness and mellifluity, the torrent of superb verbiage which disguised the paucity of his thought, was however an important influence on Victorian versifiers:

> She loves — but knows not whom she loves,
>   Nor what his race, nor whence he came; —
> Like one who meets, in Indian groves,
>   Some beauteous bird without a name,
> Brought by the last ambrosial breeze,
> From isles in th' undiscovered seas,
> To show his plumage for a day
> To wond'ring eyes, and wing away!
>   (*Lalla Rookh*, "The Fire Worshippers")

Also influential with mid-century versifiers was his incessantly titillating preoccupation with sexual matters, carefully veiled in imprecise language, which inspired the following rhyme (probably by the Rev. John Sneyd):

> Lalla Rookh
> Is a naughty book
> By Tommy Moore,
> Who has written four,
> Each warmer
> Than the former,
> So the most recent
> Is the least decent.

This sexual element in Moore was of course in keeping with the tradition of titillation observable in gothic romances, though divorced from the harshness and threatening violence of gothic; the same kind of appeal but in a different package.

Less successful commercially than Moore, but also an important influence on the succeeding generation, was Leigh Hunt, whose *The Story of Rimini* was published in 1816. In his Preface, Hunt made a violent attack on the Augustans. He claimed that he was making "an attempt to describe natural things in a language becoming them, and to do something towards the revival of what appears to me a proper English versification." Though he was no great admirer of Wordsworth's poetry, Hunt took his ideas (of course without acknowledgement) from the Preface to *Lyrical Ballads*:

> the proper language of poetry is in fact nothing different from that of real life, and depends for its dignity upon the strength and dignity of what it speaks.[72]

Hunt's preaching however was unlike his practice, and the vocabulary he used was little different from Scott's or Byron's, apart from the employment of specially coined words like *clipsome* which, though not found in idiomatic use, were thought by Hunt to deserve currency. He was anyway less concerned with vocabulary than with the popularizing of a modified, irregular iambic pentameter couplet which he supposed was the natural medium of English poetry. As his model he claimed Chaucer, and *The Story of Rimini* achieved some fidelity to its venerable prototype in that it at least resembles a Neville Coghill paraphrase of *The Canterbury Tales*:

> Francesca from herself but ill could hide
> What pleasure now was added to her side,—
> How placidly, yet fast, the days succeeded
> With one who thought and felt as she did, —
> And how the chair she sat in, and the room,
> Began to look, when he had failed to come.
> (*The Story of Rimini* (1816 edn.), p. 69)

In spite of "an outrageous eulogy ... unprincipled and partial enough to be written by Hazlitt",[73] in *The Edinburgh Review*, Hunt's doggerel only made one edition, though it was well attended to in literary circles. Amongst his disciples was John Hamilton Reynolds, a young clerk in an insurance office who had already published one poem in the style of Byron (*Safie*, 1814) and another somewhere between Coleridge's *Christabel* and Scott's *The Lay of the Last Minstrel* (*The Naiad*, 1816), and who went on to write a third in the style of Hunt (*The Garden of Florence*). It was while he was a member of Hunt's circle that Reynolds met Keats, who adopted him as his principal literary confidant. Keats was also for a time under Hunt's influence and wrote some shorter pieces in his style, but by the time he came to write *Endymion* he was already in the process of emancipating himself from Hunt's tutelage and managed to avoid Hunt's irritating verbal mannerisms while at the same time producing a poem which owed a considerable amount in its conception and prosody to Hunt's ideas. Hunt's poetry, and his fondness for Italian subjects, may also have been an influence on Bryan Waller Procter, a wealthy solicitor writing under the pseudonym of "Barry Cornwall", who was compared by *The Edinburgh Review* to Keats,[74] and whose romance *A Sicilian Tale* was described by a disgusted Byron as "I know not what affectation of Wordsworth, and Hunt, and Moore, and Myself, all mixed up in a kind of Chaos."[75]

The lesson suggested by the popularity of the metrical romance was lost on many, though not all, of the period's many writers of full-scale epics.[76] The second volume of the Rev. George Townsend's *Armageddon* was not published since there was insufficient demand for the first, and one edition of Richard Wharton's *Roncesvalles* satisfied popular demand even though the author had the additional glamour of being a junior government minister. The more astute of the epic authors however perceived the necessity of at least making their poems readable, for all that they may have suspected that vigour and simplicity of language were inconsistent with epic grandeur. Southey relinquished the innovatory but somewhat awkward free verse stanzas he had used in *Thalaba the Destroyer* and *The Curse of Kehama* and returned to the smoothly flowing, rather characterless blank verse he had used in his first two epics, *Joan of Arc* and *Madoc*. His *Roderick the Last of the Goths* was as easy to read as, and not actually much longer than, one of Scott's metrical romances, and sold more rapidly than any of his other long poems (five editions 1814-18). James Montgomery's *The World before the Flood* (1813) and the Rev. Henry Hart Milman's *Samor* (1818) were almost as popular, though Milman enjoyed his greatest success with his verse drama *The Fall of Jerusalem* (1820).

Though there is a great difference in mood as well as format, between one of Byron's verse tales and *The World before the Flood*, or *Lalla Rookh*, let alone Keats's *Endymion*, the narrative element which these poems had in common was perhaps more significant than the features which differentiated them. If the characteristic long poem of the eighteenth century was the philosophical or descriptive essay, that of the early nineteenth century was the exotic and escapist verse tale. Moreover, much more than *Lyrical Ballads* and *The Pleasures of Hope*, the early nineteenth-century verse tale represented a departure from earlier poetic tradition. This being so, it is Scott and Byron, rather than Wordsworth, who should be regarded as the true revolutionaries of the Romantic period. The fact that they were inferior to Wordsworth as poets is nothing to the point; at the time they were much more widely read and more influential, and Wordsworth's eventual acceptance as a great poet was partly a measure of the success of their cruder efforts in creating a public that could appreciate his work.

6
Lyric Poetry

> .... though his compositions are all gross nonsense, yet they are pleasant enough in their way; and if a man likes to be tickled with straws, he may find some amusement in reading them.
>
> (*The Satirist*, vol. 1, p. 78-9, on Thomas Moore)

The characteristics of the lyric — subjectivity and intensity — to which might be added comparative brevity and simplicity — were not at all the most prominent characteristics of Augustan verse. It is true that the eighteenth-century public accorded an enthusiastic reception to Watts's *Divine Songs*, Cowper's *Olney Hymns*, the hymns of the Wesley brothers, and to the secular lyrics of Cowper and John Gay. Della Cruscan verse was mainly lyric, and the more popular for being so. When Nathan Drake, in his *Literary Hours* (1798), listed ninety-six examples of sublime, pathetic, descriptive and amatory lyrics, only nine of them were written before 1700.[1] Yet no great reputations were established by any poet who wrote mainly lyrics, except for some separate reasons. Watts's and the Wesleys' lyrics were hymns and depended on their religious relevance rather than on their intrinsic beauty for their success; Joseph Warton, Bowles and Collins became famous for writing in highly specialized verse forms, and never really achieved a mass public; Gray's *Elegy*, again, succeeded because of its subject as much as because of its execution.

Nevertheless, there was a noticeable increase in the number of lyrics produced as the century progressed. This was one of the results of the turn away from Augustanism but a no less important factor was the increase in the number of papers, magazines and periodicals printing verse contributions, which provided an ever more convenient outlet for shorter poems. The odes and sonnets legitimized by Collins and the Wartons also encouraged imitation and experimentation in more irregular forms. Moreover the Wartons' rediscovery of early Milton bore fruit in numerous poems influenced by *Il Penseroso* and *L'Allegro*:

1750-60	46 poems showing debt to *Il Penseroso* and *L'Allegro*
1760-70	71 ditto
1770-80	68 ditto
1780-90	75 ditto
1790-1800	61 ditto.[2]

Sonnets, though rare till the 1770s, became during the final quarter of the eighteenth century even more numerous, nearly 600 being published by *The Gentleman's Magazine* and *The European Magazine* alone between 1780 and 1800, and over 1,500 appearing in books in the same period.[3] Yet even by the end of the 1780s, with the Della Cruscan craze in full spate, it could hardly be said that lyric verse was widely acknowledged as one of the most proper poetic genres. *The Monthly Review* pointed out:

> Small poems, however admired at the time of their publication, are apt to be neglected; and, in the course of a few years, to be lost, or at least to become extremely scarce, unless preserved and multiplied by collections.[4]

but the same periodical contributed heartlessly to this process of attrition by dismissing short poems with remarks such as: "If the Author should ever compose a poetical work of more consideration than this small performance, it would, no doubt, be worth criticising."[5]

In its treatment — and indeed choice — of subject matter moreover, the lyric merely followed the course mapped out by longer poems, whether in nature worship:

> Hail, beauteous stranger of the wood,
> Attendant on the spring!
> Now heav'n repairs thy rural seat,
> And woods thy welcome sing.
>   (Michael Bruce, *Ode to the Cuckoo*, c. 1766)

or in melancholy:

> Whoe'er thou art whom chance may bring
> To this sequestered spot,
> If then the plaintive Syren sing,
> Oh softly tread beneath her bower,
> And think of Heaven's disposing power,
> Of man's uncertain lot.
>   (Mark Akenside, *To the Evening Star*, 1772)

Yet prosodically there was a considerable tradition of experimentation which reached its technical peak in the 1790s with Robert Southey, whose poems however were generally inferior as *poems* almost directly in proportion to their metrical virtuosity, as for example in *The Widow*, written in sapphics:

> Cold was the night wind, drifting fast the snow fell,
> Wide were the downs and shelterless and naked,
> When a poor Wanderer struggled on her journey,
>   Weary and way-sore,

or in *The Soldier's Wife*, written in dactyls:

> Weary way-wanderer, languid and sick at heart,
> Travelling painfully over the rugged road,
> Wild-visaged Wanderer! God help thee wretched one!

or in *The Dead Friend*:

> Not to the grave, not to they grave, my Soul,
>   Follow thy friend beloved!
>   But in the lonely hour,
>   But in the evening walk,
> Think that he companies thy solitude;
>   Think that he holds with thee
>   Mysterious intercourse;
> And though remembrance wake a tear
>   There will be joy in grief.

There was however an enduring preference for the simpler forms, particularly the iambic quatrain, the diction of which did not change during the eighteenth century, or indeed during the nineteenth:

> In Hours of Bliss we oft have met,
> They could not always last;
> And though the present I regret,
> I'm grateful for the past.
>   (William Congreve, *Song*, 1710)

In the 1800s the simple lyric of this kind took on a new significance with the success of Moore and Byron. In their shorter poems they provided the same atmosphere of vicarious drama, the same scope for the reader to project himself into what he was reading, as they did in their verse narratives. Yet though they both dealt chiefly with love in their lyrics, and thus touched on the fondest preoccupation of their age, their love lyrics were in no sense a substantial advance either in language or sentiment on earlier performances, except in that Moore's verses were rather more lubricious than had been quite normal for some time past, and in that both Moore and Byron frequently indulged in verbal and conceptual conceits of a kind which eighteenth-century taste had tended to condemn as beneath the dignity of poetry:

> Chloris, I swear, by all I ever swore,
> That from this hour I shall not love thee more —
> 'What! Love no more? Oh! why this alter'd vow?'
> Because I cannot love thee *more* — than *now*!
> (Moore, *The Surprise*)

and :

> The tears that from *my* eyelids flow'd
> Were lost in those which fell from *thine*.
> (Byron, *To Caroline* ("Thinkst then I saw thy beauteous eye"))

In the Preface to his pseudonymous *The Poetical Works of the late Thomas Little Esq.* (which went through five editions 1801-4 and ten more by 1822) Thomas Moore claimed that "the early poets of our own language were the models which Mr LITTLE selected for his imitation", but a perusal of his verse is unlikely to induce anyone to take this statement seriously (though some of his stanzas are reminiscent of the work of Sir John Suckling, and, moreover, at least one reader thought "he steals from Dr Donne"[6]). The main influence on Moore's style, if we discount the love of verbal excess which according to the prejudices of the day was natural to the Irish, was the Della Cruscans, but his taste for verbal conceits seems to have been derived from the contemporary tradition of fugitive *vers de société*. Rhymes of this type, written by clever young men in the highest walks of society, normally had a small circulation confined to the salons of London's West End, and were rarely printed, their merit often depending largely on whether one knew the author or the person addressed. A rather superior specimen of the genre was *To The Lady Anne Hamilton* by Moore's friend William Robert Spencer:

> Too late I staid, forgive the crime,
>   Unheeded flew the hours;
> How noiseless falls the foot of Time,
>   That only treads on flow'rs!
>
> What eye with clear account remarks
>   The ebbing of his glass,

> When all its sands are di'mond sparks,
> That dazzle as they pass?
>
> Ah! who to sober measurement
> Time's happy softness brings,
> When birds of Paradise have lent
> Their plumage for his wings?

Moore's adoption of this idiom of elegantly turned emptinesses was a vital contribution to his success. The enormous popularity of the novels of Barbara Cartland and Georgette Heyer in the mid-twentieth century testifies to the enduring readership appeal of the dashing patrician lover, with all the smart mannerisms and brittle sophistication of the *beau monde*. The same archetypal figure had no less fascination for the domestic servants, apprentices, clerks, subalterns and bored daughters of businessmen who made up Thomas Moore's original readership;[7] and the success in the 1800s of novels dealing with high society by such writers as Fanny Burney and Thomas Skinner Surr (head of the drawing office at the Bank of England and author of such works as *The Magic of Wealth, Splendid Misery* and *Winter in London*) shows that Moore was not alone in exploiting this market. By evoking the love-life of the leisured patrician, Moore was able to cast over his verse all the grace and glamour which his readers ardently craved. In addition he struck a note of suppressed sensuality which could not fail to be irresistible to readers many of whom were unmarried, somewhat reluctantly chaste, and totally ignorant of the physical realities of sexual passion:

> Why that little wanton blushing,
> Glancing eye, and bosom flushing?
> Flushing warm, and wily glancing,
> All is lovely, all entrancing!
>
> (Moore, *Sweet Seducer*)

> Damp was the chill of the wintry air,
> But it made us cling closer, and warmly unite;
> Dread was the lightning, and horrid its glare
> But it show'd me my Julia in languid delight.
>
> (Moore, *Love in a Storm*)

Reading Moore's poetry, said Hazlitt, "we literally lie 'on the rack of restless ecstasy,' "[8] but that was precisely its attraction. *The Edinburgh Review* condemned Moore for "stimulating his jaded fancy for new images of impurity, with as much melancholy industry as ever outcast of the muses hunted for epithets or metre."[9] Another reader complained:

His love, putting the tedium of Rosa's and Celia's diamonds, rubies, and *hortus siccus* whereof they are composed, out of the question, is generally immodest; and he hath taught all the boarding-school girls and other misses of the present day to screech indecency as well as political reformation.[10]

Southey called him "that lump of lasciviousness",[11] though personally Moore was a model of correct behaviour and eventually became a devoted husband. Later in life he shed "tears of deep contrition" at having ever published *The Poetical Works of the late Thomas Little esq.*,[12] and several poems (including those quoted from above) were suppressed in the 1841 edition of his works; but by then Moore was an assured success with *Lalla Rookh* and several collections of songs in his *Irish Melodies* series to his credit, and no longer had any need for the less reputable means by which he had first achieved celebrity.*

Byron's lyrics were, to adopt the vocabulary of the day, more "manly", though he was referred to as "a young Moore", and by *The Satirist* as "a feeble Moore".[13] His juvenile poems were printed in four separate collections, each with successive additions, as *Fugitive Pieces, Poems on Various Occasions, Hours of Idleness,* and (as a second edition of *Hours of Idleness*) *Poems Original and Translated.* Nearly all the copies of *Fugitive Pieces* were destroyed, and *Poems on Various Occasions* was circulated only among Byron's friends; *Hours of Idleness* and *Poems Original and Translated* were printed for public sale but enjoyed only a modest success. His *Hebrew Melodies* (1815) also made only two editions, one with music, one without. Owing to the scandal of his wife's desertion however, a collection published in 1816, *Fare Thee Well, or Poems on his Domestic Circumstances,* became a bookselling phenomenon. The British Library possesses two editions, by two separate publishers, published in Bristol, one from New York, one from Dublin and eight from London (by three different publishers) — all dated 1816. Another London edition in the British Library, dated 1817, claimed on the title page to be the twenty-third edition — and not one of these issues had Byron's authorization. Thus this one collection of lyrics, published without the author's permission, outsold even his most popular verse narratives.

---

* Moore's poetry was actually less suggestive than that of one of his imitators, David Carey, whose *Poems, Chiefly Amatory* were published in 1807 with a frontispiece showing a woman in bed with a bared breast and nipple peeping through her erotically disarrayed clothing.

Though Moore and Byron had no important influence on the subject and treatment of the lyric, except in so far as they were the first to succeed in exploiting the mass market for love poetry, and though they were in most respects very far from being prosodic experimenters in the way Southey was, they did have a lasting impact on the quatrain tradition in that it was they who popularized the anapaestic tetrameter.

In this present age of contempt of prosody, the anapaestic tetrameter will not be immediately identified as an epoch-making literary phenomenon, yet in fact the adoption of the anapaest was of great importance in nineteenth-century poetry. The use of anapaests imposes severe limitations on the vocabulary, and consequently on the thought, of the poet; at the same time it has such a lulling, musical rhythm, that the lack of meaning in the verses seems less important than the beauty of their sound. In short, anapaests put sound before sense. The fact that so many Victorian poetasters loved to write anapaests was part symptom, part cause, of the relative poetic aridity of the ninety years following Byron's death. The anapaest both encouraged and enabled the Victorians and Edwardians to commit poetic suicide. Even when they wrote in different measures they still strove for the same empty, hypnotic lilt. That is not to say that if the anapaest had never become popular, nineteenth-century poetry would have been better than it was, but the form was certainly intimately bound up with the actual performance of the nineteenth-century poets. And in writing anapaests, these poets were by and large taking their example from Byron, Moore, and their earliest imitators.

Matthew Prior's *The Secretary* (1696) had been the first entirely anapaestic poem in the English language, and John Byrom's *Pastoral*, published in *The Spectator* in 1714 had been the first poem in the metre to achieve widespread popularity. Shenstone's *The Scholar's Relapse* (c. 1744) had been in anapaestic tetrameters, and his better known *Pastoral Ballad* (1743) in anapaestic trimeters. The latter was occasionally imitated, as late as the 1790s, as for example in William Perfect's *January* (from his *Poetic Effusions, Pastoral, Moral, Amatory, and Descriptive,* 1797):

> How painted with ice is the air!
> The woodlands bespangled with frost,
> A portrait pellucid prepare,
> Whose beauties in terror are lost.

Goldsmith and Anstey used the anapaest too, though only as a medium for light humour, but they, Byrom, and Shenstone were the only notable eighteenth-century practitioners. Then, in 1796, "Monk" Lewis adopted it for narrative verse in *Alonzo the Brave, and Fair Imogine*. Some of Moore's earlier anapaestic poems were also short narrative pieces, for example *Reuben and Rose* ("The darkness that hung upon Williamberg's walls"), but he also employed it for the love lyric, as in *To Rosa* ("Say, why should the girl of my soul be in tears"). At about the same time, Wordsworth tried it as an alternative to the ballad measure in *The Reverie of Poor Susan*, Campbell used it for declamation in *Lochiel's Warning*, and the Scots weaver poet Robert Tannahill employed it for rural description in *The Storm* :

> Now the dark rains of Autumn discolour the brook,
> And the rough winds of Winter the woodlands deform.

Byron included some anapaestic poems in *Hours of Idleness* such as *The First Kiss of Love* and two of his poems *To Caroline*, and later wrote what is perhaps the best known attempt in the form, *The Destruction of Sennacherib*. The *Fare Thee Well* collection of 1816 included anapaestic stanzas *To Augusta*, and after 1816 the form became increasingly popular. Among those who took up the anapaest with particular enthusiasm was Bernard Barton, the veritable prototype of the nineteenth-century minor poet, whose pedestrian lyrics had a remarkable popularity in the 1820s (doubtless because of their tone of Christian earnestness). Barton's adoption of the anapaestic tetrameter (e.g. in *The Sea* and *The Valley of Fern*), is indicative of how rapidly the metre had become established : in his other poems he showed himself to be somewhat unadventurous and conservative in his choice of metre, with a penchant for ungainly Spenserians; it is worth noting on the other hand that Coleridge, Southey and Shelley, all of whom were serious experimenters in prosodic forms, did not use the anapaestic in any of their mature work.

The other most important development of the early nineteenth-century lyric was one scarcely touched on by Moore and Byron : an altered attitude to imagery. It is true that some of the best lyrics of the period, such as the Rev. Charles Wolfe's *The Burial of Sir John Moore at Corunna* or Wordsworth's *The Solitary Reaper*, are almost devoid of imagery. Wordsworth's short lyrics often present single experiences of the sort which are essentially beyond comment; his concluding stanzas, for example,

> For oft, when on my couch I lie
> In vacant or in pensive mood,
> They flash upon that inward eye
> Which is the bliss of solitude;
> And then my heart with pleasure fills,
> And dances with the daffodils,
> *(I wandered lonely as a cloud)*

or,

> And, as I mounted up the hill,
> The music in my heart I bore,
> Long after it was heard no more,
> *(The Solitary Reaper)*

seem to be afterthoughts which add little to the poems beyond a rather banal moral on the recruitment of psychic energies from the experiences described, which though important to Wordsworth's way of thinking, rather underestimate the true significance of the incidents in question. In most lyrics by other poets of the period however the communication of a definite point or moral seems much more central, and very often this communicable point is the extended exposition of a single metaphor or simile, as for example in John Clare's *Falling Leaves*:

> How frail the bloom, how short the stay,
>   That terminates us all!
> To-day we flourished green and gay,
>   Like leaves, to-morrow fall.
>
> Alas! how short is four score years,
>   Life's utmost stretch — a span;
> And shorter still, when past, appears
>   The vain, vain life of man.
>
> These falling leaves once flaunted high,
>   O pride! how vain to trust:
> Now wither'd on the ground they lie,
>   And mingled with the dust.

The large number of poems written of this type show that the short lyric was increasingly being identified as principally a vehicle of imagery. This process was taken to its furthest extent by Shelley, in whose shorter poems, similes and metaphors, some so complex as to defy paraphrase, withdrew the reader's attention from the poems' very firmly maintained literal meaning. In *Ode to the West Wind*, for example, the autumn leaves are identified both as fleeing ghosts and as plague-discoloured people, the seeds are first winged riders in chariots and then buried corpses, the buds are driven forth like flocks to feed, the clouds are like leaves, are angels, are a Maenad's hair, the wind is a dirge, the night sky is a vast vaulted sepulchre, the forest is a lyre, Shelley's thoughts are like the leaves, or like ashes, and the whole poem achieves a rich confusion of evocation which is about as far away from the ordered diction of the eighteenth century as it is possible to get.

In Shelley's lyrics, as in Keats's odes, it is possible to see the surfacing of a lyric tradition separate from and alternative to the simple quatrain tradition exploited by Moore and Byron with such commercial success. The simple lyric, because simple, had to hang on to literalness; the pellucid exposition of the analogy between human life and leaves in Clare's *Falling Leaves* is scarcely more an original exercise in imagination than the amatory conceits of Thomas Moore. For a more complex and highly structured idiom, therefore, Shelley, Keats, and even Wordsworth (in *Ode, Intimations of Immortality*) returned to the practice of formal experimentation initiated by Collins and the Wartons two generations earlier, and it was no coincidence that Keats developed for the Wartons' own principal models, Spenser and Milton, an admiration equal to that felt by the Wartons themselves. From Spenser and Milton, Keats derived that curiously lush neo-classicism which differs from that of the Wartons only in its greater immediacy and sensuousness; for where the Wartons merely enumerated discrete components of the scenes they describe, Keats focused on the details of one single image, used as a kind of synecdoche for a number of associated images, and thereby brings the whole picture to life:

> Let, then, winged Fancy find
> Thee a misstress to thy mind,
> Dulcet-eyed as Ceres' daughter,
> Ere the God of Torment taught her
> How to frown and how to chide,
> With a waist and with a side
> White as Hebe's, when her zone
> Slipped its golden clasp and down
> Fell her kirtle to her feet,
> While she held the goblet sweet,
> And Jove grew languid. . . .
> (*Fancy*, ll. 78-89)

Shelley too sometimes came close to resembling the Wartons:

> I have made my bed

> In charnels and in coffins
>
> (*Alastor* 1. 23-4)

and he too owed much to Milton, and not infrequently echoed his phraseology.

Shelley and Keats were however exceptional, and their careers coincided with a general turning away from the Wartons' and Collins's tradition of longer and more highly structured lyric forms, as if these fell too short of the ideal of lyric simplicity. This movement away from length and complexity is shown by the decline in the numbers of poems of the *L'Allegro/Il Penseroso* type:

1790-1800	61 poems published influenced by *L'Allegro* and *Il Penseroso*
1800-10	40 ditto
1810-20	6 ditto.[14]

The last success of the Warton school was Henry Kirke White, whose youthful struggles to raise himself from his plebeian origins and early death as a Cambridge undergraduate appealed to the morbid sentimentality of the period and secured a market for ten editions of his *Remains* between 1807 and 1823. As well as being a remarkably proficient sonneteer, Kirke White wrote odes *To an Early Primrose, To Contemplation, To the Genius of Romance* and *To Midnight*; though he wrote of Thomas Warton's *Pleasures of Melancholy*, "there are few pieces which I have perused with more exquisite gratification", it appears to have been Joseph Warton who was the chief influence on his odes, and it may be that it is Joseph who is referred to in *Lines on Reading the Poems of Warton*, written when Kirke White was fourteen:

> O Warton! to thy soothing shell,
> Stretch'd remote in hermit cell,
> Where the brook runs babbling by,
> For ever I could listening lie. . . .

Kirke White seems to have been regarded by his immediate posterity more as a tragic instance of promising genius cut down in early youth than as a poet of any significance; Keats and Shelley, by surviving to a slightly older age, lived long enough to be neglected in their own lifetimes, and public indifference to their poetry continued for some years after their deaths. Perhaps it was the case that while the long poem retained its viability, writers whose best work was in shorter poems could never be regarded as significant. Furthermore, whereas in the eighteenth century the language of the lyric had been different, simpler and more direct than that of longer poems, in the early nineteenth century the diction of the newly established form of longer poem, the verse tale, conformed much more to that of the simpler lyric, and one of the initial objections to Keats and Shelley was that *their* lyrics were too difficult to understand, that is, more difficult than longer poems. According to the standards of the day, Keats was "full of extravagance and irregularity, rash attempts at originality, interminable wanderings, and excessive obscurity",[15] and Shelley was "much too obscure and intricate for the generality of his readers";[16] *Adonais*, the poem Shelley wrote on Keats after the latter's death, was described as "pure nonsense . . . unintelligible stuff",[17] there were said to be "five readable lines in the entire",[18] and its stanzas were "altogether unconnected, interjectional, and nonsensical".[19] It was only gradually during the century following their deaths that the view became established that lyric poetry might well deal with perceptions and insights which could not be expressed in a language immediately comprehensible at first reading.

7
The New Poetry and the Reading Public in the 1800s

> But there must be a resemblance which does not depend upon their own will, between all the authors of any particular age. They cannot escape from subjection to a common influence which arises out of an infinite combination of circumstances belonging to the times in which they live, though each is in a degree the author of the very influence by which his being is thus pervaded.
>
> (Shelley, Preface to *The Revolt of Islam*)

There are two types of explanation for the rapid establishment in public favour of the metrical romance and the accompanying increase in popularity of the lyric. The first type of explanation argues that British society in the 1800s was especially susceptible to changes in cultural fashion, and presupposes that the specific characteristics of new cultural fashions were less important than the mere fact of their novelty. It has been suggested that receptivity to extreme changes in fashion is a symptom of general restlessness in a society; for example research on the yearly alteration of the fashionable length for women's dresses indicates that in periods of social upheaval and intellectual uncertainty, dress lengths alter much more markedly from year to year than in periods of tranquillity.[1] It could be that social upheaval also generates instability in much more self-conscious cultural forms, such as poetry, and that the changes in poetic taste in the early nineteenth century are an example of this process.

Britain in the 1800s presented a strange paradox. It was a stable, even dynamic society; unmistakable evidence of this was the massive investment between 1800 and 1815 in housebuilding, industrial plant, agricultural improvements, and major public works such as dockyards. It is obvious that people would not have invested on the scale they did if they had not been confident of the future. Yet at the same time the country was periodically gripped by fear — fear of a French invasion

(Britain was at war with France for most of the period 1793-1815); fear of lower-class disorder; fear of the paralysis of effective government by faction struggles in Parliament. Indeed it was precisely because the country was relatively flourishing that threats of French invasion or domestic sedition seemed so terrifying; a nation already *in extremis* is not afraid of dangers that have yet to materialize. The rapid advance of industrialization, which was a demonstration of economic resources astonishing in a country engaged in a war extending simultaneously over four continents, was perceived by some as an undermining of the basic structure of society, by others as a triumph of civilization. Agricultural dearth and famine were still regarded as very real dangers, yet during the food shortages of 1800 the government refused on doctrinaire grounds to take effective measures, and left the work of relief to private individuals — who, significantly, were not slow in coming forward. For all its fundamental solidity and capacity to absorb change, Britain was undoubtedly a nation under pressure both socially and culturally.[2] And it may be that it was because of this sense of social and cultural stress that the reading public were so eager for novelty — any kind of novelty — in the poetry they read. Perhaps it is possible to go even further, and see the gothic fantasies and pseudo-Renaissance extravagances as nothing but the hysterical symptoms of a society unbalanced by rapid change, uprooted from hitherto valid cultural norms that had been based on conditions that no longer existed, and desperately searching for a new symbolic idiom, a new framework of reference that would provide justification and explanation for the transformations that were taking place.

Itself created by change, the revolution in literary fashion may also have owed its apparent extent and completeness to the fact that it coincided with alterations in the structure of the reading public; that is, the emergence of the verse romance may not have been in itself any more significant than, say, the rise of the gothic novel or the revival of the sonnet, but may have given the impression of totally transforming reading habits simply because reading habits were being transformed at the same period as a result of very different factors. One of the most remarkable aspects of the careers of Scott, Byron (and earlier Bloomfield) was the size and rapidity of their sales. Their success was (in the case of Scott and Bloomfield) both very sudden and very short-lived, as if they were able to satisfy all possible demand in a matter of months. This is in contrast to the career of earlier best-sellers like Thomson and Young, whose poetry, while selling moderately quickly at first, remained in demand at only a slightly lower level for many years after its first appearance. This rather suggests (what is confirmed by other evidence) that increased facility of communications meant that the fame of a best-selling poem spread much more quickly from one end of the country to another. Moreover, the reading public, as well as being more unified by improved communications, was also larger than it had been in the days of Thomson and Young. The total population of the country had increased 55 per cent since 1750, and even supposing a slight overall decline in literacy rates — the evidence for which is inconclusive — there must have been half as many more people able to read in 1810 as there had been in 1750. Furthermore a higher proportion of the population had access to reading material. The real incomes of a sizeable proportion of the population were higher (as a result of the progress of industrialization) than they had been two generations earlier, enabling more people to afford the luxury of their own books. Nor was it necessary to purchase a volume in order to be able to read it. Gentlemen's subscription libraries had opened in most large provincial towns from 1758 onwards[3] and book clubs had become common in the 1780s and 1790s,[4] while booksellers' circulating libraries, which had been only in their infancy in the 1720s, had come to number several hundreds by 1800; London alone had twenty-six, at least one of which claimed to have 100,000 books for loan.[5] In addition there was an increase in the number of reviews printing long extracts from the books they discussed; between 1793 and 1809 the old established *The Monthly Review* and *The Gentleman's Magazine* were joined by *The British Critic*, *The Monthly Magazine*, *The Anti-Jacobin Review*, *The Edinburgh Review*, *The Eclectic Review*, and *The Quarterly Review*, as well as a large number of more ephemeral periodicals. The growing popularity of reading is evident in the increased circulation of newspapers: each sheet of newspaper paid $3\frac{1}{2}$ pence stamp duty, and the amount of revenue collected from this source more than doubled in England and Wales between 1797 and 1814:

Year	Revenue from newspaper stamps
1797	£144,940 14s. 10d
1807	£245,388 4s. 9d
1814	£304,962 8s. 10d[6]

At the same time the reading public remained a largely middle- and upper-class entity. The decline during the late eighteenth century of the chapbook,[7] formerly the main species of literature available to the poor, and the large number of poets who emerged from the working classes — weavers like Robert Tannahill, Robert Millhouse and John Blackner, shoemakers like William Gifford, Robert Bloomfield, David Service, Joseph Blacket, John Struthers and Charles Crocker, pedlars like William Nicholson[8]— does suggest that more orthodox forms of literature were making at least a marginally greater penetration among the poorest sectors of society; but the anecdote of how John Clare, at the age of thirteen, painfully scraped together eighteen pence to buy a copy of Thomson's *The Seasons,* saving sixpence from his wages and borrowing sevenpence from his mother and fivepence from friends at the public house where he was a servant, and then, on his next free day walked seven miles to the nearest bookshop in Stamford, only to find it was closed because it was a Sunday,[9] illustrates the difficulties the working-class reader still faced in his search for books.

Explanations along these lines, having little or no reference to the internal characteristics of the new type of poetry, may either be taken as sufficient in themselves, or else as contributing to an alternative system of explanation in which change is most fully to be understood in terms of the distinctive features of the new poetry.

The most potent single element in the new poetry was the personality and charisma of Byron. Yet we are so accustomed to seeing Byron as one of the accidental attributes of the Regency period that we underestimate the extent to which he fitted in with a whole complex of cultural values which were virtually unique to his lifetime. Byron was born into an era which was increasingly in love with itself. Though in literature the example of the dead was — till Byron himself emerged — preferred to the practice of the living, in most other fields of human endeavour the Britons of the reign of George III regarded themselves as living in a golden age. Porson was regarded as the greatest British Greek scholar of all times, Reynolds as the greatest painter; Pitt and Fox as political orators, were thought to "rival those of Greece and Rome".[10] The admirals Nelson and St Vincent received far more public adulation than ever came the way of Blake or Hawke, and yet they were quite eclipsed by Wellington, who became a field marshal at only forty-four, the age at which Marlborough had still been only a major-general. More monuments to famous soldiers and sailors were erected at public expense — by parliamentary vote or local subscription — in churches and town squares than at any time previously, and even today the surviving memorials of the wars of George III many times outnumber those of the times of William III and George II. A new heroic style of historical painting emerged, of which the chief exponents were Benjamin West and John Singleton Copley, to commemorate the great men of the period. In part this triumphant self-awareness derived from a novel sense of national mission. It was not merely that Britain had led Europe in the struggle against Napoleon; the British were convinced that they were *morally* superior. Britain, it was claimed, was "the day-star of our planet":

> as if the Divine Providence had chosen it as the instrument of its benevolent purpose, to enlighten by an almost insensible progression the distant and divided families of mankind, to hold up to them the sacred lamp of religious and moral truth, to harmonize them by the example of mild and liberal institutions.[11]

But perhaps the need for great men, and great deeds, and great emotions was also a part of the taste for hyperbole and magnificence evident in the most popular poetry of the day. Byron's good looks, his hereditary title, his reputation for being a rake certainly fell in with an existing appetite for increased sensationalism and drama; he was a real man foreshadowed by fictional Lovelaces, Zelucos and Montonis.

This hunger for drama may partly be understood as a hunger for *sexual* drama. The increased cossetting of women and the increased romanticization of their lives and destinies,[12] made women — and men too — more fascinated with the possibility of sexual adventure, more ready to believe in the dangers of unbridled masculinity. The process of romanticizing female sexuality, which stemmed from the need to justify and to disguise the transformation of the socio-economic position of women, had so to speak its nemesis in the unleashing of female masochistic fantasies in the Byron cult.

But this taste for drama was also a more general phenomenon, arising from the fact that society was becoming more orderly. Kenneth Clark remarks that:

> When life is fierce and uncertain the imagination craves for classical repose. But as society becomes tranquil, the imagination is starved of action, and the immensely secure society of the eighteenth century indulged in day-dreams of incredible violence[13]

and however unsupported this may be when applied to the

1740s, it has some relevance to the early nineteenth century when despite the upheavals of the Napoleonic wars, most English people above the poorer classes led comfortable and essentially stable lives.

This restless desire for sensation may be supposed to have been most evident in younger people, and it is surely the case that the most successful poetry of this period had more natural appeal to the young than Augustan reflective verse ever could have. Though virtually unprecedented at the time, the rate of population growth was not high by the standards of, for example, twentieth-century India, and it is unlikely that there were any very marked changes in the age profile of the population as a whole, or of the reading public, but it does seem that poetry became more youth-orientated in the early nineteenth century in contrast to Augustan poetry which was (or pretended to be) the poetry of a mature élite. It was for this reason perhaps that the youth of writers like Campbell, Dermody, Shelley and Kirke White was so constantly emphasized. Perhaps the trend during the eighteenth century towards the more liberal treatment of children had contributed towards making young adults more self-assertive and more self-conscious than had been the case in earlier periods,[14] but the cultural ascendancy of youth is probably best seen as stemming from the paradoxical nature of British society at this time. On the one hand societies in a state of crisis tend to be dominated by the age-groups which actually hold the reins of government, which would tend to be the age-groups of people in their late thirties and older, and Britain was stable enough for the young not to be dominated to any great extent; on the other hand the rate of social change was rapid enough to bring out differences of attitude between people of different generations so that younger people were to a large extent mentally and culturally emancipated from the influence of their elders.

The contradictory features of British society at this period may also have been the origin of the sense of individual alienation which is one of the key themes linking Byron to those of his contemporaries who superficially least resembled him, particularly Wordsworth and Coleridge. The alienation of the individual seems characteristic of essentially confused and disorientated societies; the sense of alienation arises from a perception of a discrepancy between one's own view of inescapable reality and the majority view; yet for this sense of alienation to be expressed publicly there needs to be an awareness of the existence of a large minority of like-minded people who also find themselves at odds with the majority. The most prevalent self-image of British society in the 1800s was undoubtedly one of optimism, though it is possible to detect a certain uneasiness in the bluster with which this optimism was expressed:

> When we contemplate the height of Glory to which this Nation has arrived by a series of Naval Victories to which the History of the World affords no parallel; when we consider the extent of our Commerce, the wonderful increase of our National Wealth; when we examine the progressive improvement of Learning and the Arts among us; we feel the value and importance of the English Character; our hearts expand with confidence and hope, and we glance forward to succeeding years of prosperity and happiness.[15]

But there were many who perceived only signs of deterioration:

> While Mechanic Arts, Manufactures, Agriculture, Commerce, and all those products of knowledge which are confined to gross — definite — and tangible objects, have, with the aid of Experimental Philosophy [i.e. Science], been every day putting on more brilliant colours, the splendour of the Imagination has been fading: Sensibility, which was formerly a generous nursling of rude Nature, has been chased from its ancient range in the wide domain of patriotism and religion with the weapons of derision by a shadow calling itself Good Sense: calculations of presumptuous Expediency — groping its way among partial and temporary consequences — have been substituted for the dictates of paramount and infallible Conscience.[16]

The number of people who dissented from the majority optimism was large enough for Shelley (in his Preface to *The Revolt of Islam*) to be able to claim that "gloom and misanthropy have become characteristic of the age in which we live".[17] The period was rich in classic expositions of the theme of personal isolation and alienation from society: Godwin's novel *Caleb Williams* and his daughter's *Frankenstein*, Maturin's *Melmoth the Wanderer*, Coleridge's *The Rime of the Ancient Mariner*, Shelley's *Alastor*, and above all, the poems of Wordsworth:

> O Heavens! how awful is the might of Souls,
> And what they do within themselves, while yet
> The yoke of earth is new to them, the world
> Nothing but a wild field where they were sown.
>   (*Prelude*, Bk. 3, l. 178-81)

In *Resolution and Independence*, Wordsworth had a momentary vision of the potential nightmarishness of solitude:

> In my mind's eye I seemed to see him pace
> About the weary moors continually,
> Wandering about alone and silently,

and there is an even more horrific evocation of total isolation in the second stanza of *A Slumber Did My Spirit Seal*:

> No motion has she now, no force;
> > She neither hears nor sees;
> Rolled round in earth's diurnal course,
> > With rocks, and stones, and trees.

Yet in general Wordsworth seemed to embrace solitude willingly for the sake of his own spiritual development:

> Points have we all of us within our souls
> Where all stand single; this I feel, and make
> Breathings for incommunicable powers.
> > > > (*Prelude*, Bk. 3, l. 186-8)

Byron however was perhaps more typical in that he represented isolation simply as man's inevitable predicament, even when surrounded by his fellows:

> Then loathed he in his native land to dwell,
> Which seemed to him more lone than Eremite's sad cell.
> > > (*Childe Harold's Pilgrimage*, Canto 1, stanza 4)

and much of his work — most strikingly *The Siege of Corinth*, *Manfred* and *The Prisoner of Chillon* — was a dramatic representation of different forms of isolation enforced by circumstances rather than by choice.

To some extent this emphasis on isolation may be a natural development from the sensitivity to the uniqueness of experience which, as I argued in my Introduction, was characteristic of Romantic poetry. But if we admit this we merely shift the question back to the psychic origins of the idea of the uniqueness of specific experience; and it is interesting to note that the pioneers of specific vision in the 1780s, Cowper and Bowles, were both melancholics with a strong sense of individual isolation.[17]

It may be that this sense of personal isolation also stemmed in part from the hiatus between the decline of a religion which, though it stressed the individual's relationship with God, nevertheless smoothed over the differences between individual humans, and the rise of secular philosophies which demoted the individual on ideological and economic grounds. Though this was a period of religious ferment, with the spread of

Evangelicalism and Methodism, religion was certainly much less central to culture than it had been in Milton's day, and in a sense *The Prelude* is the *Paradise Lost* of a secular era; yet interestingly enough both Wordsworth and Coleridge eventually sought to come to terms with their sense of isolation by a return to institutionalized religion, and perhaps Byron would have done so too had he lived longer.

The narrative poem was the natural vehicle for exploring individual isolation in that besides providing a dramatic paradigm of individual aloneness it also focused to a much greater extent than the descriptive verse essay on the perceptions and experiences of individuals. Though the hero of the poem would be palpably only a fictional stereotype, the imaginative involvement of the reader — the projection of the reader's sense of self on to the poem's hero — could easily be achieved by the interest generated by the development of the plot. Thus though the idiom of the verse romance was quite different from that of the Wordsworthian lyric, the reader experienced the same sense of personal involvement, though in quite different ways. One of the failings of the epics written by Southey and others was that, though typical of their period's striving for grandeur, their leisurely pace and diffuseness of plot eliminated the possibility of the reader projecting himself into the narrative.

One of the most remarkable features of the early nineteenth century was that its self-obsession was so rarely translated into poetry directly, literally, or without employing an intervening medium of fake gothic or oriental colouring. As Walter Scott, himself a principal offender in this respect, pointed out in 1809 :

> There is no point in which our age differs more from those which preceded it, than in the apparent apathy of our poets and rhymers to the events which are passing over them... some of them roam back to distant and dark ages; others wander to remote countries, instead of seeking a theme in the exploits of a Nelson, an Abercromby, or a Wellesley; others amuse themselves with luscious sonnets to Bessies or Jessies; and all seem so little to regard the crisis in which we are placed, that we cannot help thinking they would keep fiddling their allegros and adagios, even if London was on fire, or Buonaparte landed at Dover.[18]

Yet perhaps this turning away from current issues was itself a means by which the men and women of the early nineteenth century came to terms with the contradictions of their own society. Referring to the wars and dynastic upheavals which convulsed Europe in the wake of the French Revolution, Thomas Moore wrote:

> it will, at least, be conceded, that the free loose which had been given to all the passions and energies of the human mind, in the great struggle of that period, together with the constant spectacle of such astounding vicissitudes as were passing, almost daily, on the theatre of the world, had created, in all minds, and in every walk of intellect, a taste for strong excitement, which the stimulants supplied from ordinary sources were insufficient to gratify; — that a tame deference to established authorities had fallen into disrepute, no less in literature than in politics, and that the poet who should breathe into his songs the fierce and passionate spirit of the age, and assert, untrammelled and unawed, the high dominion of genius, would be the most sure of an audience toned in sympathy with his strains.[19]

But the point about readers of poetry was surely that they *were* readers, i.e. people who were not so completely embroiled in the tumult of the times that they did not have leisure and money for books and poetry. They were bystanders looking on from a comparatively safe distance, and poetry provided them, not with a clearer perception or a more profound understanding of what was happening to their world, but with a tranquillizing succession of parallels and analogies, a kind of paradigmatic representation of the way in which their own society — often, their own particular group in society — was so much more fortunate and prosperous and secure than any other. People read partly in order to escape from the tensions of their lives and partly in order to find a new perspective or commentary on these tensions. The avoidance of contemporary realities in Scott's and Byron's poetry seems to have provided them with exactly the escape and exactly the perspective they were looking for.

8
The Renewal of Interest In Elizabethan and Jacobean Playwrights

> The best old poetry has so much the air of being written for all time, that it wants little but modern orthography, and the present age wants nothing but powers equal to its production, to make it pass for the effusion of yesterday.
>
> (*The Quarterly Review*, vol. 4 (1810), p. 176)

The popularity of the verse romances of Scott, Byron and Moore was only one indication of early nineteenth-century readers' eagerness to find parallels in other times and places for the dramatic events of their own day; another aspect of their fascination for the archaic and the exotic was an increasing interest in the Elizabethan period, and especially in the literature of that time.

In August 1810 *The Quarterly Review* announced that, "The reign of Elizabeth, and not that of Anne, was without doubt the Augustan age of English poetry",[1] and exactly a year later *The Edinburgh Review,* after noticing the "late restoration to some degree of favour and notoriety" of some of the early English playwrights, claimed that: "The era to which they belong, indeed, has always appeared to us by far the brightest in the history of English literature,— or indeed of human intellect and capacity."[2] By 1815, the merits of the Elizabethans had become part of the critics' stock in trade, to be expended where and when convenient:

> The language [of Southey's *Roderick, the last of the Goths*] is such as the best authors of the best era of our literature would acknowledge, nor can we give it higher praise than to say its standard worth would be admitted in the mint of Queen Elizabeth's age.[3]

As will be shown in the next chapter, the increasing fashionableness of the Elizabethans and Jacobeans was associated with criticism of the Augustans. But it is worth asking whether the Elizabethan revival contributed anything more than polemical material to the change in public taste.

First of all, it must be admitted that the revival was exaggerated. Spenser, though the favourite of Southey and Leigh Hunt, received no greater (or lesser) degree of attention than he had in the age of Shenstone and the Wartons. Shakespeare's sonnets, though praised by Coleridge and Wordsworth, remained neglected. The Jacobean lyric poets, though selected editions of Carew, Herrick and others were published, were still condemned for their metaphysical conceits, even by critics as large-minded as Hazlitt and Coleridge,[4] and where, as in *The Poetical Works of the late Thomas Little Esq.*, they were adduced as models, the ascription was patently unjustified. It was only the Elizabethan and Jacobean drama which enjoyed any significant vogue, but even this was to a lesser degree than was pretended. Gifford's edition of Massinger did not, for example, rescue that author "from oblivion", as was claimed.[5] It is true that in the early eighteenth century Massinger had been so little known that Nicholas Rowe had passed off *The Fair Penitent* (which he had adapted from Massinger's *The Fatal Dowry*) as entirely his own work, but there had later been two inaccurate editions of Massinger, in 1759 (later reissued with a new title page) and in 1777. Copies of these editions were probably hard to come by in 1800, but the author himself enjoyed a modest reputation after 1759. There had been at least five editions of Ben Jonson in the eighteenth century, and three of Beaumont and Fletcher. Tourneur's *Atheist's Tragedie* had been reprinted twice in the 1790s. Dodsley's *A Select Collection of Old Plays*, which included work by John and Thomas Heywood, Sackville and Norton, Kyd, Marston, Middleton, Rowley, Shirley, Ford, Dekker, and Marlowe went through two editions in 1744 and a third in 1780. True there had been no complete editions of Webster, Dekker, Marston or Shirley in the eighteenth century, but the early years of the nineteenth did not supply this omission. All the first twenty years of the new century contributed to knowledge of the old dramatists was a series, *The Ancient British Drama*, commenced in 1810, a volume of extracts chosen by Charles Lamb, new editions of Jonson, Beaumont and Fletcher, Ford and Massinger, and, of course, an enormous quantity of Shakespeare. Considering the increase of book production during those twenty years, this was a somewhat poor advance on the eighteenth century's record of editing.

Nor were the new editions greeted with unqualified approval.

Weber's edition of Ford in 1811, and of Beaumont and Fletcher in 1812 were condemned for their inaccuracy (a circumstance which, according to the psychiatric theories of the day, was responsible for Weber going mad in 1813, and dying insane). *The Monthly Review* criticized both Weber and Gifford for exaggerating the merits of the authors they edited, objected to "all the overstrained panegyrics which it is the fashion to lavish on the works of our older dramatists", and accused Gifford in particular of bringing Massinger forward, if not as Shakespeare's professed rival, "yet in such terms of high-flown panegyric as to imply even a preference over Shakespeare himself".[6] *The Edinburgh Review*, though acknowledging that the old dramas, "even setting Shakespeare aside, are among the highest boasts of English literature",[7] nevertheless sneered at "that indiscriminate rage for editing and annotating by which the present times are so happily distinguished".[8] The same periodical, in a review of Gifford's Juvenal, made such a vicious attack on the same editor's Massinger that Gifford responded hysterically in the Advertisement to the second edition of his Massinger in 1813. And even Gifford's own *The Quarterly Review* referred disparagingly to "that appetite for reprints, which is one of the symptoms of the bibliomania now so prevalent".[9]

In spite of this back-biting, the merits of the old playwrights became generally accepted. This was not merely because they had a kind of novelty after two centuries of neglect, or because the public had a taste for the antique and gothic. The old dramas had an earnestness, a tragic solemnity, that went beyond that of the most serious productions of the Augustan era, and as the Augustans came to be regarded as more and more superficial (as will be discussed in the next chapter) so the Elizabethans and Jacobeans came to be regarded as embodying the opposite characteristics, which were more in accord with early nineteenth-century taste. Lamb, in his Preface to *Specimens of the English Dramatic Poets* (1808), clearly spelt out what the public looked for in the old dramas:

> The kind of extracts which I have sought after have been, not so much passages of wit and humour, though the old plays are rich in such, as scenes of passion, sometimes of the deepest quality, interesting situations, serious descriptions, that which is more nearly allied to poetry than to wit, and to tragic than to comic poetry.

The revival of interest in the Elizabethans and Jacobeans was in fact an important contributor to the dethronement of the Augustans (the "wit" and "comic poetry" school, as they came to be regarded).

This revival was something of a negative process however in that it contributed to the new tide of poetry (Wordsworth, Campbell, Scott, Byron, etc.) only by weakening rival standards; for signs of positive influence on new poetry one looks almost in vain. It is true that, no sooner had the merits of the old playwrights been admitted, than it became part of the cant of criticism — especially in *The Edinburgh Review* — to speak of the current generation of poets as mere imitators, thus:

> Southey, and Wordsworth, and Coleridge, and Miss Baillie have all of them copied the manner of our older poets; and, along with this indication of good taste, have given great proofs of original genius. The misfortune is, that their copies of those great originals, are all liable to the charge of extreme affection. They do not write as those great poets would have written: they merely mimic their manner, and ape their peculiarities.[10]

Even the saccharine and etiolated verses of "Barry Cornwall's" *A Sicilian Story* did not escape the accusation of being an imitation of the old dramatists: "His style is chiefly moulded, and his versification modulated on the pattern of Shakespeare, and the other dramatists of that glorious age — particularly Marlowe, Beaumont and Fletcher, and Massinger."[11] Francis Jeffrey, editor and principal literary critic of *The Edinburgh Review* even went so far as to claim for himself some of the credit for establishing the Elizabethans and Jacobeans as fashionable models: "That imitation of our older writers, and especially of our older dramatists, to which we cannot help flattering ourselves that we have somewhat contributed, has brought on, as it were, a second spring in our poetry."[12] This systematic misrepresentation of contemporary poetry, once initiated by Jeffrey, was continued in the same periodical by an even more intolerant critic, Macaulay:

> We look on the beauties of the modern imitations with feelings similar to those with which we see flowers disposed in vases, to ornament the drawing-rooms of a capital. We doubtless regard them with pleasure, with greater pleasure, perhaps, because in the midst of a place ungenial to them, they remind us of the distant spots in which they flourish in spontaneous exuberance. But we miss the sap, the freshness, and the bloom.[13]

Such statements should perhaps be viewed as Parthian shots, for *The Edinburgh Review* remained hostile to all the most original poets of the time, even after their poetic ideals had been converted into generally accepted formulae. The very notion of Southey or Coleridge owing anything in their poetry to the Elizabethans and Jacobeans, beyond what any literate person might derive from familiarity with his native language, is ludicrous, and could only have occurred to prejudiced critics. In Wordsworth's case the accusation went nearer to the truth, but only by chance, for when Jeffrey named Worthsworth as a copier of the old poets, in 1811, none of his longer blank verse contemplative poems, with their frequent Shakespearian echoes, had yet appeared in print. Only in the case of Joanna Baillie, the least important of the four poets accused of imitation in the first passage quoted above, was Jeffrey's sneer justified.

Joanna Baillie's chief literary preoccupation was with writing plays, and it was in the field of drama that Elizabethan influence was most likely to reveal itself. Yet as Allardyce Nicoll has demonstrated, the very considerable interest shown by the theatre of the time in Shakespeare and his contemporaries involved a search neither for dramatic models to emulate nor for fundamental ideas from which to gain inspiration.[14] Shelley's *The Cenci* was greatly influenced by Shakespeare, without being an imitation, but it was an exception.[15] The characteristic early nineteenth-century adaptation of Shakespeare was the travesty. King Lear for example, was staged as *King Lear and his Daughters Queer,* and there was also an attempt to present it in contemporary terms as *The Lear of Private Life.* Some of Shakespeare's plays were also put on as melodramas. The few attempts made to write imitation Shakespearian plays did not originate with the theatrical world; and though Joanna Baillie gained considerable critical acclaim for her efforts, not all of them were ever put on the stage and Charles Lamb's *John Woodvill* (1802) was never acted. Moreover, for all her efforts, Joanna Baillie's notions of fidelity to Shakespeare were superficial and mechanical in the extreme. Many of her scenes were derived from Shakespeare,[16] and she constantly attempted to reproduce the texture of Shakespeare's language by employing unfamiliar adjectives and by varying her iambic lines with initial trochees and feminine endings:

De Montfort I know resentment may to love be turn'd;
    Tho' keen and lasting, into love as strong:
    And fiercest rivals in th'ensanguin'd field
    Have cast their brandished weapons to the ground,
    With gen'rous impulse fir'd. I know right well
    The darkest, fellest wrongs have been forgiven

	Seventy times o'er from blessed heavenly love:
	I've heard of things like these; I've heard and wept,
	But what is this to me?
Jane	All, all my brother!
	It bids thee too that noble precept learn,
	To love thine enemy!
De Montfort	Th' uplifted stroke that would a wretch destroy,
	Gord'd with my richest spoil, stain'd with my blood,
	I would arrest, and cry, "Hold! Hold! have mercy!"

(De Montfort, Act 3, sc. 2)

But the all-revealing epithet, the splendid imagery, the vivid characterization, let alone the complex dramatic patterns and the underlying concepts which were the vital part of Shakespeare's work were beyond Joanna Baillie's power of execution; probably beyond even her power of recognition. And when her work was the best that could be done in the way of imitating Shakespeare in drama, serious Shakespearianism in other forms of poetry was not to be looked for.

What really mattered about the revival of interest in the Elizabethans was their utility as an embodiment of certain critical standards; their polemical convenience, in fact. Just as in the 1740s the Wartons appealed to Spenser and early Milton as their authority for their poetic experiments, so men like Southey in the early nineteenth century set up Elizabethan and Jacobean drama as a corpus of classical values alternative to Augustan couplet verse. Thus even if the direct influence of the old playwrights on actual literary creation was nil, their impact on critical values was of major importance.

9
The Dethronement of the Augustans

> Fix on some well-known name and bit by bit
> Pare off the merits of his worth and wit:
> On each alike employ the critic's knife,
> And when a comment fails, prefix a life;
> Hint certain failings, faults before unknown,
> Review forgotten lines, and add your own;
> Let no disease, let no misfortune 'scape,
> And print, if luckily deformed, his shape:
> Thus shall the world, quite undeceived at last,
> Cleave to their present wits, and quit the past,
> Bards once revered no more with favour view
> But give their modern sonneteers their due,
> Thus with the dead may living merit cope,
> Thus Bowles may triumph o'er the shade of Pope.
>
> (Lord Byron, *English Bards, and Scotch Reviewers*, 1st edn. only, 1 247 foll. This passage is actually by John Cam Hobhouse.)

The setting up of the Elizabethan and Jacobean playwrights as rivals of the Augustans was only one part of a general campaign of denigration conducted by the poetic innovators of the first two decades of the nineteenth century against those poets whom they regarded as exemplifying the "old" standards they were struggling to displace. As well as referring to even older models, the advocates of the new-style poetry also appealed to general principles which the Augustans were alleged to have contravened. Yet to present the literary controversies of the early nineteenth century in these terms, as the rivalry between "new" and "old" poetic schools, tends to disguise the fact that the example of the "old" school was embodied in what was only a very recent orthodoxy. The idea that the Augustans were the only proper models for poetic writing, set forth by Francis Jeffrey in the very first issue of *The Edinburgh Review* in 1802 was quite novel. The Augustans had of course been imitated, and they had even been held up as *bad* models, as for example

THE DETHRONEMENT OF THE AUGUSTANS

by Cowper (see page 46) but a systematic theory asserting the exclusive virtue of imitation came only with Jeffrey.

It is worth pointing out that Jeffrey was a Scot, for it was the case that most educated Scots of the period still spoke Lallans and were unduly self-conscious about the English language. As Dugald Stewart explained,

> An author who lives at a distance from the acknowledged standard of elegance, writes in a dialect different from that in which he is accustomed to speak; and is naturally led to evade, as much as possible, the hazardous use of idiomatic phrases.... Hence, in all the lighter and more familiar kinds of writing, the risk of sacrificing ease and vivacity, and what Dr Johnson calls *genuine Anglicanism,* in order to secure correctness and purity.[1]

James Beattie had put it even more succinctly:

> We who live in Scotland are obliged to study English from books, like a dead language, which we understand, but cannot speak; avoiding, perhaps, all ungrammatical expressions, and even the barbarisms of our country, but at the same time without communicating that neatness, ease, and softness of phrase, which appear so conspicuously in Addison, Lord Lyttleton [sic], and other elegant English authors.[2]

Nothing is more common in the private writings of Scots authors of this period than reference to English stylistic models. This painful striving for classical correctness was hardly likely to induce a tolerance for linguistic experimentation and originality of phrase. This was especially so in the case of Francis Jeffrey; it was surely not a man who believed that each age needed to develop its own distinctive idiom who wrote in 1802:

> Poetry has this much, at least, in common with religion, that its standards were fixed long ago, by certain inspired writers, whose authority it is no longer lawful to call in question.

and in 1805 referred approvingly to that ambition,

> which aspires at distinction through a just graduation of honours, and, looking at first with veneration to those who have previously attained the heights of fame, ventures by degrees to follow their footsteps, and to emulate or surpass their achievements.[4]

Reference to "models" and "schools" became commoner in critical parlance than at any earlier period, and it was not confined merely to *The Edinburgh Review.* Thus the rival *Quarterly* on Rogers:

It was as the faithful, diligent disciple of Pope and Goldsmith, that Mr Rogers became deservedly a favourite of the public, and it is to the imitation of these splended and captivating, but safe and correct models of excellence, that he seems most fitted by the bent of his genius, and the direction of his studies.[5]

The assessment of authors in terms of their resemblance to other authors was a peculiarly early nineteenth-century fashion which directly derived from the establishment of a canon of models and archetypes. Comparison was often employed to dazzle rather than to illuminate. Of Crabbe for example it was once said: "He imagines his stories with the humour and truth of Chaucer and tells them with the copious terseness of Dryden, and the tender and thoughtful simplicity of Cowper",[6] as if he had no other merit than of combining the merits of others. This desire for analogy extended even to the mode of criticizing critics. For example, Thomas Campbell wrote of Joseph Warton's *Essay on Pope*: "It is very entertaining, and abounds with criticism of more research than Addison's, of more amenity than Hurd's or Warburton's, and of more insinuating tact than Johnson's."[7] With a style of criticism thus dependent on a canon of classics, the Augustans came to represent not merely the poetic principles they seemed to embody, but also the particular technique of applying these principles in criticism.

Of the Augustans, it was Pope who was set up as the most important universal model. During the 1780s a popular, though rather pointless, topic of controversy was whether Pope or Dryden was the greater poet.[8] Rogers and other serious writers of verse gave their preference to Dryden, but it was Pope who obtained the suffrage of public opinion. Consequently, the merits of the Augustans became equated with the merits of Pope, and it was the assault on the reputation of Pope which was the keynote of the repudiation of Augustan standards.

Pope was constantly reviled in his own lifetime,[9] but the first significant criticism of Pope to concentrate on his work rather than on his personality did not appear till 1756, twelve years after his death, when Joseph Warton published the first volume of his *Essay on the Writings and Genius of Pope*. In the Dedication Warton wrote, "The sublime and the pathetic are the two chief nerves of all genuine poesy. What is there transcendently Sublime and Pathetic in Pope?" and later, having acknowledged the excellence of Pope's wit and satire, claimed "WIT and SATIRE are transitory and perishable, but NATURE and PASSION are eternal".[10] These principles subsequently became the basis of early nineteenth-century criticisms of Pope. Warton's choice of *Windsor Forest, The Rape of the Lock,* and *Eloisa to Abelard* as the three poems that would maintain Pope's reputation was largely endorsed by Warton's posthumous disciples, though it even influenced Johnson whose critical prejudices were by no means sympathetic to Warton's views.

It was not till fifty years later that these ideas were embodied in a more extreme form, by Bowles and Southey. It is often assumed that Wordsworth and Coleridge were hostile to Pope. This is scarcely true. Wordsworth (in his *Essay Supplementary to the Preface,* 1815) objected to the descriptive technique in Pope's *Iliad,* and sneered at him in passing in his second letter on *Epitaphs* — "Pope, whose sparkling and tuneful manner had bewitched the men of letters of his contemporaries, and corrupted the judgment of the nation through all the ranks of society"[11] — but he never published any wholesale condemnation of Pope, and was even prepared to admit his merits, and those of Dryden:

> I have a very high admiration for the talents both of Dryden and Pope, and ultimately, as from all good writers of whatever kind, their country will be benefited greatly by their labours.[12]

His views on Pope gradually hardened into hostility during his middle age, but only because of the influence of changing general opinion; and the strongest objections to Pope that he ever expressed were, by the time of their expression, no more than the critical commonplace of the day:

> if the beautiful, the pathetic, and the sublime be what a poet should chiefly aim at, how absurd it is to place those men among the first poets of this country.[13]

> I do not name Pope, for he stands alone — as a man most highly gifted — but unluckily he took the Plain, when the Heights were within his reach.[14]

By the time Wordsworth passed these remarks, his own career as a poet was virtually over. In his famous *Preface* to *Lyrical Ballads,* written a generation earlier when at the height of his creative powers, he did not merely omit to criticize Pope — who was comparatively innocent of the crime of false diction which the *Preface* condemned — but singled out, as the classic poetical malefactor, Gray, whose *The Bard* was compared favourably by Warton to both Pope's and Dryden's efforts at sublimity.[15]

Coleridge, though he privately "spoke with contempt of Gray, and with intolerance of Pope,"[16] was even kinder than Wordsworth to Pope in his public utterances. He objected to Pope's versification and epigrammatic style, but publicly praised his *Iliad* as "that astonishing product of matchless talent and ingenuity."[17]

Southey was by far the most outspokenly hostile of the so-called "Lake School", but as his public condemnation came out at a crucial stage in the controversy, we will defer discussion of his views to their chronological place.

The first blow against Pope in the early nineteenth century was delivered by the sonneteering parson, the Rev. William Lisle Bowles. Bowles had been educated at Winchester, when Joseph Warton was headmaster, and at Trinity College, Oxford, of which Joseph Warton's younger brother Thomas was a fellow. Bowles's poetic tastes were however probably the result less of direct proselytizing than of an accidental congruence of mentality. Nevertheless, just as Thomas Warton's River Lodon series of sonnets inspired Bowles's effusions to the Itchen and the Cherwell, so Joseph Warton's *Essay on Pope* helped Bowles formulate his critical ideas in his edition of Pope's Complete Works which he published in 1806.

Despite the chastened sentimentality of his more successful poems, and despite his clerical profession, Bowles was a coarse-mannered eccentric who attacked Pope with such aggressive gusto that his contemporaries wondered at his motives for undertaking his edition in the first place. His aspersions on Pope's private character, though notorious at the time, have no significance as literary criticism; but in his concluding remarks Bowles borrowed from Joseph Warton's discussion of the true nature of poetry and altered the entire emphasis of what Warton had written. Warton had merely argued that Pope had not attempted the highest and truest form of poetry; Bowles consigned his victim to a totally inferior order of poets for not making the attempt. Where Warton had given credit for ingenuity, Bowles denounced its application. Where Warton had thought the sylphs in *The Rape of the Lock* equal in fancy to the fairies in *A Midsummer Night's Dream,* Bowles questioned,

> how can Warton think, that in fancy they equal *anything of the kind*? but there is no comparison between beings who
> — "pluck the wings from painted butterflies
>   To fan the moon beams" &c
> And those
> — "who invention bestow
>   To change a flounce".[18]

Where Warton had argued that some subjects were essentially

THE DETHRONEMENT OF THE AUGUSTANS 153

more poetical Bowles claimed that a poem was necessarily less or more poetical, according to how poetical its subject was, thereby travestying Warton's argument by making it more categorical:

> A description of a forest is more *poetical* than a description of a cultivated Garden: and the *Passions* which are portrayed in the Epistle of an Eloisa, render such a Poem more *poetical*, (whatever might be the difference in merit in point of execution,) *intrinsically* more poetical, than a Poem founded on the characters, incidents, and modes of *artificial life*; for instance, the Rape of the Lock.[19]

In the following year, 1807, Southey published his *Specimens of the Later English Poets*. Southey, who privately told Rogers that "he had read Spencer through about *thirty* times, and that he could not read Pope through *once*,"[20] adopted and developed various criticisms of Pope in the Preface to his anthology. From Warton and Bowles he took his assumptions about the true nature of poetry:

> Whatever praise may be given to them [the Augustans] as versifiers, as wits, as reasoners, they may deserve, but versification, and wit, and reason do not constitute poetry. The time which elapsed from the days of Dryden to those of Pope, is the dark age of English poetry.[21]

From Cowper's claim that Pope

> Made poetry a mere mechanic art
> And every warbler had his tune by heart,
>   (*Table Talk* l. 656-7)

Southey developed the argument that

> He so familiarized his countrymen with the mechanism of verse, that the very facility of his versification seems to have prevented the effusions of genius, and the redundancy of poetical phrases to have superseded all originality of language. . . .
> The tune, indeed, which he set, every poetizer, whether man, woman, or child, has been singing ever since, and we are still referred to him as the perfect Poet, by those who hold that poetry is an acquirable art — the materialists of fine literature; but not one writer since his day, who has acquired the slightest popularity, has been formed upon this school.[22]

But Southey's most important contribution to the Pope issue — a master-stroke that one might not have expected from a man whose first major work championed Joan of Arc against English prejudice — was to accuse Pope of writing in an un-

English idiom. This idea had been familiar to eighteenth-century critics:

> Dryden and Pope took the French poets for their patterns, particularly Boileau, who followed the ancients (of whom he was a passionate admirer) as far as the prosaic genius of the French tongue would permit.[23]

Warton had merely hinted at it, taking it as a matter of course:

> he studied Boileau attentively, formed himself upon him, as Milton formed himself upon the Grecian and Italian Sons of Fancy.[24]

It was Southey who was the first to turn the influence of Boileau into a grounds for accusation, as if trying to cash in on wartime xenophobia:

> since the days of Boileau, who communicated to Racine that notable precept of making the second line of a couplet first, it has been the fundamental article of critical belief in France. Pope was completely a Frenchman in his taste; he imported *l'art de parler toujours convenablement*, the etiquette and *bien séance*, the court language and full-dress costume of verse.[25]

By the time these views became public in 1807, the acknowledged doyens of the heroic couplet school were Rogers and Campbell. These two men were nominally, as we shall see, champions of Pope and were regarded as exponents of his style. Individual lines of Rogers's *The Pleasures of Memory* could pass muster as written by Pope — after all, not every line of Pope, if taken out of context, would unequivocally proclaim its authorship — but the general tone of Pope was lacking, and Rogers was incapable of, if he did not deliberately avoid, the antithetical compactness which was characteristic not only of Pope's satires, but even of *Windsor Forest* and *Eloisa to Abelard*. Rogers's contemporary and fellow couplet writer, Payne Knight, wrote of Pope:

> The ... desire of condensing into one couplet what had better have been extended into two or three, has sometimes made him debase the solemnity and dignity of the didactic moralist, by a sudden and unexpected transition to the levity, and even the vulgarity, of the satirist, as in the following: —
> > Rewards that either would to virtue bring
> > No joy, or be destructive *of the thing,*
>
> And
> > What nothing earthly gives, or can destroy,
> > The soul's calm sunshine, and the heartfelt joy,

> Is virtue's prize: a better would you fix?
> *Then give humility a coach and six.*

The pert flippancy of the last of these four lines so ill accords with the calm and beautiful solemnity of the two first, that it quite spoils the effect of the passage.[26]

And in expressing himself thus, Payne Knight evidently spoke for Rogers as well, and for the other couplet writers of the time. It was not that the men of 1800 were less humorous than those of 1700, but they were less broad-minded in their view of what constituted a fitting treatment of solemn topics.

Campbell's non-resemblance to Pope went even further than Rogers's or Payne Knight's. Some of his individual couplets recalled Pope with their deftness (if not with their wistfulness of tone) thus:

> While Memory watches o'er the sad review
> Of joys that faded like the morning dew.
> *(The Pleasures of Hope,* Pt. 2, ll. 45-6)

or

> .... though my winged hours of bliss have been
> Like angel-visits, few and far between.
> *(The Pleasures of Hope,* 4th and subsequent edns.,
> Pt. 2, ll. 375-6)

Yet Campbell's alternation of frenzy and sentimentality was the complete opposite of the Augustan's calm objectivity. One merely has to glance at a page of *The Pleasures of Hope,* with its profusion of dashes and exclamation marks, to see how distant its author was from his great predecessor. Originally of course, neither Rogers nor Campbell had any idea of trying to write like Pope. Their model, if they had one, was Goldsmith, though the heroic couplet was a sufficiently easy medium to be attempted without the guidance of particular models. Rogers and Campbell were, in short, undeliberate and unselfconscious neo-Popians. It was only when they had been overtaken by the attacks on Pope delivered by Bowles and Southey, that they declared their allegiance to Pope. But by then they had already helped to undermine Pope's cause by writing in an essentially un-Popian manner. This was particularly true of Campbell, who nevertheless was to take the more prominent role in defending Pope. Merely by having published *The Pleasures of Hope,* which reinforced a popular taste antipathetic to Pope, Campbell helped defeat the cause he afterwards espoused.

Campbell further damaged Pope's cause in his review of Bowles's edition of Pope in *The Edinburgh Review* in January 1808. He castigated Bowles and his theories:

> in this judgement upon the merits of Pope, we conceive Mr Bowles to have failed, and the cause of his failure to be derived from principles of criticism by no means peculiar to himself, but which have obtained too great an influence over the public taste of our age.[27]

Yet in his subsequent remarks Campbell showed that his poetic standards were roughly similar to Bowles's though more confused in their application. When he referred to "real poetry, according to the strictest notion of the term", Campbell seemed to be referring to the Warton-Bowles definition, for he went on to specify "the moral sublime, in the excitement of high and dignified emotion", "the sprightliness of a versatile fancy", and "the fervour of passion, the power of exciting and expressing emotion",[28] only the second of which Bowles would have rejected as being of inferior importance. These three qualities Campbell found in Pope; but it was surely true that "the moral sublime" and "the fervour of passion", though discoverable, were not common in Pope, and certainly not characteristic of him, whereas other qualities neglected by Campbell represented the essence of Pope's major poetic achievement. Campbell in fact damned Pope by praising his less important aspects, and, as if even that were too generous, he added: "let it be understood, that we do not believe him possessed of that diviner spirit, that energy and enthusiasm, which are required for the epic, the tragic, or the lyric muse."[29]

This was the first extensive treatment of Pope in *The Edinburgh Review,* and marked already a change of heart, for articles by Francis Jeffrey in early issues of the review had extolled Pope by implication in the course of denunciations of Wordsworth and Southey.[30] Within less than a year *The Edinburgh Review* had adopted one of the most useful weapons against Pope (though without initially applying it against that poet) and expatiated on the "corrupt imitation of the French stage" in the Augustan period.[31] In October 1813 however the accusation of foreign influence was laid fair and square at Pope's door:

> The school of Dryden and Pope... is neither the most poetical nor the most national part of our literary annals... they rather approached the elegant correctness of our Continental neighbours, than supported the daring flight which, in the former

THE DETHRONEMENT OF THE AUGUSTANS 157

age, had borne English poetry to a sublimer elevation, than that of any other modern people of the West.[32]

Significantly these remarks came in the course of a review of *The Voyage of Columbus*, the poem that marked Samuel Rogers's first movement away from the late-Augustan style.

The Quarterly Review was even more hostile to Pope. Though its editor, William Gifford, was a poetic conservative (and author of couplet satires such as *The Baviad*) and though he kept his contributors on a much tighter rein than Jeffrey did in the case of *The Edinburgh Review*, nevertheless *The Quarterly* numbered Southey amongst its contributors. Early issues of the periodical indicated what its views on Pope were; Martin Archer Shee, author of *Rhymes on Art* (1805) and *Elements of Art* (1809), was accused of being "too fond of antithesis".[33] Pope's lines were mentioned as suffering from "monotonous structure".[34] Then, in October 1814, a review of Chalmers's edition of the English poets, apparently written by Southey, delivered a full-scale attack. Southey criticized the moonlight description in Pope's version of the *Iliad*, and went on to say,

> from Dryden to Thomson, there is scarcely a rural image drawn from life to be found in any of the English poets, except Gay and Lady Winchelsea.[35]

A few months later Wordsworth took up some of Southey's ideas in his *Essay Supplementary to the Preface*. But, as usual with him, Southey took a more extreme line than Wordsworth later did by criticizing the late Augustans as follows:

> Taking Pope for their master, they culled every thing that was vicious in his style for imitation, and what was good they spoilt by misapplying it.[36]

However, public taste was not formed entirely by the academic lucubrations of critics and editors. While their opinions were being formulated, poetic fashion was developing apace. In the first dozen years of the nineteenth century, the popularity of Campbell and Bloomfield and Cowper, the continuing vogue of Thomson, and the tremendous success of Scott, were all contributing to the establishment of poetic norms closer to Warton's and Bowles's than to Pope's. Just as, at an earlier period, Joseph Warton's critical values had been extrapolated from the established Milton and Shakespeare canon, so similar standards could be derived from the most popular poetry of the years following 1800. The sublime and the pathetic, nature and passion, were all to be found in Scott; the sublime and pathetic particularly in Campbell; nature was to be found in Thomson, Cowper and Bloomfield.

The establishment of sublimity, pathos, nature and passion as the characteristics of true poetry, coincided with the establishment of a new kind of poetic diction which was simpler, more direct, more emphatic, more variable and musical, but less fanciful, less dependent on rhetorical artifice. The new diction prevailed because of its congruity with the new subject matter and because it was, in itself, new and appealed to the public's appetite for innovation. The only form which saw no substantial movement away from Augustan modes was the verse satire, which was of course a genre which Pope had made peculiarly his own, but even here such works as Lady Anne Hamilton's *Epics of the Ton* (1807) and the political satires of Peter Pindar and Eaton Stannard Barrett served to discredit Pope by the very feebleness of their imitation:

> What! shall my muse in silent numbers bound,
> Rest undisturb'd while nations rage around?
> Or, rous'd to writing, make her dainty theme
> A rose, a mistress, or a purling stream?
> Like *Party-prints*,* steal caustic from her lays,
> And oint with unguents of ignoble praise?
> Calm shall she see the fever'd placeman rave,
> Knaves act the fool and fools enact the knave;
> Old men grow boys, and boys (t'excel the type)
> Turn, like a medlar, rotten while unripe?
> (Barrett, *All The Talents*, 1807 edn., p. 4)

The advance of these few years was shown by Campbell's second major poem, *Gertrude of Wyoming*, published in 1809. Ten years previously, *The Pleasures of Hope* had resembled a moral epistle by Pope in three ways; it was philosophical — though the philosophy and its chaotic expression differed immeasurably from Pope's — it was in heroic couplets, and some of its lines clung to the memory as aphorisms. *Gertrude of Wyoming* had none of these characteristics. It was a narrative, in Spenserians, and very few of its lines were memorable for their pregnant brevity. In addition, the sentimentality and false pathos already remarkable in *The Pleasures of Hope* as the features most distinguishing it from Augustan verse were carried much further in *Gertrude of Wyoming*. The poem in

---

* *Party-prints* refers to newspapers supporting different political parties.

fact, though written by a defender of the old standards, embodied all the new poetic values.

A similar shift in principles was shown by Rogers. In his fragmentary epic *The Voyage of Columbus*, published in 1812, his saccharine diction became more forcible, almost Campbellesque:

> COLUMBUS err'd not. In that awful hour,
> Sent forth to save, and girt with Godlike power,
> And glorius as tne regent of the sun,
> An angel came! He spoke, and it was done!

Moreover, Rogers's new subject matter was more "romantic" than had been the case with *The Pleasures of Memory* — a heroic voyage into the unknown rather than a comfortable journey back to experiences which had already been lived through. He even, in the second canto, made an uncharacteristic excursion into the praeternatural:

> The pilot smote his breast; the watchman cried
> "Land!" and his voice in faltering accents died.
> At once the fury of the prow was quelled;
> And (whence or why from many an age withheld)
> Shrieks, not of men, were mingling in the blast;
> And armed shapes of god-like stature passed!
> Slowly along the evening sky they went,
> As on the edge of some vast battlement;
> Helmet and shield, and spear and gonfalon
> Streaming a baleful light that was not of the sun.

The Quarterly Review was unimpressed, giving the opinion that,

> Tired of pleasing, he is ambitious to astonish and transport his readers. The consequences of failure are harshness and abruptness, instead of variety in the versification — obscurity for grandeur, and in some instances, mere baldness, where he intended to exhibit the native force of simple unadorned expression.[37]

But Rogers was not deterred by such comments. In the following year he published *Jacqueline*, a Provençal tale bound in the same volume as his young friend Byron's verse romance *Lara*. The story — a daughter, promised to a rich neighbour, elopes with the son of a family enemy but is forgiven — was tame by Byronic standards, but the language and diction were reminiscent of Rogers's young associate:

> Oh what the madd'ning thoughts that came?

> Dishonour coupled with his name!
> By Condé at Rocroy he stood;
> Ty Turenne, when the Rhine ran blood.
> Two banners of Castile he gave
> Aloft in Notre Dame to wave;
> Nor did thy cross, St Louis, rest
> Upon a purer, nobler breast.
>
> (*Jacqueline*, Pt. 1, ll. 33 foll.)

In his next poem, *Human Life* (1819), Rogers reverted to the eighteenth-century philosophical mode, and was even old-fashioned enough to prefix the verse with an Argument (a custom which had already fallen out of use), which was as follows :

> Introduction — Ringing of Bells in a neighbouring Village on the Birth of an Heir — General Reflections on Human Life — the Subject proposed — Childhood — Youth — Manhood — Love — Marriage — Domestic Happiness and Affliction — War — Peace — Civil Dissension — Retirement from Active Life — Old Age and its Enjoyments — Conclusions.

This sounded fairly similar to the treatment of *The Pleasures of Memory*; but the verse that followed was very different from that of Rogers's earlier poem. Though he returned to the heroic couplet, his lines were now far more irregular, his ideas at once more sentimental and more would-be profound:

> Ah who, when fading of itself away,
> Would cloud the sunshine of his little day?
> Now is the May of Life. Careering round,
> Joy wings his feet, Joy lifts him from the ground!
> Pointing to such, well might Cornelius* say,
> When the rich casket shone in bright array,
> "These are MY Jewels!" Well of such as he,
> When Jesus spake, well might his language be,
> "Suffer these little ones to come to me."
>
> (*Human Life*, 1819 edn., pp. 22-3)

At times his expression became so rapturous that — by eighteenth-century standards at least — it became almost unintelligible:

> And Milton's self (at that thrice-honour'd name
> Well may we glow — as men, we share his fame)
> And Milton's self, apart with beaming eye,

---

* Mother of the Gracchi in Roman history.

> Planning he knows not what — that shall not die.
> (*Human Life*, 1820 edn., p. 26)*

Rogers's effusions were merely a symptom of the times, for his sales were modest compared with those of Byron. The two major factors in the continuing movement away from Augustanism in the second decade of the century were Byron, and the Elizabethan and Jacobean revival. In the case of the Elizabethans and Jacobeans, their identification in the public mind with the naval triumphs of the Elizabethan era caused them to be regarded as the writers of an earlier Golden Age which alone was comparable to the epoch of Nelson and Wellington; their essential Englishness gave them an important advantage over Pope, now seen as the embodiment of foreign influences; and their greater antiquity gave them the authority of classics, in an age which, despite its own sense of mission and achievement, was still classically minded.

One poet and critic, indeed, claimed to base his own practice principally on these older models. Leigh Hunt, in his Preface to *The Story of Rimini* combined an attack on "Pope and the French school of versification" with an exposition of his adaptation of the older standards. Hunt was perhaps better at destruction:

> I do not hesitate to say however that Pope and the French school of versification have known the least on the subject, of any poets perhaps that ever wrote. They have mistaken mere smoothness for harmony, and in fact wrote as they did, because their ears were only sensible of a marked and uniform regularity. One of the most successful of Pope's imitators, Dr Johnson, was confessedly insensible to music.[38]

His blueprint for "the revival of what appears to me a proper English versification" was less cogent, and the poem which exemplified his views was altogether unimpressive. Even so, *The Edinburgh Review* thought it similar to "that pure and glorious style that prevailed among us before French models and French rules of criticism were known in this country".[39]

Two years later Hunt announced:

> The downfall of the French school of poetry has of late been increasing in rapidity; its cold and artificial compositions have given way like so many fantastic figures of snow; and imagination breathes again in a more green and genial time.[40]

He attributed this to three causes: "political convulsions",

---

* These lines are an expansion of a couplet in the first two editions.

Wordsworth's "new school", and "the renewed inclination for our older and great school of poetry, chiefly produced, I have no doubt, by the commentators on Shakespeare, though they were certainly not aware what fine countries they were laying open."[41]

Curiously enough Hunt grouped Dryden with Spenser, Milton, Ariosto, Shakespeare and Chaucer as "the great masters of modern versification". The comparative merits of Dryden and Pope were still being canvassed at this period, but such a disparate estimate of the two Augustans was most unusual. Hunt's protégé Keats was also contemptuous of Popian versification:

> With a puling infant's force
> They swayed about on a rocking horse
> And thought it Pegasus.
> *(Sleepy and Poetry,* ll. 180-2)

but in *Lamia* he was influenced by Dryden in the direction of a tighter metrical structure, in spite of the fact that Hunt held up Dryden as a model of irregularity and colloquialism. In his sonnet "If by dull rhymes our English must be chained", moreover, Keats argued for a systematic pruning and reworking of one's verse, an idea that was much more in accordance with neo-classical than with "Romantic" practice:

> Misers of sound and syllable, no less
> Than Midas of his coinage, let us be
> Jealous of dead leaves in the bay wreath crown;
> So, if we may not let the Muse be free,
> She will be bound with garlands of her own.

Another poet who seemed as anxious as Leigh Hunt to return to Renaissance models was Edward, Lord Thurlow, who published large quantities of execrable verse of unusual disharmoniousness. Among his other redactions and imitations of old English models was a version of Chaucer's *Knight's Tale* and an attempt at a continuation of Shakespeare's *The Tempest*, Thurlow also published an edition of Sir Philip Sidney's *The Defence of Poesy* (1810) but he did not share Hunt's taste for literary polemic.

It was in 1818 that the first reaction to the cry against Pope set in. *The Quarterly Review* attempted to defend his precision of language:

> he is supposed to want feeling, because he abounds in sense. Were some of his finest passages to be translated into the mystical language of the modern school, the eyes of many would be opened, who are now blind to his superlative merits.[42]

THE DETHRONEMENT OF THE AUGUSTANS 163

This opinion was endorsed by Rogers:

> People are now so fond of the *obscure* in poetry, that they can perceive no *deep thinking* in that darling man Pope, because he always expresses himself with such admirable clearness.[43]

And it was in that year that Hazlitt — then a contributor to *The Edinburgh Review* — lectured at the Surrey Institution on the English poets, and revived the Wartonian assessment (as distinct from Bowles's version) of Pope's station in the poetic scale of merit.

> Dryden and Pope are the great masters in the artificial style of poetry in our language... and though this artificial style is generally and justly acknowledged to be inferior to the other, yet those who stand at the head of that class ought, perhaps, to rank higher than those who occupy an inferior place in the superior class.[44]

In a subsequent lecture, Hazlitt sneered at the poetry of the later eighteenth century: "Our poetical literature had, towards the close of the last century, degenerated into the most trite, insipid, and mechanical of all things, in the hands of the followers of Pope and the old French school of poetry" and made a violent attack on Campbell's verse — "the decomposition of prose is substituted for the composition of poetry". He seemed intent on sacrificing Pope's so-called imitators in order to establish a more just appreciation of Pope himself.[45]

Though these lectures were subsequently published, Hazlitt at this time had little influence; the lectures themselves were delivered

> before audiences with whom he had but "an imperfect sympathy". They consisted chiefly of Dissenters, who agreed with him in hatred of Lord Castlereagh, but who "loved no plays"; of Quakers, who approved him as the opponent of slavery and capital punishment, but who "heard no music"; of citizens, devoted to the main chance, who had a hankering after "the improvement of the mind", but to whom his favourite doctrine of its natural disinterestedness was a riddle; of a few enemies, who came to sneer; and a few friends, who were eager to learn and admire.[46]

"The comparative insensibility of the bulk of his audience"[47] meant that Hazlitt's views were not immediately transmitted to a wider public. Yet the year after this lecture course was given, a substantial campaign to defend Pope got under way.

In the lead was Campbell, whose *Specimens of the British Poets* (1819) was prefaced by an *Essay on English Poetry*. This was not altogether flattering to Pope, in that it criticized him for being too antithetical and for lacking variety in his pauses, but it rejected with a sneer the argument that the Augustans wrote in a foreign style — "they are armed with a noble provocative to English contempt, when they have it to say, that those poets belong to a French school"[48]— and it devoted nine pages to dealing with Bowles's by now hackneyed criticisms. This provoked a pamphlet from Bowles, *The Invariable Principles of Poetry: in a letter to Thomas Campbell*. In 1820, Isaac d'Israeli's review of Spence's *Anecdotes* in the July number of *The Quarterly Review* provoked Bowles to publish *A Reply to the Charges Brought by the Quarterly Reviewer* in *The Pamphleteer*, and in the course of the following two years Bowles also published *Observations on the Poetical Character of Pope, A Vindication of the late editor of Pope's Works* and *An Address to Thomas Campbell Esquire* in successive numbers of *The Pamphleteer*. Meanwhile Byron published his two open letters to John Murray in defence of Pope, which were answered by Bowles in a separate pamphlet entitled *Two Letters to the Right Hon. Lord Byron*. *The Pamphleteer* also printed Martin McDermot's *Letter in Vindication of Pope* which was reviewed by Campbell in *The New Monthly Magazine*. Other reviews also added to the debate at various stages; amongst the contributors was Hazlitt who used the controversy as an opportunity to make a splenetic attack on Byron. The various arguments hardly deserve summarizing, they were at such an obtuse level of criticism.[49] Bowles maintained that poetry lay in the subject, his opponents that it lay in the treatment of subjects. The truth, surely, lay somewhere between the two viewpoints, though Bowles's position was much the more absurd, as it dispensed with the element of artistic achievement in poetry. The poverty of Bowles's controversial position was such that, though he was defending the prevalent poetic taste, only one other writer apart from Hazlitt came forward to assist him, and that anonymously. This "Fabius"— such was the pseudonym — attempted a naïve *argumentum ad hominem* against Campbell:

> Will posterity, indeed, prefer the "Eloisa" to "Gertrude" — the "Rape of the Lock" to the "Exile of Erin" — and the "Essay on Man" to the "Pleasures of Hope"?

and asserted bluntly that "Pope finished with great skill and with unquestionable genius, but all his subjects are unpoetical".[50]

Yet though Bowles lost every wordy battle, he won the war;

or rather, it was won for him by his opponents, since the most prominent of Pope's defenders, Byron and Campbell, were two of the most influential practitioners of the newer poetic style. And whatever views were taken on the true nature of poetry, even Pope's admirers conceded that after all he was only "the very highest in the second rank", and incapable of the heights of Homer, Milton and Shakespeare.[51] And, more important still, even the defenders of Pope ceased to recommend him as the most proper model for imitation, and it became fashionable to condemn the later Augustan period as "that flattest and tamest period of English heroic poetry when the imitators of Pope had racked his sweetness to the very lees, and poverty and meanness were almost universally mistaken for a chaste and classic simplicity."[52]

It is perhaps the chief literary and historical importance of the Pope controversy that, both at the time and subsequently, it served to distort the truth about the poetic development of the late eighteenth and early nineteenth century. Pope was given the status, which he only partially deserved, of the most characteristic poet of the earlier eighteenth century; at first Wordsworth and Southey were judged, by reference to Pope, as more rashly innovating than they actually were; later when innovation became the fashion, the predecessors of Wordsworth and Southey were blamed for bearing much more of a resemblance to Pope than was altogether the case. A lot of bad, and some good, poetry was buried in this polemical chaos. The Pope issue had a catapult effect; it restrained the first movement, and then caused Romanticism to spring forward with all the greater force from having been held back. The very idea of a Romantic Revival, or a Romantic Revolution, or even of a Romanticism distinct from Augustan neo-classicism, was a product of this catapult effect on the minds of contemporaries, and of scholars ever since.

Nevertheless, the dethronement of the Augustans was less an autonomous contribution to the developing poetic fashion than a product of it. The Augustans were not brought down by the logic of Bowles or Hunt or Southey; for such a task their handful of rather superficial ideas were clearly inadequate, without the assistance of more potent factors. The Augustans were brought down by the taste for Campbell, Scott and Byron; the critical attack on them was merely an academic endorsement of an irresistible swing in public taste.

Conclusion

Deem not, devoid of elegance, the sage,
By fancy's genuine feelings unbeguil'd,
Of painful pedantry the poring child;
Who turns, of these proud tomes, th' historic page,
Now sunk by time, and Henry's fiercer rage.
Think'st thou the warbling muses never smil'd
On his lone hours? Ingenuous views engage
His thoughts, on themes, unclassic falsely styl'd,
Intent. While cloister'd piety displays
Her mouldering roll, the piercing eye explores
New manners, and the pomp of elder days,
Whence culls the pensive bard his pictur'd stores.
Nor rough, nor barren, are the winding ways
Of hoar antiquity, but strewn with flowers.

(Thomas Warton, *Sonnet Written in a blank leaf of Dugdale's Monasticon*)

In a sense the Romantic period of English poetry lacks chronological symmetry. There was a break between the poetry of the eighteenth century and the poetry of the 1800s — a break which I have suggested was represented by the poetry of Scott rather than by that of Wordsworth — but there was no corresponding break to mark the end of the period. Yet by 1825 most of the poets who had achieved prominence during the previous thirty years either were middle-aged men with their best work behind them, or were dead. Of the older generation, Coleridge wrote only a few short insignificant pieces of verse after 1802; Wordsworth had published *Ecclesiastical Sketches* and *Memorials of a Tour on the Continent 1820* in 1822 but was to produce no more work till *Yarrow Revisited* in 1835; Campbell published his *Theodric* in 1824 but thereafter did not produce another long poem till just before his death twenty years later; Crabbe's last collection of verse narratives, *Tales of the Hall*, had come out in 1819. Scott, of course, was establishing a whole new career as a historical novelist: Southey and Moore too were turning much more to writing prose; Southey published his last book-length poem, *A Tale of Paraguay* in 1825,

CONCLUSION

while Moore, after publishing *Loves of the Angels* in 1823, scrapped his next verse tale, later publishing it as a prose narrative, and settled down to writing biographies; Rogers published his last major poem, *Italy*, in 1822, and Blake, having completed his *Jerusalem* in 1820, produced his last (and very short) illuminated poem *The Ghost of Abel* in 1822. Only James Montgomery and the forerunner of them all, the Rev. William Lisle Bowles, were still going strong. As well as *A Final Appeal to the Literary Public, relative to Pope* published in 1825, Bowles was to produce a reflective poem, *Banwell Hill*, in 1828, and a verse drama *St John In Patmos* in 1835. Of the younger generation, Keats died in 1821, Shelley was drowned in 1822, and Byron died in 1824. A number of their less talented but not altogether unpromising contemporaries seem to have decided that verse was all very well for adolescents but would not do for mature men; Keats's friend John Hamilton Reynolds abandoned verse in favour of law, as did Bryan Waller Procter; Thomas Dale, having paid his way through university with the profits of his *The Widow of Naïn* became a popular preacher, and the Rev. Henry Hart Milman, after publishing his fourth and last verse drama (*Anne Boleyn*, 1826), devoted himself to working on his controversial *The History of the Jews* (1829).

Of those who had died young, both Shelley and Keats had received more from the existing tradition of poetry than they had given back. Shelley's *Alastor* was a medley of echoes of Wordsworth, Southey and Coleridge and his debt to them can be traced in many of his other poems; Keats escaped from his brief phase of imitating Leigh Hunt by turning to the sixteenth- and seventeenth-century poets who were recommended by Hunt as correct models. The influence of other poets became less evident in their work as their powers developed, and had they lived their resemblances — anyway more a matter of detail than of general similarity — to other poets would have been eliminated. Perhaps they would have become in their turn the model for imitation by cocksure young men who at the same time pretended to despise them (as had happened with Wordsworth). As it was they died before they had made any real impact beyond the circle of those who knew them personally.

With Byron it was quite different. Like one of those hugely successful pop-stars of the 1960s of whom he was in so many ways the precursor, Byron had achieved his phenomenal popularity while still young enough to be uncertain of his real talents; and nourished by success he had continued to change and develop until he had begun to outgrow his public. The metrical romance genre, to which he owed most of his fame, ceased to satisfy him. It was not the best vehicle for expressing ideas and attitudes, for density of language or sonorous declamation in the grand style. In his verse drama *Manfred* (1817), Byron tried to raise the posturings of the metrical romance to a higher level, by presenting them in a more static format. During the next six years, as well as producing another verse romance, *Mazeppa*, Byron cast around uneasily for a new idiom that would suit him. He published six more plays, three longish satirical poems, and a verse tale, *The Island*, which attempted to combine sentimentality, action and burlesque; he toyed with the idea of producing another instalment of *Childe Harold's Pilgrimage*; and he wrote successive cantos of his travesty epic *Don Juan*. In this latter work, according to the consensus of twentieth-century critical opinion, he found the style of poetry which best suited his genius; whether this would have been his own considered opinion and what he would have tried next if he had lived, we shall never know. His readiness to involve himself with the Greek struggle for independence, after fifteen years of adult life spent avoiding responsibility and commitment, at least suggests that he had it in mind to take a rest from poetry.

It is not inappropriate that Byron's death should virtually mark the end of the period of development in poetry into which he had been born. It had been Byron who had consummated the changes in poetry foreshadowed in the second quarter of the eighteenth century, brought closer in the 1790s and finally launched by Scott in 1805. The loss of direction evident in his career in the last years of his life was symptomatic of the loss of direction of the whole movement of poetic change with which he had been involved. Byron died at just the right moment to signalize the end of an era — but the era would have ended whether he had died or not.

It was perhaps no accident that the loss of impetus in poetic change from the early 1820s onward coincided with the lessening of the tensions which had characterized the first two decades of the century. Lower-class political agitation, which had been gaining momentum since before the end of the Napoleonic Wars reached a kind of climax with the Peterloo massacre in 1819 and the Cato Street Conspiracy in 1820 and thereafter faded away. The economy was recovering from the post-war slump — industrial production increased 55 per cent between 1820 and 1830 — and the middle classes found themselves entering on a new age of prosperity. In Parliament the Whig

CONCLUSION

opposition was no longer seen as a threat to the stability of government, as it had been no more than a dozen years earlier, and was coming to be regarded as part of the constitutional framework — the phrase *His Majesty's Opposition* was coined by Byron's friend Hobhouse in 1826. The government itself seemed more firmly entrenched than it had been during the war years, and embarked on a miscellaneous programme of legal and commercial reforms. More important than any of this was a growing sense of adjustment to the new economic order that had been emerging over the past sixty years. The founding of the Political Economy Club in 1820 and the publication of a number of text books on economics such as James Mill's *Elements of Political Economy* (1821) and John Ramsay McCulloch's *The Principles of Political Economy* (1825) were indications of an increasingly widespread recognition of the dominant position industry and commerce now had in British life. Dreams of

> Old, unhappy, far-off things
> And battles long ago

were beginning to seem somewhat irrelevant and were ceasing to have any but a subordinate place in Britons' view of the world.

Any explanation of the hiatus in poetic change in the mid-1820s in terms of the altered socio-economic climate of the decade would be of a piece with the explanation suggested earlier for the triumph of the metrical romance, and it has to be admitted that till we know much more than we do about the laws governing the process of cultural change suggestions of this sort can only be tentative. Even when it is admitted that culture reflects the society which produces it, it may be that this reflection is not equally precise and detailed in every age; the nature of the relationship between culture and society might vary from period to period. At the same time it might be that there are certain elements in art and literature which are constant, such as, let us say, the desire to convert the transience of experience into permanence. These two hypotheses, taken together, provide us with the concept of an on-going, substantially autonomous tradition of culture which is only periodically brought within the orbit of socio-economic influences. Even today, after a hundred years of sophisticated scholarly research, we know our past only in shreds and patches, and the reality of socio-economic and of cultural conditions in any given period are so inadequately understood, even leaving out of consideration the possible range of connections between them, that it would be impossible to say, supposing socio-economic influences were not constant in degree, which phases of culture were more intimately influenced than others.

It might be that the early eighteenth century, the period this book takes as its starting point, was a period of uniquely close inter-reaction of culture and society; the whole neo-classical tradition might have been an unprecedentedly total effort by that period to buttress itself against the threat of political, social and economic disintegration, and it might be that Romanticism was less the symptom of new socio-economic influences coming into play than a process of relaxation from the unaccustomed rigidities and self-disciplines of neo-classicism, a return to normality after the extremes of repression and tension, a revival (with all their drama and exoticism) of the age-old central traditions of culture after two generations during which they had been smothered by political and social crisis. The truth about this and other periods of decisive change will only be understood by studying the various forms of culture far more systematically than has been done hitherto. In the case of poetry, this means looking at the bad and indifferent poets as well as at the good. For too long the poetic geniuses, the Wordsworths and the Shelleys, have been studied in splendid isolation, and the third-raters, the Campbells and Montgomerys who are frequently more representative of their age have been ignored: it is time the balance was redressed, and that is what this book has tried to do.

Notes
(All books cited were published in London unless otherwise stated)

INTRODUCTION
1. See for example Mary Jacobus, *Tradition and Experiment in Wordsworth's* Lyrical Ballads, 1798 (Oxford, 1976).
2. *Pamphleteer*, vol. 10, p. 443 (May 1815).
3. William Hazlitt, *Lectures on the English Poets* (1818), in P. P. Howe, ed., *Complete Works of William Hazlitt* (21 vols., 1930-34), vol. 5, p. 161.
4. Leigh Hunt, *Foliage* (1818), p. 10.
5. *Examiner*, 15 July 1821, Sketch of Bowles.
6. Shelley to C. Ollier, letter 15 October 1819, in F. L. Jones, ed., *The Letters of Percy Bysshe Shelley* (2 vols., Oxford, 1964), vol. 2, p. 127.
7. A. Beljame, *The Men of Letters and the English Public in the Eighteenth Century*, trans. E. O. Lorimer (1948), espec. pp. 385-6; A. S. Collins, *The Profession of Letters, 1780-1835* (1928), pp. 115, 247; J. W. Saunders, *The Profession of English Letters* (1964), pp. 116 foll.
8. C. A. G. Goede, *The Stranger in England* (3 vols., 1807), vol. 2, pp. 120-21.
9. Leigh Hunt, *Lord Byron and some of his Contemporaries* (1828), pp. 18-21, 32-7.
10. Cf. Raymond Wiliams, *The Country and the City* (1973).
11. N. Frye, "Blake after Two Centuries", in M. H. Abrams, ed., *English Romantic Poets* (New York, 1960), p. 65.
12. N. Frye, "The Drunken Boat" in Frye, ed., *Romanticism Reconsidered* (New York, 1963), p. 16.
13. M. H. Abrams, *Natural Supernaturalism* (1971), p. 411.
14. ibid., p. 13.
15. Wordsworth, *Essay Supplementary to the Preface* (first published in 1815 edition of Wordsworth's poems).
16. Norman Callan, "Augustan Reflective Poetry", in B. Ford, ed., *Pelican Guide to English Literature*, vol. 4, *From Dryden to Johnson* (1963), pp. 346-71, 353. Cf. J. R. Sutherland, *A Preface to Eighteenth-Century Poetry* (Oxford, 1948), pp. 77-80.
17. Joseph Warton, *An Essay on the Writings and Genius of Pope*, vol. 1 (1756), p. 43-4.
18. ibid., p. 44.
19. Samuel Taylor Coleridge, *Biographia Literaria* (2 vols., 1817),

vol. 2, p. 24; Everyman edition (1956), p. 181.
20. F. W. Bateson, *English Poetry and the English Language* (3rd edn., Oxford, 1973), p. 45.
21. *Edinburgh Review*, vol. 9 (1806-7), p. 354.
22. *Eclectic Review*, vol. 4, no. 1 (1808), p. 35.
23. *Edinburgh Review*, vol. 1 (1802-3), p. 63.
24. *Quarterly Review*, vol. 9 (1813), p. 207.
25. W. Cowper, *Poems,* ed. J. Montgomery (Glasgow, 1824), introduction, p. xxvi.
26. G. Gilfillan, ed., *The Poetical Works of W. L. Bowles* (1855), introduction, p. vi.

CHAPTER 1: ENGLISH POETRY IN THE EIGHTEENTH CENTURY
1. *Edinburgh Review*, vol. 27 (1816), p. 1.
2. Cf. R. L. Edgeworth, *Essays on Professional Education* (1809), pp. 47-9, and Sydney Smith in *Edinburgh Review*, vol. 15 (1809), pp. 40-53.
3. *Edinburgh Review*, vol. 9 (1806-7), p. 348.
4. Cf. Lawrence Stone, "Literacy and Education in England 1640-1900", in *Past and Present,* 42 (1969), pp. 69-139, espec. 104 and 110.
5. Thomas Campbell, *Specimens of the British Poets* (7 vols., 1819), vol. 6, p. 189-90.
6. Richard Cumberland, *Memoirs* (1806), p. 258.
7. Poem by Carlisle in *Daily Universal Register,* 10 Sept, 1785.
8. Nathan Drake, *Literary Hours* (1798), p. 64.
9. Samuel Rogers, *Table Talk,* ed. A. Dyce (1856), p. 149.
10. Cf. D. Lovett, "Shakespeare as a Poet of Realism in the Eighteenth Century", *ELH* 2 (1943), pp. 267-89.
11. Lord Holland, *Further Memoirs of the Whig Party,* ed. Lord Stavordale (1905), p. 129; cf. *Richard III*, Act 2, sc. i, 1. 92.
12. H. G. de Maar, *A History of Modern English Romanticism* (2 vols., Oxford, 1924), vol. 1, pp. 19 foll.; R. D. Havens, *The Influence of Milton on English Poetry* (Cambridge, Mass., 1922), pp. 13-15.
13. Havens, op. cit., p. 4 n.4.
14. Samuel Johnson, *The Lives of the Poets,* Milton; cf. Havens, op. cit., pp. 3-33.
15. Ann Yearsley, *Poems on Several Occasions* (1785), Prefatory letter to Mrs Montagu (by Hannah More), p. vi.
16. *Quarterly Review*, vol. 11 (1814), p. 78.
17. Cf. Bateson, op. cit, pp. 60-61.
18. T. Twining, *Aristotle's Treatise on Poetry, Translated: With Notes . . . and Two Dissertations, on Poetical and Musical Imitation* (1789), p. 35.
19. James Beattie, "On Poetry and Music, as they Affect the Mind", in *Essays* (Edinburgh, 1776), p. 374. (N.B. there is another

edition of 1776, also containing this essay but omitting "An Essay on the Nature and Immutability of Truth" — the passage quoted is on pp. 36-7 of this edition.)
20. Cf. John Chalker, *The English Georgic* (1969), pp. 90-140.
21. Cf. The Elder Seneca, *Controversiae* (2 vols., Cambridge, Mass., and London, 1974), Bk. 7.1.15. (I am indebted to Miss J. A. Fairweather of Girton College for assistance on this point.) The device is also found — though not in the context of the delights of rural retirement — in Horace's *Epistles*, Bk. 1, epistle V11.
22. Cf. M.-S. Röstvig, *The Happy Man* (2 vols., Olso, 1954-8), *passim*.
23. *Edinburgh Review*, vol. 18 (1811), p. 282.
24. Cf. Burns's letters *passim*; E. Blunden, ed., *Sketches in the Life of John Clare* (1931), pp. 57-9; T. F. Dibdin, *Reminiscence of a Literary Life* (2 vols., 1836), vol. 1, p. 85; James Hurdis, *The Village Curate* (1788); Thomas Gisborne, *Walks in the Forest* (1794); and see also Havens, op. cit., pp. 126-7.
25. W. Hazlitt, "My First Acquaintance with Poets", in *The Liberal*, no. 3 (1823) and P. P. Howe, ed., *Complete Works of William Hazlitt* (21 vols., 1930-34), vol. 17, p. 12. The index in this edition refers to three other occasions in Hazlitt's work where he repeated this anecdote.
26. Kenneth Clark, *The Gothic Revival* (1928), p. 53.
27. Mary Bayley, burnt at the stake for petty treason (i.e. murdering her husband) at Portsmouth in 1784, was the last woman to be executed in England in this fashion; L. O. Pike, *A History of Crime* (2 vols., 1873-6), vol. 2, p. 379.
28. Shakespeare, *The Tempest*, Act IV, sc. i, 1. 182; Richard Carpenter, *Experience, Historie, and Divinitie* (1642), III, chap. 5, p.53 (sig. Dd 3); William Dampier, *A New Voyage Round the World* (1697), p. 14.
29. Coleridge, *Biographia Literaria*, vol. 2, p. 258 (not in Everyman edition).
30. R. Lonsdale, ed., *The Poems of Thomas Gray, William Collins and Oliver Goldsmith* (1969), notes on Gray's *Elegy*.
31. *European Magazine*, 1790, p. 333, and Joseph Farington, *The Farington Diary*, ed. J. Greig (8 vols., 1922-8), vol. 1, p. 165, 27 Sept. 1796.
32. Rogers, *Table Talk*, p. 34.
33. *Annual Register*, 1795, Chronicle, p. 32.
34. James Hervey, *Meditations among the Tombs*, addition in 6th edition and subsequently, p. 2.
35. Clark, *Gothic Revival*, pp. 53-4.
36. Cf. C. T. Houpt, *Mark Akenside* (Philadelphia, 1944), p. 71.
37. D. Fairer, "The Poems of Thomas Warton the Elder", in *Review of English Studies* n.s., XXVI (1975), pp. 287-300 and 395-406.
38. Havens, op. cit., p. 431.

39. T. Warton's edition of Milton's *Poems upon Several Occasions* (1785), p. x.
40. This poem is attributed to Edmund Smith, who had died in 1710. Though it was claimed to be an imitation of Spenser on its title page, its rhyme scheme was ababbccc. It was probably not by Smith himself, but merely based on one of his Latin odes, though Smith's admiration of Spenser is evident in his *A Poem to the Memory of Mr John Philips* (1709).
41. Thomas Warton, *Observations on The Fairy Queen of Spenser* (2nd edn., 2 vols., 1762), vol. 2, p. 264. The phrase is not in the first edition.
42. R. D. Altick, *The English Common Reader* (Chicago, 1957), p. 50.
43. Cf. W. D. McClintock, *Joseph Warton's Essay on Pope* (Chapel Hill, 1933), pp. 19-22, J. Kinsley, "The Publication of Warton's 'Essay on Pope'", in *Modern Language Review*, No. 44 (1949), pp. 91-3, and Joan Pittock, "Joseph Warton and his Second Volume of the 'Essay on Pope'", in *Review of English Studies*, n.s. XVIII (1967), pp. 264-73.
44. Joseph Warton, *An Essay on the Writings and Genius of Pope*, vol. 1, (1756), p. x.
45. ibid., p. 334 (concluding sentence of the first volume of the *Essay*).
46. Robert Southey, *Specimens of Later English Poets* (3 vols., 1807), vol. 1, p. xxxii.
47. Cf. V. E. Neuburg, *The Penny Histories* (1968), pp. 1 foll., 18-20.
48. R. S. Crane, *The Idea of the Humanities* (2 vols. Chicago and London, 1967), vol. 1, pp. 214-87 ("Anglican Apologetics and the Idea of Progress, 1699-1745").
49. Cf. P. Fussell, "Patrick Brydone: The Eighteenth-Century Traveler as Representative Man", in W. G. Rice, ed., *Literature as a Mode of Travel* (New York, 1963), pp. 53-67, espec. 57-8.
50. Edward Gibbon, *Miscellaneous Works*, ed. John, Lord Sheffield (2 vols, 1796), vol. 1, p. 129.
51. Ann Radcliffe, *The Mysteries of Udolpho* (4 vols, 1794), vol. 2, p. 332.
52. Cf. Crane, op. cit., vol. 1, pp. 188-213 ("Suggestions towards a Genealogy of the 'Man of Feeling'").
53. Cf. A. R. Humphreys, " 'The Friend of Mankind' (1700-60) — An Aspect of Eighteenth-Century Sensibility", in *Review of English Studies*, 24 (1948), pp. 203-18.
54. Burns to J. Murdoch, 15 Jan. 1783, in J. de Lancey Ferguson, ed., *The Letters of Robert Burns* (2 vols., Oxford, 1931), vol. 1, p. 14.
55. Havens, op. cit., p. 434.
56. Raymond Williams, *The Country and the City* (1973), pp. 74-9.
57. Dorothy Wordsworth to Jane Pollard, 10-12 July 1793, in E. de Selincourt, C. L. Shaver *et al.*, *The Letters of William and*

Dorothy Wordsworth (Oxford, 1967-   ), vol. 1, pp. 100-101.
58. Cf. Robert Millhouse, *The Song of the Patriot* (1826), John Struthers, *The Poor Man's Sabbath* (1804), *The Peasant's Death* (1806), *The Plough* (1818), and Charles Crocker, *The Vale of Obscurity* (1830).

Chapter 2: THE 1780s
1. Wiliam Hayward Roberts. *Judah Restored* (2 vols., 1774), vol. 1, p. xvi.
2. William Mason, *The English Garden*, Bk. 4 (1781), p. 53 ("General Postscript").
3. James Boswell, *The Life of Samuel Johnson* (2 vols., 1791), vol. 1, p. 342 (vol. 1, p. 391 of Everyman edition).
4. Cf. A. M. Wilkinson, "The Decline of English Verse Satire in the Middle Years of the Eighteenth Century", in *Review of English Studies*, n.s. III (1952), pp. 222-33.
5. Cf. Campbell, *Specimens of the British Poets*, vol. 5, pp. 216-17, vol. 7, pp. 360-61, and *Edinburgh Review*, vol. 11, p. 409.
6. John Wilson, *The Recreations of Christopher North* (3 vols., 1842), vol. 3, p. 230.
7. Anonymous, *Ode to Lansdown Hill* (1785); Lord Crawford, *Richmond Hill* (1777). Cf. R. A. Aubin, *Topographical Poetry* (New York, 1936).
8. W. Roberts, *Memoirs of the Life and Correspondence of Mrs Hannah More* (4 vols., 1834), vol. 2, p. 77.
9. W. M. Hargreaves-Mawdsley, *The English Della Cruscans and Their Time 1733-1828* (The Hague, 1967), p. 29.
10. ibid., p. 41.
11. ibid., p.48. Quotation is from Merry's "Distant Prospect of Rome" (*Florence Miscellany*, p. 86).
12. Cf. *Blackwood's Edinburgh Magazine*, vol. 10 (1821), p. 696.
13. Rogers, *Table Talk*, p. 258 n.
14. W. L. Bowles, *Scenes and Shadows of Days Departed: A Narrative Accompanied with Poems of Youth and some other Poems of Melancholy and Fancy* (1837), p. xiv.
15. Preface to Coleridge's untitled selection of sonnets bound up with Bowles's sonnets; cf. Samuel Taylor Coleridge, *Complete Poetical Works*, ed. E. H. Coleridge (2 vols, Oxford, 1912), vol. 2, p. 1139.

Chapter 3: THE AGE OF LYRICAL BALLADS
1. Lord Byron, *English Bards and Scotch Reviewers* (2nd edn., 1809), 1. 894. Cf. Thomas James Mathias, *The Pursuits of Literature* (1794), Dialogue 1, note to 1. 101 (1. 77 in later editions).
2. Mathias, loc. cit.
3. Cf. N. Fruman, *Coleridge, the Damaged Archangel* (1972), pp. 253-4.

4. Rogers, op. cit., p. 16.
5. ibid., p. 18.
6. ibid.
7. ibid., p. 58.
8. *Annual Review*, vol. 1 (1802), p. 660; see also *Quarterly Review*, vol. 4 (1810), p. 516-17, for later comparisons with Goldsmith.
9. *Monthly Review*, vol. 17 (1795), p. 355.
10. *British Critic*, vol. 6 (1795), p. 185.
11. Cf. Jacobus, *Tradition and Experiment in Wordsworth's* Lyrical Ballads, p. 168.
12. *Edinburgh Review*, vol. 24 (1814), p. 1; also cf. *The Album*, vol. 1, p. 215.
13. *British Critic*, new series, vol. 11 (1819), p. 592.
14. C. H. Herford, *The Age of Wordsworth* (1897), p. 158; W. J. Courthope, *A History of English Poetry* (6 vols., 1903-26), vol. 6 *passim*; G. Saintsbury, *A History of English Criticism* (1911), pp. 315, 327; cf. Margaret Oliphant, *The Literary History of England, in the end of the Eighteenth and beginning of the Nineteenth Century* (3 vols., 1882), and C. E. Vaughan, *The Romantic Revolt* (1907).
15. M. L. Barstow, *Wordsworth's Theory of Poetic Diction* (New Haven, 1917), p. xii.
16. G. M. Harper, *William Wordsworth, His Life, Works and Influence* (2 vols., 1916), vol. 1, pp. 424-5.
17. M. H. Needleman and W. B. Otis, *An Outline History of English Literature* (2nd edn., 1939), vol. 2, p. 444.
18. M. Drabble, *Wordsworth* (1966), pp. 9 and 20.
19. W. J. B. Owen, "Wordsworth's Preface to Lyrical Ballads", in *Anglistica*, no. 9 (1957), p. 12.
20. J. Scoggins, "The Preface to Lyrical Ballads, a Revolution in Dispute", in H. Anderson and J. S. Shea, eds., *Studies in Criticism and Aesthetics 1660-1800* (Minneapolis, 1967), p. 397.
21. Coleridge, *Biographia Literaria*, vol. 2, p. 96 (Everyman edn., p. 246); for what follows, compare vol. 2, pp. 69-70 (Everyman edn., p. 222).
22. Rogers, *Table Talk*, p. 205.
23. Hazlitt, "My First Acquaintance with Poets", loc. cit.
24. Note by Wordsworth c. 1836 in Mss of Barron Field's *Memoirs* of him, printed in W. Knight, ed., *Letters of the Wordsworth Family* (3 vols, Boston and London, 1907), vol. 3, p. 122.
25. Wordsworth to Walter Scott, 7 Nov. 1805, in De Selincourt, Shaver *et al.*, op. cit., vol. 1, p. 641.
26. Cf. Jacobus, op. cit.
27. R. D. Mayo, "The Contemporaneity of Lyrical Ballads", *PMLA*, vol. 69 (1954), no. 1, pp. 486-522.
28. *British Critic*, vol. 15 (1800), p. 605.

29. Coleridge, *Biographia Literaria*, vol. 1, pp. 84-5 (Everyman edn., pp. 48-9).
30. *Notes and Queries*, 4th series, vol. 3, p. 580 quoted; vol. 4, p. 85 identified.
31. Southey to Taylor, 5 Sept. 1799, in J. W. Robberds, *A Memoir of the Life and Writings of William Taylor, of Norwich* (2 vols., 1843), vol. 1, p. 223.
32. Mary Jacobus, "Southey's Debt to *Lyrical Ballads*", in *Review of English Studies*, n.s. XXII (1971), pp. 20-36.
33. Southey to G. C. Bedford, 19 Aug. 1801, in C. C. Southey, *Life and Correspondence of the Late Robert Southey* (6 vols., 1850), vol. 2, p. 160.
34. Thomas de Quincey, *Recollections of the Lake Poets* (1948), p. 52; cf. Southey to Taylor, 11 Jan. 1803, in Robberds, op. cit., vol. 1, p. 440.
35. Robberds, op. cit., vol. 1, p. 199; cf. A. D. Harvey, "The English Epic in the Romantic Period", in *Philological Quarterly*, 55 (1976), pp. 241-59, espec. 255-6.
36. Sir Samuel Egerton Brydges, *Autobiography, Times, Opinions, and Contemporaries* (2 vols., 1834), vol. 1, p. 186.
37. Rogers, *Table Talk*, p. 251.
38. *The Album*, vol. 1 (1822), p. 211.
39. Campbell, *Specimens of the British Poets*, vol. 6, pp. 43-8, 129-31.
40. Beattie, *Life and Letters of Thomas Campbell*, vol. 3, p. 226.
41. National Library of Wales, Mss NLW 4814D, Southey to Wynn, 18 Feb. 1804.
42. J. P. Collier, *Seven Lectures on Shakespeare and Milton by the Late S. T. Coleridge* (1856), p. xxvi. For Coleridge's own insatiable borrowing, see Fruman, *Coleridge, the Damaged Archangel, passim.*
43. Rogers, *Table Talk*, p. 251n. Cf. E. J. Morley, ed., *Henry Crabb Robinson on Books and their Writers* (1938), p. 90.
44. Dorothy Wordsworth to Catherine Clarkson, 23 Feb. 1811, in De Selincourt, Shaver *et al.*, op. cit., vol. 2, p. 467.
45. Thomas Moore, *Memoirs, Journal and Correspondence*, ed. Lord J. Russell (8 vols., 1853-6), vol. 7, p. 197, 10 Aug. 1837; the occasion was one of Rogers's literary dinner parties.
46. Leigh Hunt, sketch of Campbell, in *The Examiner*, 21 Aug. 1821; cf. L. H. and C. W. Houtchens, eds., *Leigh Hunt's Literary Criticism* (New York, 1956), pp. 160, 643.
47. Thomas Telford to the Rev. Archibald Alison, 5 July 1802, in Beattie, op. cit., vol. 1, p. 395.

Chapter 4: THE GREAT AGE OF RURAL POETRY
1. Cf. Röstvig, *Happy Man*, vol. 2, pp. 387, 418, where it is suggested that there was a shift from an emphasis on man's active initiative in his dealings with nature to an emphasis on the effect of nature on man.

2. *Daily Universal Register*, 6 Jan. 1785.
3. J. D. Chambers and G. E. Mingay, *The Agricultural Revolution* (1966), pp. 110-12.
4. F. K. Brown, *The Fathers of the Victorians* (Cambridge, 1961), pp. 332-9.
5. Cf. A. D. Harvey, "First Public Reactions to the Industrial Revolution", in *Etudes Anglaises*, XXXI (1978), pp. 273-93.
6. C. W. Chalklin, *The Provincial Towns of Georgian England* (1974), pp. 3-16, 26.
7. W. Albert, *The Turnpike System in England 1663-1840* (1972), p. 45.
8. P. S. Bagwell, *The Transport Revolution from 1770* (1974), pp. 41-60.
9. William Windham, *Diary*, ed. H. Baring (1866), p. 20.
10. Rayner Unwin, *The Rural Muse* (1954), p. 92.
11. ibid.
12. Robert Bloomfield to George Bloomfield, 15 June 1800, in W. H. Hart, ed., *Selections from the Correspondence of Robert Bloomfield* (1870), p. 6.
13. ibid., 31 Oct. 1801, p. 15.
14. Thomas Green, *Extracts from the Diary of a Lover of Literature* (Ipswich, 1810), p. 207.
15. Mary Russell Mitford to R. L. Mitford, in A. G. d'Estrange, *The Life of Mary Russell Mitford* (3 vols., 1870), vol. 1, pp. 98-9.
16. Unwin, *Rural Muse*, p. 103.
17. Beattie, *Life and Letters of Thomas Campbell*, vol. 1, p. 242.
18. T. S. Grimshawe, *A Memoir of the Rev. Legh Richmond, A.M.* (5th edn., 1829), p. 296.
19. *Edinburgh Review*, vol. 2 (1803), pp. 81-4.
20. ibid., vol. 13 (1808-9), p. 276.
21. ibid., vol. 11 (1807-8), p. 411. This was one of the two reviews Campbell wrote for Jeffrey of *The Edinburgh Review*.
22. ibid., vol. 11, p. 168.
23. H. W. Hamilton, *Doctor Syntax* (1969), p. 260.

Chapter 5: THE METRICAL ROMANCE
1. H. Whitfield, *A Picture from Life* (2 vols, 1804), vol. 1, pp. 158-9.
2. Cf. A. D. Harvey, "Clarissa and the Puritan Tradition", in *Essays in Criticism*, XXVIII (1978), pp. 38-51, espec. 49.
3. *Northampton Mercury*, 25 Oct. 1800, 28 Feb. 1807, 26 May 1810, 1 Sept 1810; *Annual Register*, 1804, p. 421.
4. *Annual Register*, 1807, pp. 379-82.
5. Green, *Diary of a Lover of Literature*, p. 4, 23 Sept. 1796.
6. For a different but perhaps not incompatible interpretation of the sexual element in *Christabel*, see J. Spatz, "The Mystery of Eros: Sexual Initiation in Coleridge's 'Christabel' ", *PMLA* 90 (1975), pp. 106-16.

7. Coleridge to ?, Dec. 1811, in E. L. Griggs, ed., *Collected Letters of Samuel Taylor Coleridge* (6 vols., Oxford, 1956-71), vol. 3, pp. 355-61.
8. Morley, *Crabb Robinson on Books*, p. 47.
9. Cf. G. Saintsbury, *History of English Prosody* (3 vols., 1906-10), vol. 3, p. 64.
10. Cf. J.-M. Carre, *Goethe en Angleterre* (Paris, 1920), pp. 40-42.
11. Cf. A. D. Harvey, "The English Epic in the Romantic Period", *Philological Quarterly*, 55 (1976), pp. 241-59.
12. Morley, op. cit., p. 47.
13. J. G. Lockhart, *Memoirs of the Life of Sir Walter Scott* (7 vols., 1837), vol. 2, p. 35.
14. ibid., vol. 2, pp. 292-3.
15. *Monthly Review*, vol. 62 (1810), p. 178, and vol. 76 (1815), p. 268.
16. *Edinburgh Review*, vol 16 (1810), p. 270.
17. Charlotte Brontë to Ellen Nussey, 4 July 1834, in C. K. Shorter, *The Brontës, Life and Letters* (2 vols., 1908), vol. 1, p. 111.
18. Sir Walter Scott, *Poetical Works* (11 vols., Edinburgh, 1830), vol. 4, pp. ix-x, Introduction to *The Lady of the Lake*.
19. Cf. U. Amarasinghe, *Dryden and Pope in the Early Nineteenth Century* (Cambridge, 1962), pp. 14-16.
20. Cf. Lockhart, op. cit., vol. 2, p. 132 (Scott to Southey, Nov. 1807), and vol. 4, p. 92 (conversation with Washington Irving).
21. Southey to Taylor, 22 Oct. 1805, in Robberds, op. cit., vol. 2, p. 104.
22. Rogers, *Table Talk*, p. 193.
23. Collier, op. cit. p. xxv. Cf. Coleridge's letter to Wordsworth, October 1810, in Griggs, op. cit., vol. 3, pp. 290-95.
24. Morley, op. cit., p. 82.
25. Wordsworth to Rogers, 12 Jan. 1813, in De Selincourt, Shaver *et al.*, op, cit., vol. 3, p. 70.
26. E. Railo, *The Haunted Castle* (1927), pp. 33-5.
27. E. J. Trelawney, *Records of Shelley, Byron and the Author* (2 vols., 1878), vol. 2, p. 102. Cf. Dedication to Canto 4 of *Childe Harold's Pilgrimage*.
28. E. D. Hirsch, "Byron and the Terrestrial Paradise", in F. W. Hilles and H. Bloom, eds., *From Sensibility to Romanticism* (New York, 1965), p. 455.
29. Cf. Trelawney, op. cit., and Hunt, *Lord Byron and some of his Contemporaries*.
30. Jeffrey to Robert Morehead, 6 Aug. 1798, in H. Cockburn, *Life of Lord Jeffrey* (2 vols., Edinburgh, 1852), vol. 1, p. 100.
31. J. Holland and J. Everett, *Memoirs of the Life and Writings of James Montgomery* (7 vols., 1855-6), vol. 2, pp. 28-9.
32. ibid., p. 184, Montgomery to Daniel Parken, Nov. 1807. "Splendour and foppery" are not very evident in *The Wanderer*

but when Montgomery wrote this letter, he was working on *The West Indies,* which was very different in its style.

33. *Edinburgh Review,* vol. 9 (1806-7), p. 347.
34. ibid., pp. 348-9.
35. Lord Byron, *English Bards and Scotch Reviewers* (2nd edn.), 1.418n.: "Poor MONTGOMERY! though praised by every English Review, has been bitterly reviled by the EDINBURGH. After all, the Bard of Sheffield is a man of considerable genius: his 'Wanderer of Switzerland' is worth a thousand 'Lyrical Ballads' and at least fifty 'Degraded Epics'." Like most of Byron's critical pronouncements, this one seems to have been inspired chiefly by contrariness.
36. Southey to Murray in S. Smiles, *Memoir and Correspondence of John Murray* (1891), p. 198.
37. For Keats, cf. E. V. Weller, *Keats and Mary Tighe* (New York, 1928), and C. W. Gillam, "Keats, Mary Tighe and Others", in *Notes and Queries,* 199 (1954), pp. 76-9. For Barton, cf. his *Verses, written in a blank leaf of "Tighe's Psyche"* and his numerous attempts at Spenserians (which are, however, more reminiscent of Beattie than of Mary Tighe), e.g. *A Widow's Tale, Meditations in Great Bealings Church-Yard* and *A Day in Autumn.*
38. Mitchell Library, Glasgow, Ms 75/3/a, unidentifiable press-cutting signed E. P., circa 1810.
39. Cf. A. M. Bierstadt, "Gertrude of Wyoming", in *Journal of English and German Philology,* 20 (1921), pp. 491-501.
40. Mary Russell Mitford to R. L. Mitford, 3 March 1811, in L'Estrange, *Life of Mary Russell Mitford,* vol. 1, p. 119.
41. Byron's Diary, 9 Jan. 1821, in R. E. Prothero, ed., *Letters and Journals of Lord Byron* (6 vols., 1898-1901).
42. Byron to Moore, 3 May 1821, in ibid., vol. 5, p. 274.
43. Byron to Murray, 15 Sept. 1817, in ibid., vol. 4, p. 169.
44. Byron's Diary, 24 Nov. 1813, in ibid., vol. 2, p. 343.
45. Byron to Moore, 5 Sept. 1813, in ibid., vol. 2, p. 260.
46. Countess of Blessington, *Conversations of Lord Byron* (1834), p. 353.
47. Moore, *Diary,* vol. 3, p. 34, 15 Oct. 1819.
48. Hunt, *Lord Byron and his Contemporaries,* pp. 45-6.
49. Byron to Augusta Leigh, 23 Feb. 1824, in Prothero, op. cit., vol. 6, p. 332.
50. Byron's Diary, 24 Nov. 1813, in ibid., vol. 2, p. 343.
51. Byron's Diary, 12 Jan. 1821, in ibid., vol. 5, pp. 167-8. Byron used the same analogy with the Athenian statesman Aristides, with reference to Pope, in his second letter to John Murray in the Pope-Bowles controversy in 1821.
52. Byron to Moore, 29 Feb. 1816, in ibid., vol. 3, p. 267.
53. Byron to Coleridge, 18 Oct. 1815, in L. A. Marchand, ed., *Byron's Letters and Journals* (1973-), vol. 4, pp. 318-19 (not in Prothero edition). Cf. Byron to Murray, 4 Nov. 1815, in Prothero,

op. cit., vol. 3, p 246.
54. Morchard Bishop, ed., *The Table Talk of Samuel Rogers* (1952), Appendix, p. 240 (passage cancelled by Dyce in his own edition).
55. E. H. Coleridge, ed., *The Poetical Works of Lord Byron* (7 vols., 1898-1904), vol. 3, p. 496, quoting Murray's recollection of Byron's opinion.
56. Byron to Moore, 10 Jan. 1815, in Prothero, op. cit., vol. 3, p. 169.
57. Thomas Medwin, *Journal of the Conversations of Lord Byron* (1824), p. 237.
58. J. O. Hayden, *The Romantic Reviewers, 1802-24* (1969), p. 145.
59. Moore, *Diary*, vol. 3, p. 161, 27 Oct. 1820.
60. Medwin, op. cit., p. 237.
61. Thomas de Quincey, *Recollections of the Lake Poets* (1948), p. 326n.; cf. W. Jerdan, *Autobiography* (4 vols., 1852-3), vol. 4, pp. 5-7, and Alaric Watts, "Lord Byron's Plagiarisms", in *Literary Gazette*, vol. 5 (1821), pp. 121-4, 137-9, 150-52, 168-70, 201-3.
62. Rogers, *Table Talk* (Dyce's edition), p. 234.
63. *Quarterly Review*, vol. 27 (1822), p. 476. The reviewer was either William Gifford or Reginald Heber.
64. *Edinburgh Review*, vol. 21, p. 299; vol. 23, p. 198; vol. 27, p. 277; vol. 28, p. 418; vol. 30, pp. 95 and 99.
65. D'Israeli to Murray, Dec. 1815, in Smiles, op. cit., p. 358.
66. *Monthly Review*, vol. 95 (1821), p. 96.
67. *Tatler*, 14 Jan. 1831.
68. Blessington, op cit., p. 321.
69. William Wordsworth, *Prose Works*, ed. A. B. Grosart (3 vols., 1876), vol. 3, p. 462, reminiscence by Christopher Wordsworth.
70. Bryan Waller Procter, *An Autobiographical Fragment and Biographical Notes* (1877), p. 154. For the essayist Hazlitt's application of a similar metaphor to Moore, see *The Spirit of the Age* (1825), in Howe, *Complete Works of Hazlitt*, vol. 11, p. 171.
71. Henry Crabb Robinson, *Diary, Reminiscences, and Correspondence*, ed. T. Sadler (3 vols., 1869), vol. 3, p. 218, 4 June 1843.
72. Leigh Hunt, *The Story of Rimini* (1816), p. xv.
73. Morley, op. cit., p. 186.
74. *Edinburgh Review*, vol. 34 (1820), pp. 206, 211.
75. Byron to Murray, 4 Jan. 1821, in Prothero, op. cit., vol. 5, p. 217.
76. Cr. Harvey, "English Epic . . .", in *Philological Quarterly*, 55, pp. 241-59 *passim*.

Chapter 6: LYRICAL POETRY
1. Nathan Drake, *Literary Hours* (1798), p. 378.
2. Havens, op. cit., p. 469.
3. ibid., p. 499.
4. *Monthly Review* (original series), vol. 81, pp. 312-13 (1789).
5. ibid., vol. 79 (1788), p. 279.

6. Sharpe to Miss Pitman, Nov. 1812, in W. K. R. Bedford, ed., *Letters from and to Charles Kirkpatrick Sharpe, Esq.* (2 vols., 1888), vol. 2, p. 37.
7. Cf. *Edinburgh Review*, vol. 9 (1806-7), p. 348.
8. W. Hazlitt, *The Spirit of the Age* (1825) in Howe, op. cit., vol. 11, p. 171.
9. *Edinburgh Review*, vol. 8 (1806), p. 457.
10. Sharpe to Pitman, Nov. 1812, in Bedford, op. cit., vol. 2, p. 37.
11. National Library of Wales, Mss NLW 4814D, Southey to Wynn, 18 Feb. 1804.
12. Rogers, *Table Talk*, pp. 281-2.
13. Byron to J. M. B. Pigot, 13 Jan. 1807, in Prothero, op. cit., vol. 1, p. 113; *Satirist*, vol. 1, p. 79.
14. Havens, op. cit., p. 469.
15. *Edinburgh Review*, vol. 34 (1820), p. 203.
16. *General Weekly Register*, 30 June 1822.
17. *Blackwood's Edinburgh Magazine*, vol. 10 (1821), p. 697.
18. ibid.
19. *Literary Gazette*, vol. 5 (1821), p. 772, col. 3.

Chapter 7: THE NEW POETRY AND THE READING PUBLIC IN THE 1800s
1. J. Richardson and A. L. Kroeber, "Three Centuries of Women's Dress Fashions: A Quantitative Analysis", in *Anthropological Records*, 5, no. 2 (1940).
2. Cf. A. D. Harvey, *Britain in the Early Nineteenth Century* (1978), passim.
3. T. Kelly, *Early Public Libraries* (1966), p. 126.
4. ibid., pp. 137-9.
5. ibid., p. 145, and H. M. Hamlyn, "Eighteenth-Century Circulating Libraries in England", in *The Library*, 5th series, vol. 1 (1947), pp. 197-222.
6. *Parliamentary Papers*, 1826-7, vol. XVII, p. 24.
7. V. E. Neuburg, *The Penny Histories* (1968), p. 59.
8. For Robert Tannahill, see p. 127 in this volume and his *Poetical Works* (1825 and 1870); for Millhouse, see p. 43 and n.58 (ch. 1), and *The Song of the Patriot* (1826); for Blackner, see unpublished poem on the Battle of Marengo in Notts County Record Office (he had a local celebrity as editor of *The Nottingham Review* and author of *The History of Nottingham*, 1816); for William Gifford, see his *Memoir* (1826); for Bloomfield, see pp. 83-5; for David Service, see p. 116 and *The Caledonian Herd-Boy* (Yarmouth, 1802) and *The Wild Harp's Murmurs* (Yarmouth, 1806); for Blacket, see *The Remains of Joseph Blacket* (2 vols., 1811); for John Struthers, see p. 43 and n.58 (ch. 1) and his *Poetical Works* (1850); for Charles Crocker, see p. 43 and n.58 (ch. 1) and anon., *Sketches of Obscure Poets* (1833); for William Nicholson, see his *Tales in Verse* (2nd edn., 1828).

9. F. Martin, *The Life of John Clare* (1865), pp. 24-6.
10. Uvedale Price, *A Letter to H. Repton, Esq.* (1795), p. 107.
11. Thomas, Lord Erskine, *Armata* (1817 edn.), p. 24; cf. Harvey, "English Epic...", in *Philological Quarterly*, 55, espec. p. 243.
12. Cf. Harvey, "*Clarissa* and the Puritan Tradition", in *Essays in Criticism*, xxviii, espec. pp. 44 foll. See also M. LeGates, "The Cult of Womanhood in Eighteenth-Century Thought", in *Eighteenth-Century Studies*, vol. 10 (1976-7), pp. 21-39.
13. Kenneth Clark, *The Gothic Revival* (1928), p. 53.
14. J. H. Plumb, "The New World of Children in Eighteenth-Century England", in *Past and Present*, 67 (1975), pp. 64-95.
15. *Gentleman's Magazine*, vol. 75 (1805), pt. 1, p. iii.
16. W. Wordsworth, *Concerning the Relations of Great Britain, Spain and Portugal... and Specifically as Affected by the Convention of Cintra* (1809), in W. B. J. Owen and L. J. W. Smyser, eds., *The Prose Works of William Wordsworth* (3 vols., Oxford, 1974), vol. 1, pp. 324-5.
17. Cf. Cowper's *The Task*, Book 3, ll.108 foll., and Bowles's sonnets *To a Friend* and *Bereavement* and *Monody, written at Matlock*, ll.111 foll.
18. *Quarterly Review*, vol. 2 (1809), p. 426-7. Scott's remarks on this subject were not entirely fair; see for example Coleridge's *Fears in Solitude* (1798). See also Betty T. Bennett, ed., *British War Poetry in the Age of Romanticism: 1793-1815* (New York, 1977).
19. Thomas Moore, *Letters and Journals of Lord Byron: With Notices of his Life* (2 vols., 1830), vol. 1, p. 343.

Chapter 8: THE RENEWAL OF INTEREST IN ELIZABETHAN AND JACOBEAN PLAYWRIGHTS

1. *Quarterly Review*, vol. 4 (1810), p. 166.
2. *Edinburgh Review*, vol. 18 (1811), p. 275.
3. *Quarterly Review*, vol. 13 (1815), p. 112.
4. Cf. opening paragraphs of Hazlitt's third lecture on the Comic Writers, on Cowley, Butler, Suckling, Etherege, etc., P. P. Howe, *Complete Works of Hazlitt*, vol. 6, pp. 49 foll.; Coleridge, *Biographia Literaria*, vol. 1, pp. 23-4 (Everyman edn., p. 12).
5. Henry Weber, ed., *The Dramatic Works of John Ford* (2 vols., Edinburgh, 1811), p. vii.
6. *Monthly Review*, vol. 67 (1812), p. 242.
7. *Edinburgh Review*, vol. 13 (1808-9), p. 120.
8. ibid., vol. 18 (1811), p. 275.
9. *Quarterly Review*, vol. 4, (1810), p. 165.
10. *Edinburgh Review*, vol. 18 (1811), p. 283.
11. ibid., vol. 33 (1820), p. 144.
12. ibid., vol. 34 (1820), p. 203.
13. ibid., vol. 47 (1828), p. 13.
14. J. Allardyce Nicoll, *A History of Early Nineteenth-Century Drama, 1800-1850* (2 vols., Cambridge, 1930), vol. 1, pp. 88 foll.

15. Cf. Beach Langston, "Shelley's Use of Shakespeare", in *Huntingdon Library Quarterly*, 12 (1948-9), pp. 163-90.
16. H. S. Cathcart, *The Life and Work of Joanna Baillie* (New Haven, 1923), p. 73. Cf. *Annual Review*, vol. 1 (1802), p. 689, where Joanna Baillie sneered at Lamb's Shakespearian echoes in her ungenerously facetious review of *John Woodvill*. For comments on her attitude in this review, see Southey to Taylor, 22 March 1804, in Robberds, op. cit., vol. 1, p. 489, and Taylor to Southey, 27 March 1804, ibid., vol. 1, p. 491.

Chapter 9: THE DETHRONEMENT OF THE AUGUSTANS
1. Dugald Stewart, *Account of the Life and Writings of William Robertson, D.D., F.R.S.E.* (1801), p. 51; the allusion is to Johnson's life of Addison.
2. Sir William Forbes, *An Account of the Life and Writings of James Beattie, LL.D.* (2 vols., Edinburgh, 1806), vol. 2, p. 17.
3. *Edinburgh Review*, vol. 1 (1802-3), p. 63.
4. ibid., vol. 7 (1805-6), p. 1.
5. *Quarterly Review*, vol. 9 (1813), p. 212.
6. John Wilson Croker, *Correspondence and Diaries*, ed. L. J. Jennings (3 vols., 1884), vol. 1, p. 146, Croker to Murray, 18 July 1819.
7. *The British Poets* (100 vols., 1822), vol. 68, p. 219, J. W. Singer's Life of Joseph Warton.
8. Amarsinghe, *Dryden and Pope in the Early Nineteenth Century*, p. 56n.
9. Cf. J. V. Guerinot, *Pamphlet Attacks on Alexander Pope 1711-1744* (1969).
10. Joseph Warton, *Essay on the Writings and Genius of Pope*, p. 334.
11. Wordsworth, Second letter on *Epitaphs*, in Owen and Smyser, eds., op. cit., vol. 2, p. 75.
12. Wordsworth to Scott, 18 Jan. 1808, in De Selincourt and Shaver *et al.*, op. cit., vol. 2, p. 191.
13. Note by Wordsworth c. 1836 in Mss of Barron Field's *Memoirs* of him, printed in W. Knight, ed., *Letters of the Wordsworth Family* (3 vols., Boston and London, 1907), vol. 3, p. 122.
14. Wordsworth to Dyce, 12 Jan. 1829, in E. de Selincourt, ed., *The Letters of William and Dorothy Wordsworth: The Later Years* (3 vols., Oxford, 1939), vol. 1, p, 346.
15. Alexander Pope, *Works*, ed. Joseph Warton (9 vols., 1797), vol. 1, p.1xviii; John Dryden, *Poetical Works* [ed. anonymously by H. J. Todd from materials left by Joseph and John Warton etc.] (4 vols., 1811), vol. 2, p. 259n.
16. Hazlitt, "My First Acquaintance with Poets", loc. cit.
17. Coleridge, *Biographia Literaria*, vol. 1, p. 18 (Everyman edn., p. 9).
18. Alexander Pope, *Works*, ed. William Lisle Bowles (10 vols.,

1806), vol 1, pp. 317-20n.
19. ibid., vol. 10, pp. 363-4 (Bowles's "Concluding Observations on the Poetic Character of Pope").
20. Rogers, *Table Talk*, p. 208.
21. Southey, *Specimens of the Later English Poets*, vol. 1, p. xxxix.
22. ibid., p. xxx.
23. James Beattie, Essays (1776), p. 757 ("Remarks on the Utility of Classical Learning").
24. Pope, *Works*, ed. Warton, vol. 1, p. lxviii.
25. Southey, op. cit., vol. 1, p. xxx.
26. Richard Payne Knight, *The Progress of Civil Society* (1796), pp. vi-vii.
27. *Edinburgh Review*, vol. 11 (1807-8), p. 407.
28. ibid., vol. 11, p. 409.
29. ibid., vol. 11, p. 412.
30. ibid., vol. 7 (1805-6), p. 2.
31. ibid., vol. 13 (1808-9), pp. 120 foll.
32. ibid., vol. 22 (1913-14), p. 33.
33. *Quarterly Review*, vol. 3 (1810), p. 416.
34. ibid., vol. 4 (1810), p. 517.
35. ibid., vol. 12 (1814-15), p. 87.
36. ibid., vol. 12, p. 88.
37. ibid., vol. 9 (1813), p. 213.
38. Hunt, *The Story of Rimini*, pp. xiii-xiv. Earlier, in his *The Feast of the Poets* (1811), Hunt had written (11.17-18):
> Pope spoiled the ears of the town
> With his cuckoo-song verses, half up and half down.
39. *Edinburgh Review*, vol. 26 (1816), p. 476.
40. Hunt, *Foliage*, p. 9.
41. ibid., p. 10.
42. *Quarterly Review*, vol. 19 (1818), pp. 432-3.
43. Rogers, *Table Talk*, p. 29.
44. Hazlitt, *Lectures on the English Poets*, in Howe, op. cit., vol. 5, p. 68.
45. ibid., vol. 5, pp. 161 and 149.
46. W. C. Hazlitt, *Memoirs of William Hazlitt* (2 vols., 1867), vol. 1, p. 236, report of T. N. Talfourd.
47. ibid.
48. Campbell, *Specimens of the British Poets*, vol. 1, p. 259.
49. Cf. Amarasinghe, *Dryden and Pope in the Early Nineteenth Century*, H. A. Beers, *A History of Romanticism in the Nineteenth Century* (1902), and J. J. van Rennes, *Bowles, Byron and the Pope Controversy* (Amsterdam, 1927).
50. "Fabius", "A Letter to the Right Hon. Lord Byron", in *The Pamphleteer* (1821), vol. 18, p. 580.
51. *Quarterly Review*, vol. 32 (1825), p. 311.
52. ibid., vol. 25 (1821), p. 426.

Appendix

Numbers of Editions of Poetry Published in British Isles 1795-1825

This list is taken from the British Museum Catalogue and *The New Cambridge Bibliography of English Literature*. The size of editions varied from 500 to 6,000 though 1,000 was usual, but this list should give a rough idea of relative popularities.

The older poets had in fact a greater circulation than is here suggested, as secondhand bookstalls were very common.

The list is of authors; I have included Complete Works (of authors who were principally writers of verse), Poetical Works, and separately published poems other than those issued as thin pamphlets. A figure might involve a number of different poems published in the same year, or several editions of the same poem. A single edition published in a year is not shown.

Pre 1700 authors are written: THUS
Pre 1800 authors are written: Thus
Wordsworth, Coleridge, Byron, Shelley: *THUS*
Their contemporaries: *Thus*

1795		Bowles	2
MILTON	4	*Mathias*	2
Young	3	Rogers	2
SHAKESPEARE	2		
Thomson	2	1797	
Macpherson	2	SHAKESPEARE	2
Akenside	2	*Mathias*	2
Goldsmith	2	*Southey*	2
Rogers	2		
		1798	
1796		*Mathias*	3
MILTON	4	Young	2
Collins	3	Cowper	2
SHAKESPEARE	2	Burns	2

APPENDIX

1799		SHAKESPEARE	2
Campbell	3	MILTON	2
MILTON	2	Macpherson	2
Mathias	2	Burns	2
		Bloomfield	2
1800			
Watts	5	*1806*	
Bloomfield	3	SHAKESPEARE	3
SHAKESPEARE	2	MILTON	3
MILTON	2	Pope	3
Gray	2	*Montgomery*	3
		Scott	3
1801		Macpherson	2
Burns	4	Beattie	2
SHAKESPEARE	2	Goldsmith	2
Bloomfield	2	Cowper	2
Bowles	2	*Bloomfield*	2
		Grahame	2
1802		*Moore*	2
Thomson	5		
Bloomfield	3	*1807*	
SHAKESPEARE	2	SHAKESPEARE	5
MILTON	2	Pope	3
Rogers	2	Gray	3
		Beattie	3
1803		Watts	2
SHAKESPEARE	4	Burns	2
MILTON	4	*BYRON*	2
Thomson	3		
Cowper	2	*1808*	
Burns	2	*Scott*	6
Campbell	2	MILTON	4
Moore	2	Thomson	4
Walker	2	Collins	3
		Burns	3
1804		*Crabbe*	3
Goldsmith	3	*Grahame*	3
MILTON	2	*BYRON*	3
Burns	2	SHAKESPEARE	2
Moore	2	DRYDEN	2
		Pope	2
1805		Young	2
Thomson	5	Watts	2
Scott	4	Johnson	2

APPENDIX

Gray	2	Moore	11
Cowper	2	Scott	8
		Crabbe	4
1809		Montgomery	3
Croker	4	MILTON	2
BYRON	3	*Thurlow*	2
MILTON	2		
Montgomery	2	*1814*	
		BYRON	24
1810		SHAKESPEARE	9
Scott	12	*Thurlow*	3
Cowper	4	Gray	2
Crabbe	4	Cowper	2
Croker	4	Burns	2
Thomson	3	*Southey*	2
Pope	3	*Montgomery*	2
Gray	3	Scott	2
Beattie	3	*Crabbe*	2
Campbell	3		
Moore	3	*1815*	
MILTON	2	SHAKESPEARE	16
Collins	2	*Scott*	10
Bloomfield	2	BYRON	9
Rogers	2	Cowper	4
BYRON	2	*Southey*	4
		Bloomfield	3
1811		Burns	2
Scott	6	*Rogers*	2
Watts	3	*Montgomery*	2
SHAKESPEARE	2	WORDSWORTH	2
Thomson	2		
		1816	
1812		BYRON	22
BYRON	5	SHAKESPEARE	6
Crabbe	5	*Crabbe*	3
Watts	4	*Southey*	3
Macpherson	3	COLERIDGE	3
Bloomfield	3	Goldsmith	2
Goldsmith	2	Burns	2
Grahame	2	Watts	2
Rogers	2	*Scott*	2
Scott	2		
		1817	
1813		*Moore*	8
BYRON	14		

MILTON	6	Cowper	2
BYRON	6	Burns	2
Cowper	5	*Campbell*	2
Southey	4	*Clare*	2
Thomson	2	*Dale*	2
		Grahame	2
1818		Scott	2
SHAKESPEARE	20		
BYRON	14	*1822*	
Moore	11	*BYRON*	13
MILTON	2	Burns	5
Watts	2	*Milman*	3
Barton	2	*Thurlow*	3
Southey	2	SHAKESPEARE	2
Milman	2	MILTON	2
		Goldsmith	2
1819		Cowper	2
BYRON	10	Pope	2
Rogers	3	*Rogers*	2
SHAKESPEARE	2	*Moore*	2
Cowper	2	*Barton*	2
Burns	2	*Bloomfield*	2
Dale	2		
Hogg	2	*1823*	
		BYRON	23
1820		*Moore*	7
SHAKESPEARE	4	SHAKESPEARE	5
BYRON	4	MILTON	3
Cowper	3	Burns	3
Cornwall	3	Akenside	2
Clare	3	Beattie	2
Dale	3	*Scott*	2
Thomson	2		
Goldsmith	2	*1824*	
Barton	2	*BYRON*	17
Bloomfield	2	SHAKESPEARE	4
Milman	2	Pope	3
		Cowper	3
1821		MILTON	2
BYRON	9	Thomson	2
SHAKESPEARE	5	Goldsmith	2
SHELLEY	3	Burns	2
MILTON	2	*Campbell*	2
Gray	2	*Barton*	2

APPENDIX

Bloomfield	2	*Kirke White*	4
		Cowper	3
1825		*Campbell*	2
BYRON	12	*Scott*	2
SHAKESPEARE	6	*Montgomery*	2

Index of Artists and Writers

(Those other than British poets are identified with a brief description.)

Addison, Joseph (1672-1719), 12, 17, 18, 20, 21, 32
Akenside, Mark, *M.D.* (1721-70), 32, 35, 36, 60, 68, 83;
  poetry quoted, 121
Anstey, Christopher (1724-1805), 126
Ariosto, Ludovico, *Italian poet* (1474-1533), 162
Austen, Jane, *novelist* (1775-1817), 20

Baillie, Joanna (1762-1851), 82, 146-7;
  poetry quoted, 146-7
Barrett, Eaton Stannard (1786-1820), 158;
  poetry quoted, 158
Barton, Bernard (1784-1849), 108, 127
Beattie, James, *LL.D.* (1735-1803), 20, 41, 42-3, 87, 149;
  poetry quoted, 43
Beaumont, Francis, *dramatist* (1584-1616), 143, 144
Blacket, Joseph (1786-1810), 135
Blackner, John, *miscellaneous writer* (1770-1816), 135
Blair, Rev. Robert (1699-1746), 14, 28, 29, 30, 31, 33;
  poetry quoted, 29
Blake, William (1757-1827), 1, 2, 3, 4, 99, 167
Bland, Rev. Robert (1779?-1825), 101
Bloomfield, Robert (1766-1823), 68, 69, 77, 83-5, 86, 87, 100, 133, 135, 157, 158;
  poetry quoted, 84, 85
Bowles, Rev. William Lisle (1762-1850), 44, 55-7, 68, 90n, 106, 120, 139, 151, 152-3, 155, 156, 157, 163, 164-5, 167;
  critical opinions quoted, 152-3;
  poetry quoted, 56
Brontë, Charlotte, *novelist* (1816-55), 101-2, 105
Bruce, Michael (1746-67),
  poetry quoted, 121
Brydges, Sir Samuel Egerton, *miscellaneous writer* (1762-1837), 39, 40
Burke, Edmund, *political writer* (1729-97), 4-5
Burney, Frances, *novelist* (1752-1840), 124
Burns, Robert (1759-96), 1, 27, 41, 44, 52, 58, 68, 77, 79, 87-8, 88n
Byrom, John (1692-1763), 126, 127
Byron, George Gordon, 6th Baron (1788-1824), 1, 3, 5, 6, 7, 13, 42, 59, 72, 75, 89, 90, 101, 103-5, 106, 108, 109, 110-15, 117, 118, 122-3, 125-6, 127, 129, 133, 135, 136, 137, 139, 140, 141, 142, 145, 159, 161, 164, 165, 167-8, 169;
  critical opinions quoted, 111-14, 115, 118;
  poetry quoted, 110, 113, 123, 139

Cambridge, Richard Owen (1717-1802), 35
Campbell, Thomas (1777-1844), 1, 2, 6, 12, 14, 45, 49, 69, 70-5, 76, 77, 85, 86, 101, 102, 103, 106, 107, 108-9, 127, 137, 145, 154, 155-6, 157, 158, 163, 164, 165, 166;
  critical opinions quoted, 88, 150;
  poetry quoted, 71-5, 109
Carew, Thomas (1595?-1639?), 143
Carey, David (1782-1824), 76, 125n
Carey, Henry (d. 1743), 54
Carlisle, Frederick Howard, 5th Earl of, (1748-1825), 20
Carpenter, Richard, *theologian* (d. 1670), 29
Chalmers, Alexander, *miscellaneous writer* (1759-1834), 157
Chateaubriand, François René, Vicomte de, *French miscellaneous writer* (1678-1848), 109
Chatterton, Thomas (1752-70), 37
Chaucer, Geoffrey (1340?-1400), 117, 162
Churchill, Rev. Charles (1731-64), 41
Clare, John (1793-1864), 27, 43, 87, 129, 135;
  poetry quoted, 128
Claude Lorraine, *French painter* 1600-82), 23-4, 25
Coleridge, Hartley (1796-1849), 70
Coleridge, Samuel Taylor (1772-1834), 1, 3, 5, 12, 44, 49, 56, 62, 63, 65, 66, 70, 75, 98-9, 102, 106, 109, 110, 112, 113, 127, 137, 138, 140, 143, 146, 151, 166, 167;
  critical opinions quoted, 11, 29, 57, 67, 68-9, 74, 103, 151-2;
  poetry quoted, 54-5, 98
Collins, William (1721-59), 20, 21, 30, 32, 33, 35, 53, 60, 101, 120, 129
Collyer, Mary, *translator* (d. 1763), 22
Combe, William (1741-1823), 89-90;
  poetry quoted, 89
Congreve, William (1670-1729),
  poetry quoted, 122
Copley, John Singleton, *painter* (1737-1815), 136

INDEX OF ARTISTS AND WRITERS

"Cornwall, Barry". *See* Procter, Bryan Waller
Cottle, Joseph (1770-1853), 82, 99; *poetry quoted*, 82
Courtier, Peter L. (b. 1776), 76
Cowper, William (1731-1800), 1, 11, 44, 45, 48-51, 52, 57, 58, 64, 66, 78, 85, 87-8, 120, 139, 153, 157, 158; *poetry quoted*, 46, 48, 49-50, 153
Crabbe, Rev. George (1754-1832), 6, 45, 78-9, 87, 110, 150, 166; *poetry quoted*, 78-9
Crocker, Charles (1797-1861), 43, 135
Croker, John Wilson (1780-1857), 101
Crowe, Rev. William (1745-1829), 51; *poetry quoted*, 51
Cumberland, Richard (1732-1811), 99

Dale, Thomas (1797-1870), 115, 167
Dampier, William, *circumnavigator* (1652-1715), 29
Darwin, Erasmus, *M.B.* (1731-1802), 45, 58-9; *poetry quoted*, 59
Dekker, Thomas, *dramatist* (1570?-1641?), 143
Denham, Sir John (1615-69), 37
De Quincey, Thomas, *miscellaneous writer* (1785-1859), 5, 11, 70
Dermody, Thomas (1775-1802), 61, 137
Dibdin, Thomas Frognall, *bibliographer* (1776-1847), 27
D'Israeli, Isaac, *miscellaneous writer* (1766-1848), 114, 164
Dodsley, Robert (1703-64), 36, 41, 143
Drake, Nathan, *essayist* (1766-1836), 95, 120
Dryden, John (1631-1700), 22, 23, 47, 102, 150, 151, 162
Dunbar, James, *historian* (d. 1798), 39
Dyer, John (1700?-58), 27, 39

Edwards, Thomas (1699-1757), 36
Este, Rev. Charles (1753-1829), 52
Evans, Lewis E. (fl. 1830), 76

Fergusson, Robert (1750-74), 52
Fletcher, John, *dramatist* (1579-1625), 143, 144
Ford, John, *dramatist* (fl. 1639), 143, 144

Gay, John (1685-1732), 18, 120
Gessner, Salomon, *Swiss poet* (1730-88), 22, 55
Gibbon, Edward, *historian* (1737-94), 39
Gifford, William (1756-1826), 54, 135, 143, 144, 157

Gilfillan, Rev. George, *miscellaneous writer* (1813-78), 13, 56
Gilpin, Rev. William, *writer on picturesque* (1724-1804), 78, 83
Gisborne, Rev. Thomas (1758-1846), 27, 58
Glover, Richard (1712-85), 45
Godwin, William, *novelist* (1756-1836), 138
Goethe, Johann Wolfgang von (1749-1832), 55, 99
Goldsmith, Oliver (1728-74), 40, 41-2, 43, 47, 60, 61, 73, 76, 77, 101, 106, 115, 126, 155; *poetry quoted*, 41
Grahame, James (1765-1811), 14, 85-6; *poetry quoted*, 85-6
Grainger, James, *M.D.* (1721?-66), *poetry quoted*, 78
Gray, Thomas (1716-71), 11, 18, 20, 30-1, 53, 62, 64, 66, 115, 120, 151; *poetry quoted*, 30-1

Hamilton, Lady Ann (1766-1846), 158
Harvey, Margaret (1768-1858), 100
Hayley, William (1745-1820), 44, 48, 49, 52, 57; *critical opinion quoted*, 48; *poetry quoted*, 45
Hazlitt, William, *essayist and critic* (1778-1830), 2, 3, 27, 69, 117, 124, 143, 163, 164
Herrick, Robert (1591-1674), 143
Hervey, Rev. James, *devotional writer* (1714-58), 29-30, 32
Heywood, John, *dramatist* (1497?-1580?), 143
Heywood, Thomas, *dramatist* (d. 1650?), 143
Hodgson, Francis (1781-1852), 101
Hogg, James (1770-1835), 100, 106
Hogg, Thomas Jefferson, *biographer* (1792-1862), 11
Holford, Margaret (1778-1852), 100, 106
Holland, Henry Richard Vassall Fox, 3rd Baron, *politician and writer of memoirs* (1773-1840), 20-1
Holland, Joseph (fl. 1800), 84
Holloway, William (fl. 1800), 84
Homer, *Greek poet* (c. 800 B.C.), 1, 18, 165
Horace (Quintus Horatius Flaccus), *Roman poet* (65 B.C.-8 B.C.), 26
Hume, David, *philosopher* (1711-76), 40
Hunt, James Henry Leigh (1784-1859), 2, 3, 5, 6, 11, 12, 55, 105, 112, 113, 115, 116-17, 161, 162, 165, 167;

INDEX OF ARTISTS AND WRITERS 193

critical opinions quoted, 117, 161; *poetry quoted*, 117
Hurd, Rev. Richard, *miscellaneous writer* (1720-1808), 37
Hurdis, Rev. James (1763-1801), 14, 27, 51-2;
poetry quoted 51-2
Hutcheson, F r a n c i s, *philosopher* (1694-1746), 40

Ibbetson, Julius Caesar, *painter* (1759-1817), 79, 84

Jago, Rev. Richard (1715-81), 37, 83; *poetry quoted*, 37
Jeffrey, Francis, *critic* (1773-1850), 17, 18, 70, 106, 114, 145, 146, 148, 149, 156, 157
Jeffrey, John (fl. 1800), 76
Johnson, Samuel, *LLD.* (1709-84), 12, 20, 25, 26, 41, 61, 66, 81, 102, 111; *critical opinions quoted*, 10, 21, 36-7, 46-7, 66
Jonson, Benjamin, *dramatist* (1573?-1637), 143
Juvenal (Decimus Junius Juvenalis), *Roman satirist* (c. 60-130), 144

Keats, John (1795-1821), 1, 2, 7, 11, 12, 55, 108, 117, 118, 129, 130, 131, 162, 167;
poetry quoted, 129, 162
Klopstock, Friedrich Gottlieb, *German poet* (1724-1803), 55
Knight, Richard Payne (1750-1824), 155;
critical opinions quoted, 154-5;
poetry quoted, 46
Kyd, Thomas, *dramatist* (1558-94), 143

Lamb, Charles, *miscellaneous writer* (1775-1834), 85, 143, 144, 146
Law, Rev. Edmund, *devotional writer* (1703-87), 39
Lee, Harriet, *novelist* (1757-1851), 114
Lewis, Matthew Gregory, *novelist* (1775-1818), 95, 96, 127
Lofft, Capell (1751-1824), 83
Lovell, Robert (1770?-96), 56, 62
Lyttelton, George, later 1st Baron (1709-73), 25

Macaulay, Thomas Babington, *historian and critic* (1800-59), 145
McCulloch, John Ramsay, *economist* (1789-1864), 169
McDermot, Martin, *miscellaneous writer* (fl. 1800-24), 164
Mackenzie, Henry, *novelist* (1745-1831), 41

Macpherson, James (1736-96), 37
Mallet, David (1705?-1765),
poetry quoted, 28, 38
Marlowe, Christopher, *dramatist* (1564-93), 143
Marston, John, *dramatist* (1575?-1634), 143
Mason, William (1724-97), 46
Massinger, Philip, *dramatist* (1583-1640), 143, 144
Mathias, Thomas James (1754?-1835), 59
Maturin, Rev. Charles Robert, *novelist* (1782-1824), 138
Maurice, Rev. Thomas (1754-1824), *poetry quoted*, 83
Medwin, Thomas, *biographer* (1778-1869), 113
Merry, Robert (1755-98), 44, 52-3, 57, 62, 107;
poetry quoted, 53
Mickle, William Julius (1735-88), 37; *poetry quoted*, 37-8
Middleton, Thomas, *dramatist* (1570?-1627), 143
Mill, James, *economist* (1773-1836), 169
Millar, John, *historian* (1735-1801), 39
Millhouse, Robert (1788-1839), 43, 135
Milman, Rev. Henry Hart (1791-1868), 118, 167
Milton, John (1608-74), 18, 20, 21-2, 23, 28, 29, 30, 31, 34, 35, 53, 59, 101, 120, 129, 130, 140, 147, 157, 162, 165;
poetry quoted, 20
Mitford, Mary Russell (1787-1855), 85, 109, 110
Montgomery, James (1771-1854), 12, 14, 55, 106-8, 118, 167;
critical opinions quoted, 13, 107;
poetry quoted, 107
Moore, John, *M.D.*, *novelist* (1729-1802), 103, 105
Moore, Thomas (1779-1852), 1, 2, 6, 12, 72, 115-16, 122-5, 126, 127, 129, 141, 142, 166-7;
poetry quoted, 116, 123, 124

Newcombe, Rev. Thomas (1682?-1765), 30
Newnham, Francis (fl. 1809), 76
Nicholson, William (1782?-1849), 135
Norton, Thomas, *dramatist* (1532-84), 143

"Otway, Sylvester", i.e. John Oswald (d. 1793), 54n;
poetry quoted, 54

INDEX OF ARTISTS AND WRITERS

Parnell, Rev. Thomas (1679-1718), 28, 30
Penrose, Thomas (1742-79), 73; *poetry quoted*, 73-4
Percy, Rev. Thomas, *literary historian* (1729-1811), 38, 62, 95
Perfect, William, M.D. (d. 1809), *poetry quoted*, 126
Philips, Ambrose (1675?-1749), 25, 54
Pickering, Amelia (fl. 1788), 55
"Pindar, Peter" i.e. John Wolcot, M.D. (1737-1819), 158
Pope, Alexander (1688-1744), 12, 13, 17, 18, 19, 20, 21, 23, 24, 26, 29, 35, 36, 46, 47, 74, 101, 111, 114, 115, 150-8, 161, 162-5; *poetry quoted*, 24, 26, 32
Porson, Richard, *Grecian* (1759-1808), 135
Poussin, Nicholas, *French painter* (1594-1665), 23-4, 25
Pratt, Samuel Jackson (1749-1814), 44, 48, 49, 52, 57, 61, 78, 85, 87; *poetry quoted*, 44-5
Prior, Matthew (1664-1721), 126
Procter, Bryan Waller ("Barry Cornwall") (1787-1874), 117-18, 145, 167; *critical opinions quoted*, 116
Pye, Henry James (1745-1813), 95

Radcliffe, Ann, *novelist* (1764-1823), 19-20, 39-40, 96, 103, 105
Ramsay, Allan (1686-1758), 25
Reeve, Clara, *novelist* (1729-1807), 39
Reynolds, Frederick, *dramatist* (1764-1841), 55
Reynolds, John Hamilton (1796-1852), 117, 167
Reynolds, Sir Joshua, *painter* (1723-92), 135
Richardson, Samuel, *novelist* (1689-1761), 96
Richmond, Rev. Legh, *devotional writer* (1772-1827), 86
Ritson, Joseph, *literary historian* (1752-1803), 95
Roberts, Rev. William Hayward, D.D. (d. 1791), 46
Robertson, William, D.D., *historian* (1721-93), 39
Robinson, Henry Crabb, *diarist* (1775-1867), 70
Rogers, Samuel (1763-1855), 1, 12, 14, 31, 45, 59-62, 69, 71, 73, 75, 76, 102, 103, 112, 114, 149, 150, 153, 154, 155, 157, 159-61, 163, 167; *critical opinions quoted*, 20, 102-3; *poetry quoted*, 60-1, 159-161

Rose, William Stewart (1775-1843), 100, 111
Rosetti, Dante Gabriel (1828-82), 95n
Rowden, Frances Arabella (fl. 1801-21), 59, 76
Rowe, Nicholas (1674-1718), 143
Rowley, William, *dramatist* (1585?-1642?), 143
Russell, Rev. Thomas (1762-88), 68

Sackville, Thomas, *dramatist* (1536-1608), 143
Sanon, George (fl. 1806), 3
Scott, Walter (1771-1832), 1, 2, 13, 89, 95, 98-106, 109, 112, 113, 114, 115, 117, 118, 133, 140, 141, 142, 145, 157, 158, 165, 166, 167; *poetry quoted*, 99-100, 104
Service, David (fl. 1806), 84, 135; *poetry quoted*, 84-5
Shaftesbury, Anthony Ashley Cooper, 3rd Earl of, *philosopher* (1671-1713), 32, 40
Shakespeare, William (1564-1616), 18, 20-1, 22, 29, 35, 68, 101, 108, 112, 143, 144, 146, 147, 157, 162, 165
Shee, Martin Archer (1769-1850), 157
Shelley, Percy Bysshe (1792-1822), 1, 2, 3, 5, 6, 7, 12, 55, 75, 90, 105, 127, 128-30, 131, 138, 146, 167; *poetry quoted*, 91, 129-30
Shenstone, William (1714-63), 25, 30, 35, 37, 126, 127, 143; *critical opinions quoted*, 35
Shirley, James, *dramatist* (1596-1666), 143
Sibbald, James, *literary historian* (1745-1803), 95
Sidney, Sir Philip (1554-86), 162
Smart, Christopher (1722-71), 35
Smith, Adam, *philosopher* (1723-90), 40
Smith, Charlotte (1749-1806), 55
Sneyd, Rev. John (1764-1835), 116
Soame, Henry Francis Robert (1768-1803), 104; *poetry quoted*, 104
Sotheby, William (1757-1833), 100
Southey, Robert (1774-1843), 3, 5, 6, 13, 44, 55, 56, 61-2, 68, 69, 70, 80, 84, 87-8, 95, 99, 101, 102, 112, 113, 118, 122, 126, 127, 140, 143, 146, 151, 152, 153-4, 155, 157, 165, 166, 167; *critical opinions quoted*, 38, 67, 70, 74, 102, 108, 153-4, 157; *poetry quoted*, 11, 62, 82, 122
Spencer, William Robert (1769-1834), 95, 123; *poetry quoted*, 123-4

INDEX OF ARTISTS AND WRITERS 195

Spenser, Edmund (1552?-99), 22, 31, 35-6, 37, 42, 112, 129, 143, 147, 162
Stanley, John Thomas (1767-1850), 95
Steele, Richard, *miscellaneous writer* (1672-1729), 41
Sterne, Rev. Laurence, *novelist* (1713-68), 40-1
Stewart, Dugald, *philosopher* (1753-1828), 149
Stewart, John (fl. 1806), 76
Stoddart, John, *miscellaneous writer* (1773-1856), 98
Struthers, John (1776-1853), 43, 86, 135
Stuart, Gilbert, *historian* (1742-86), 39
Suckling, Sir John (1609-42), 123
Surr, Thomas Skinner, *novelist* (1770-1847), 124
Swift, Rev. Jonathan, *miscellaneous writer* (1667-1745), 17, 18, 20

Talfourd, Thomas Noon, *miscellaneous writer* (1795-1854), 2, 3
Tannahill, Robert (1774-1810), 127, 135;
poetry quoted, 127
Taylor, Edward (1741?-97), 55
Taylor, William, of Norwich, *miscellaneous writer* (1765-1836), 95
Thomson, James (1700-1748), 1, 10-11, 12, 18, 20, 22, 23-7, 28, 29, 30, 32, 35, 36, 40, 42, 43, 49, 51, 52, 62, 72, 77, 86, 87, 88, 90, 101, 133, 134, 135, 157, 158;
poetry quoted, 10, 23, 24
Thurlow, Edward, 2nd Baron (1781-1829), 162
Tighe, Mary (1772-1810), 108
Topham, Major Edward, *journalist* (1751-1820), 52
Tourneur, Cyril, *dramatist* (1575?-1626), 143
Townsend, Rev. George (1788-1857), 118
Trelawney, Edward John, *writer of memoirs* (1792-1881), 11, 105
Trissino, Gian Giorgio, *Italian poet* 1478-1550), 70

Vardill, Anna Jane (1781-1852), 76
Verral, Charles (fl. 1810), 76
Virgil (Publius Vergilius Maro), *Roman poet* (70 B.C.-19 B.C.), 25

Walker, Josiah (1761-1831), 3
Wallis, Rev. Richard (1753-1827), 61;
poetry quoted, 83
Walpole, Horace, *miscellaneous writer* (1717-97), 37
Wardlaw, Elizabeth, Lady (1677-1727), 38

Warton, Rev. Joseph (1722-1800), 11, 12, 14, 21, 32, 33, 34, 35, 36, 53, 60, 62, 101, 120, 121, 129, 130, 143, 147, 150, 151, 152, 153, 154, 156, 157;
critical opinions quoted, 10, 35, 36, 150;
poetry quoted, 20, 33
Warton, Rev. Thomas (1728-90), 12, 14, 21, 30, 32, 33, 34, 35, 36, 37, 53, 56, 60, 62, 101, 121, 129, 130, 143, 147, 152;
critical opinion quoted, 21;
poetry quoted, 32-3
Watts, Rev. Isaac, *D.D.* (1674-1748), 18, 120
Weber, Henry William, *literary historian* (1783-1818), 144
Wesley, Rev. Charles (1707-88), 120
Wesley, Rev. John, *evangelist* (1703-91), 120
West, Benjamin, *painter* (1738-1820), 136
West, Gilbert (1703-56), 35
West, Thomas, *topographer* (1720-79), 78
Westall, Richard, *painter* (1765-1836), 79
Whalley, Rev. Thomas Sedgwick (1746-1828), 106
Wharton, Richard (fl. 1812), 118
White, Henry Kirke (1785-1806), 14, 76, 130, 137;
poetry quoted, 130
Wilkie, David, *painter* (1785-1841), 72
Wilson, John (1785-1854), 70, 109;
critical opinions quoted, 49;
poetry quoted, 109-110
Wolfe, Rev. Charles (1791-1823), 127
Wordsworth, Dorothy, *diarist* (1771-1855), 42, 74
Wordsworth, William (1770-1850), 1, 2, 3, 5, 6, 7, 9, 11, 12, 13, 31, 42, 44, 45, 49, 51, 56, 57, 60, 62-70, 75, 76, 80, 82, 87-8, 95, 101, 102, 103, 106, 107, 109-10, 112, 113-14, 116, 118, 127-8, 29, 37, 138-9, 140, 143, 146, 151, 157, 162, 165, 166;
critical opinions quoted, 8, 38, 65-6, 67, 74, 115, 151;
poetry quoted, 68, 88n, 128, 138-9
Wrangham, Rev. Francis (1769-1842), 63

Yearsley, Ann (1756-1806), 22
Young, Rev. Edward, *D.D.* (1683-1765), 12, 18, 22, 28-9, 30, 31, 33, 35, 36, 40, 68, 73, 101, 133, 134;
poetry quoted, 29

LIBRARY OF DAVIDSON COLLEGE

Books on regular loan may be checked out for **two weeks**. Books must be presented at the Circulation Desk in order to be renewed.

A fine is charged after date due.

Special books are subject to special regulations at the discretion of the library staff.

NOV. -4. 1989